The Positive Development of Human Resources and School District Organizations

HOW TO ORDER THIS BOOK

BY PHONE: 800-233-9936 or 717-291-5609, 8AM–5PM Eastern Time

BY FAX: 717-295-4538

BY MAIL: Order Department
Technomic Publishing Company, Inc.
851 New Holland Avenue, Box 3535
Lancaster, PA 17604, U.S.A.

BY CREDIT CARD: American Express, VISA, MasterCard

The Positive Development of Human Resources and School District Organizations

Jerry J. Herman, Ph.D.
Professor and Area Head
Administration and Educational Leadership
College of Education
The University of Alabama at Tuscaloosa

Janice L. Herman, Ph.D.
Associate Professor
Educational Leadership and Instructional Support
School of Education
The University of Alabama at Birmingham

TECHNOMIC
PUBLISHING CO., INC.
LANCASTER · BASEL

**The Positive Development of Human Resources and School
District Organizations**
a TECHNOMIC®publication

Published in the Western Hemisphere by
Technomic Publishing Company, Inc.
851 New Holland Avenue
Box 3535
Lancaster, Pennsylvania 17604 U.S.A.

Distributed in the Rest of the World by
Technomic Publishing AG

Printed in the United States of America
10 9 8 7 6 5 4 3 2 1

Main entry under title:
    The Positive Development of Human Resources and School District Organizations

A Technomic Publishing Company book
Bibliography: p. 251
Includes index p. 259

Library of Congress Card No. 91-65712
ISBN No. 87762-791-6

To
Mark, Kirk, Kathy, Kristen, Steve, and Erik—young, sensitive,
and productive people who comprise a caring and
productive family organization
and to
Betsy and John Looney, and Opal and John Herman,
who provided the best of human resources

CONTENTS

vii

WHAT THIS BOOK IS ABOUT

SCHOOL DISTRICTS EXIST in a dynamic, open, and ever-changing environment. School districts' educational leaders must adjust existing organizational structures when, for example: (1) new laws and regulations are forced upon them, (2) political situations require organizational adjustments, (3) socio-economic or other demographic variables indicate significant changes within the community served by the school district, or (4) finances are significantly modified—whether increased or decreased. If the educational leaders consistently scan their external environment for trends, they will be able to project these trends and develop intervention strategies that will assist in developing and maintaining a healthy and productive organization. *Organizational development* is one of two crucial activities that effective educational leaders have mastered; the other crucial area is that of *human resource development*.

Organizational Development involves the maintenance and improvement of the total school district by: (1) monitoring the current "health" of the organization, (2) scanning the external and internal environments to determine trends and to project these trends into the future, (3) determining the desired future vision of the organization, (4) identifying the *needs* (gaps between "what is" and "what should be" or "what could be"), and (5) developing intervention strategies that will assist the educational leaders in achieving the "what should be" or "what could be" future organizational state desired.

Human Resource Development involves all activities within the educational organization or school district that have the potential

xi

of having a positive or negative effect on the humans who work within the school district. That is, the educational leaders should be conscious of the *needs* of all the employees within the organization. These needs can involve induction, assignment, training, recognition, or a myriad of other human needs. As is true of organizational development, the educational leaders should: (1) monitor those variables that affect and effect the employees, (2) identify trends and project trends into the future, (3) determine the desired future vision for the human elements of the district, (4) recognize *needs* (gaps between "what is" and "what should be" or "what could be"), and (5) devise strategies and tactics to meet the identified *needs*—whether they be related to all employees, sub-groups of employees, or individual employees.

It is quite clear that the steps involved in creating healthy and productive organizations are identical to those involved in developing happy and productive employees. The administrator who wishes to have a "winning" school building or school district must realize that as the humans within the organization change, the organization has to be modified to adjust to the changes in types of employees hired or changes in the *needs* of employees. For example, school districts and school buildings have to provide training for employees related to technological changes, curriculum changes, instructional delivery methodological changes or changes in the types of students for whom they are responsible. Human Resource Development (HRD) is a continuing responsibility of educational leaders.

On the other hand, political changes, technological changes, legal changes, financial changes, demographic changes within the community, and changes within the employees or student body will cause the alert administrator to suggest restructurings, policy changes, or whatever actions are feasible to maintain and improve the effectiveness of the total organization (school district or school building) as it adjusts to the changes required. Organizational Development (OD) is the second crucial continuing responsibility of educational leaders.

HRD activities cannot be truly successful unless the impact on the total school district or school building is considered *before* HRD activities are undertaken.

On the other hand, OD activities will not be optimally successful unless the impact on the individual employee, sub-groups of employees and the total employees are carefully anticipated *before*

OD activities are undertaken. It must be clearly understood that in any successful organization, OD and HRD activities have to be carefully integrated. To avoid planning for both the organizational and human requirements in a holistic manner is to invite misfits, non-alignment, and probable deterioration in the level of effectiveness of the school district or school building and in the levels of satisfaction and productivity of the humans within the school district or school building.

This book addresses both the OD and HRD aspects of operating a school district. More importantly, it stresses the interaction between the two areas of OD and HRD; and it identifies those helps and activities to which a school administrator must attend, if she/he is to develop and maintain both a "healthy" and productive total organization, as well as satisfied and productive employees. Finally, it recommends an HOM (Human and Organizational Management) Model as the systems plan for the future.

STRUCTURE OF THIS BOOK

Designed as a guidebook for practitioners, this work relies mainly on actual onsite experiences with human resource development activities, empowering of groups, collaborative governance, and administrative intervention strategies that promote healthy school organization. Organizational structural changes that promote both an open system and the loose coupling designs crucial to creating and maintaining a healthy organization, and to maintaining productive and happy employees, are addressed.

Although the mission of the school is to educate students well, this mission can only become a reality if there is put into place an organizational structure that promotes a positive environment. This environment must promote productivity and satisfaction among *all* categories of employees. For only through this positive interface will the school's mission be attainable.

This book is divided into chapters that individually deal with matters related to Organizational Development (OD) and Human Resource Development (HRD), and it then discusses both OD and HRD as a holistic planning system, integrating both areas. The individual chapters provide detailed discussions and activities related to: (1) developing the framework for HRD, (2) developing the framework for OD, (3) determining OD and HRD needs, (4) developing action programs to meet the identified needs, (5) fitting the employees to the organization, (6) developing and training employees, (7) involving and empowering employees, (8) developing a win-win attitude between unions and management, (9) developing and maintaining a healthy organization, and (10) anticipating future changes that will impact the planning for OD and HRD programs, strategies, and tactics. It ends by recommending an HOM (Human and Organizational Management) model as the systems plan of the future.

FOR WHOM THIS IS WRITTEN

This book is written for those practitioners who are on the front lines of school districts as continuous changes impact the people working in schools. These changes also impact the organizational structure of the school districts. The book is designed as a guide for all categories of educational administrators: superintendents, principals, and central office administrators who have the responsibility for dealing with continuous change in a manner that maintains a healthy organization, and who are also responsible for planning interventions that make for productive and satisfied employees.

The combined experience of the two authors spans most of these occupations, including teaching at the elementary, junior high, senior high, and junior college levels; serving as building principals, as central office curriculum specialists at both the elementary and secondary levels, as an assistant superintendent for instruction, as staff developers, as consultants to school district and other organizations, as a superintendent of schools for twenty years, as a state department of education researcher, as university professors, and as a university administrator. With such a wide kinship of perspective, we feel certain that this book will serve as a valuable resource for practicing administrators.

JERRY J. HERMAN
JANICE L. HERMAN

CHAPTER 1

The Framework for Human Resource Development

HUMAN RESOURCE DEVELOPMENT involves all activities within the educational organization or school district that have the potential of having a positive or a negative effect on the people who work within the school district. Those individuals charged with the responsibility for employee-related activities, whether they be called directors of human resources, directors of personnel, assistant superintendents or some other title have as their mission to attend to the activities related to employees in such a manner that the productivity and satisfaction of employees are maximized. This responsibility involves anticipating and avoiding or minimizing the impact of those activities which may negatively impact employees, and it also involves developing activities and making employee-related decisions that maximize the satisfaction and productivity levels of employees.

Human resource management "involves all management decisions and actions that affect the nature of the relationship between the organization and employees—its human resources" [1]. Traditionally, personnel departments have been isolated from line management, as an accumulating collection of independent and legally reactive functions (equal opportunity, labor relations, etc.), and in the lack of decision-making coordination between production demands and personnel needs. Coherent structure and central purpose are added when this organizational and managerial function is more broadly perceived by general managers—superintendents and central office staff—as *"the development of all aspects of an organizational context* so that they will encourage and even direct managerial behavior with regard to people" [2].

In most educational organizations, especially relatively small school districts, there is not a centralized administrator responsible for coordinating all the human resource activities. Even in large school districts that have a person or a staff who hold responsibility for Human Resource Development (HRD), many persons are involved in implementing and monitoring HRD activities. Some of the major players include: principals, staff developers, personnel specialists, superintendents, instructional specialists, trainers, and board of education members (policy makers). The enrollment size of a school district and the proportionate number of professional and classified personnel must define the need for the establishment of a differentiated Human Resource Development staff. Inefficiency in the HRD function, when one considers that salaries and benefits alone generally constitute 80 percent of all school district expenditure, is too costly in terms of service and efficiency [3]. The added HRD functions of staff development and training expand the need for a coordinated and supported HRD structure.

Regardless of the specific individual(s) who holds responsibility for HRD activities, it is clear that there are two specific phases to this responsibility. Phase One involves pre-hire decision making, and Phase Two involves all the activities from the employee point of hire to the employee point of departure from the school district. Phase Two, then, covers the entire time period during which the individual is employed. A model of HRD activities will provide a schematic detail of the major activities that are included in Phase One and Phase Two (see Figure 1.1).

PHASE ONE OF HRD

Phase One consists of activities that determine the type of person(s) to be hired and the type(s) of costs associated with attracting the type of employee(s) desired. Generally, the higher the skill level, the higher the salary, and the more attractive the fringe benefits. Supply and demand also play a large part in arriving at the pre-selection criteria.

Recruitment as a process has the major thrust of acquiring the number and type of people necessary for the current and future needs of the district, with the continuous perspective of targeting potential applicants for anticipated vacancies [4].

Certification is a continuing concern, along with affirmative action requirements. Some school districts have paid premium salaries for science and math teachers because they are in short supply. Previously, special education teachers were paid additional sums because they were in short supply. Most school districts pay teachers with advanced degrees more than they pay new hires who usually only have bachelor's degrees.

The present generation of teachers and other professional personnel, whose numbers are reflective of the great increase in employment in the field as a response to the baby boom-impacted classrooms of the 1950's and 1960's is approaching retirement, and it appears that they will be followed by fewer and less academically able ranks of personnel. The Carnegie Forum on Education and the Economy's *Report of the Task Force on Teaching as a Profession* has documented the relative academic un-

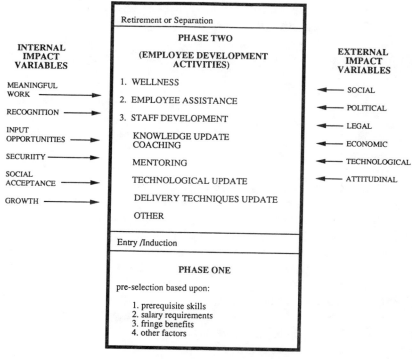

Figure 1.1 Human resource development model.

preparedness and lesser achievement of the intended education majors currently in the pipeline for the teaching labor supply of the 21st Century [5]. As a response to this anticipated (particularly minority) teacher shortage of the 1990's and the increasing lack of academically qualified teacher graduates, many new state-level alternative certification programs have been created in order to credential candidates with an undergraduate degree in a non-teacher education discipline combining an intensive course of pedagogy with technical support on the job. It is therefore likely that the HRD educational manager of the 1990s will be faced with a distinctly different professional population, technical support needs, and marketplace/recruitment realities.

The skills required to fill a particular vacant position also determine, to some extent, the pre-selection criteria. If the district wants to hire someone to head the curriculum efforts for the entire district and that person is to have both elementary and secondary experience *and* curricular/supervisory certification, the criteria will be more complex than if the district only required either elementary or secondary experience. If the district requires a master plumber or a highly trained technician, the supply will be less than if the district only required general repair training expertise of the applicants.

Whenever the district develops a vacancy or creates a new position, the persons responsible for the recruiting and hiring should do two things. First, they should analyze the skills, experiences and other information about all current employees—the development of a profile indicating the status of current human resources. (This type of information concerning all district employees should already exist in a manageable and accessible data base format.) A human resource profile for each job classification should be developed from information gathered from employees [6]. This analysis will identify what the current employees have to offer, and it will identify any areas of weakness that should be filled because of a void within the current employee group. For example, such an analysis may discover such matters as: (1) there are only women teaching in the elementary grades, (2) there are only males teaching social science at the secondary level, (3) practically all teachers have received their degrees from the same state university, (4) no teacher in the English department has had enough advanced training in literature to teach the honors and Advanced Placement courses that are to be initiated, (5) only 1 percent of the certified staff are minorities, (6) all principals are white males, and (7) only 28 percent of the teachers have advanced degrees in the field in which they teach.

Likewise, an analysis of classified employees may well turn up information of importance. For example, in reviewing dates of employment, turnover data, and documented skills, such an analysis may find that: (1) all of the "key" supervisors are within three years of retirement, and there are no plans to train replacements even in areas of shortages, (2) numerous secretaries have resigned in the past six months to take positions with a major industry that just moved into the area, that the industry is providing better fringe benefits, and the salaries paid secretaries, on average, is 35 percent higher than those paid by the school district, (3) maintenance personnel are inadequately trained to maintain the sophisticated heating and ventilation systems that were installed during the past year in the district's older school buildings, and (4) the district does not have a single food service employee who is trained as a dietician.

A human resource analysis can provide crucial information that assists in identifying pre-selection criteria. Once the data from the human resource analysis has been completed, another activity should be undertaken to identify even more detailed pre-selection criteria. The second task that should be undertaken by those who are responsible for recruiting and hiring new employees is that of identifying the Critical Success Factors (CSF's) for each vacant position. Critical Success Factors are those few items which are absolutely necessary for job performance at a very high level. This process of gathering information and distilling the essential success characteristics is also applicable to human resource forecasting and to the determination of compensation programs [7]. Once the CSF's are identified, the persons responsible for recruiting and hiring can write a district-need-structured and more customized updated job description, and subsequently advertise the position vacancy. Such techniques as observation, individual interviews, and questionnaires can be used to analyze individual jobs and to generate task requirement information [8]. These CSF's should be the focal points during the interview stage, and they should be the primary measures utilized for performance evaluation, once the person is employed.

Let's take a look at what the job description, position announcement and the interview interrogatory might well look like for a single vacancy. Since District Mighty has an increased student population and the taxpayers have voted a bond issue to build a new elementary school, our example shall be that of an elementary principal's position.

Elementary Principal's Job Description

POSITION: Elementary Principal   October 18, 19–
REPORTS TO: Director of Elementary Schools
WORK YEAR: 12 months with 20 days vacation
SALARY AND BENEFITS: Comprehensive benefits, salary range $40,000–$60,000
GENERAL STATEMENT OF DUTIES: The elementary principal is responsible for all instructional and other activities that are designed to provide for the fullest possible development of the skills of each individual student.
CRITICAL SUCCESS FACTORS: The critical factors upon which the level of performance of the elementary principal shall be evaluated include:

- The principal shall believe that *all* children can learn, and evidence shall exist that this belief is operational within the school.
- The principal shall monitor student achievement, and she/he shall see that the staff shall monitor student achievement for the purposes of improving student instruction.
- The principal shall maintain a safe and healthy environment.
- The principal shall utilize clinical and developmental supervision techniques with the staff.
- The principal shall periodically, with the assistance of others, conduct a curriculum map to determine the use of the pre-determined curriculum with the classrooms.
- The principal shall focus on instruction, and she/he shall maximize Academic Learning Time (ALT) by eliminating distractions and interruptions.
- The principal shall maintain a school climate that lets both students and employees feel wanted, cared for, valued, and one that expects high achievement of all parties.

- The principal shall maintain an open and positive communications system with students, parents, teachers, other administrators, and with members of the community in which her/his campus is located.
- The principal shall have a vision of "what should be" or "what could be" in the future, and she/he shall get others to buy into this vision or help develop it.

Once the job description is completed, the persons responsible for recruiting and hiring the elementary principal can develop a position vacancy announcement. It is critical that this process involve the administrator responsible for monitoring the district's affirmative action program, to ensure acknowledgment of receipt of application and to obtain documentation from candidates about minority status. This announcement should parallel the important information included in the job description. The position vacancy announcement would then be advertised through university placement offices, by ads in journals read by potential candidates, newspapers, and through distribution to area school districts.

Elementary Principal Vacancy

Mighty School District announces a position vacancy for an elementary principal. A comprehensive fringe package is included, and a salary will be negotiated between $40,000 and $60,000, dependent upon the training and experience of the successful candidate. The position is for 52 weeks with 20 days paid vacation. The position to begin on August 1, 19–. Applications will be accepted until April 15th.

The candidate should forward a letter expressing her/his philosophy and the five most significant accomplishments of the last five years. In addition, the candidate should forward a vita, placement papers from the universities attended, official transcripts, and a completed Mighty School District's application form.

Desired Qualifications include a doctorate, and a minimum of 3 years experience as an elementary principal. In addition, the candidate should provide evidence of knowledge and experience with the following areas:

- a system for monitoring student achievement and utilizing the results to adjust instructional programs
- an operationalized belief that *all* children can learn

- a system for periodic curriculum mapping
- an open and positive communications system with students, staff, other administrators and community members
- maintenance of a safe and healthy environment
- ability to use clinical and developmental supervisory techniques with staff members
- a clear future vision of "what should be" or "what could be" in the elementary school in which she/he is placed
- development and maintenance of a school climate that is based upon trust, caring, openness, and high expectations of the principal, staff and students
- maintenance of a structure that maximizes Academic Learning Time (ALT), eliminating interruptions and disturbances from the classroom

Once the position is advertised, the information from all candidates should be reviewed after the closing date for applicants. At this point, the five to ten candidates that seem to be the best "fit" for the criteria identified by the selection committee should be further investigated by telephone calls to them, to the references listed in their applications, and to their immediate supervisors in the districts where the candidates have worked. Following this screening, the top five might be selected, and visits to the five candidates' places of current employment are in order (these visits also may be postponed until after the interviews have been completed).

Whether the visitations are made before or after the interviews is a matter of choice. In any case, the interview provides an opportunity to check on the evidences required by the recruitment criteria. Even though a wide variety of individuals and groups, including stakeholders, may be involved in the total interview visitation, it is crucial that a focused interview of anywhere from one to three hours take place based upon the criteria that have been decided upon. It is also desirable that employees with experience in and knowledge of the particular position as well as representatives of the position's subordinates and supervisors participate in the process. The example below provides a series of structured questions that are focused on the criteria that have been established by Mighty School District. These questions would be asked after the candidate has been made to feel at ease, and her/his questions have been answered.

Elementary Principal's Interview Guide

Doctor (name of candidate), we are so pleased that you could visit Mighty School District today. As we told you on the phone, we will be asking questions directly related to those Critical Success Factors that are listed on the elementary principal's job description, which we forwarded to you.

Please take all the time you need to answer each question, and if any question is not clear, please ask us to clarify it. Would you like a cup of coffee or a glass of water before we get started?

(1) The first question has to deal with mission and vision. As our new elementary principal, what vision would you bring to us regarding what an outstanding elementary school should look like? What have you done in your current position to implement the mission you have described?

(2) What have you done in your current position to: (a) develop and maintain a safe and healthy school environment, and (b) eliminate interference with classroom Academic Learning Time?

(3) What do you know about the various methods of clinical and developmental supervision? Give us a couple of examples of how you have used these with your staff members.

(4) Do you monitor student achievement, and do you work with your staff to use these results to modify instruction? Please give us a specific example of your work with staff in this area, and tell us exactly what you do, as a principal, to monitor student achievement.

(5) When visiting your school last week it appears that you have a school climate that exemplifies trust, caring, openness and high expectations for students and employees. What do you personally do to cause that kind of climate to exist? How would you attempt to develop that type of positive school climate at your new school?

(6) Do you truly believe that *all* students can learn? If you believe, how can you get your staff to believe it also? What proof can you provide from your current school that this belief is operational?

Thank you for answering our questions. You will hear from us within two weeks. In the meantime, if you have any further questions or desire additional information, please give us a call.

Once the candidate is selected, hired, placed in position and inducted, Phase Two of the HRD process begins. Before going to Phase Two, however, we should briefly discuss induction activities. Induction includes providing information about policies, the staff, the students and the community. It also involves getting the new employee to meet people who will provide work and social contacts. Finally, it involves making the new employee feel wanted and helped by providing assistance in locating a home, getting moved, and doing whatever is necessary to get that new employee settled in and comfortable as soon as possible. The induction of a new (or reassigned) employee is an important first step, and it should not be left to chance.

A buddy system might be helpful, and this would involve having one person specifically assigned to the new employee to assist that employee in any way that would be helpful. Even if a buddy system is not utilized, a carefully planned induction process should be developed, as first impressions of the district are very important in starting the new employee "off on the right foot". Having briefly dealt with the importance of induction, let's turn to Phase Two of HRD.

PHASE TWO OF HRD

From the time the new employee starts her/his work until the time that the employee retires from the school district's service or terminates employment with the district for any cause, that employee is in the development phase of Human Resource Development. The development stage can involve three coordinated areas of activity: (1) wellness, (2) employee assistance, and (3) staff development.

Wellness

Wellness involves those programs offered employees that deal with their conditions of health. The basic rationale for wellness programs goes back to ancient times when it was believed that a "healthy body is necessary for a healthy mind." Today's version, when related to employees, might be interpreted to say that the healthier the employee, the more productive and content the employee. "Preventive health care, or wellness, is rooted in a simple premise. Create healthier people and give them access to early detection programs, and you lower their medical risk factor for many of the most serious illnesses" [9].

Usually, *wellness* encompasses several areas: health education, Employee Assistance Programs, early detection programs, and fitness programs [10]. *Wellness* programs were generally introduced by corporations, such as General Motors Corporation, as part of a broader approach called Quality of Work Life (QWL). QWL assessed the current state of work life quality, and involved employees in working together to devise programs that would continually improve the quality of their work environment. In other words, the programs focused on the identified work life needs of employees, and used those same employees to devise and enact programs that would improve their quality of work life [11].

As part of this program, *wellness* was introduced. It has now found a home in many school districts, as well as in many businesses and industries. A school district may begin its program by developing a confidential wellness survey that is taken by those employees who volunteer to complete the survey instrument. Questions about age, sex, height, weight, eating habits, sleeping habits and other pertinent health-related questions are answered by the employees who complete the confidential survey instruments. The individual results are returned to the employees, but patterns and trends are analyzed and reported to the HRD persons responsible for wellness activities.

Let's assume that the survey results indicated that 20 percent of all employees still smoked, that there were fifty-four grossly overweight bus drivers, twenty-five employees drank more than eight ounces of liquor daily, and three hundred employees did vigorous exercise less than one hour per week. The person responsible for wellness activities, with the help of a QWL steering committee (if one exists), could originate programs such as:

- A stop-smoking clinic could be organized, and public recognition could be provided those who actually stopped smoking.
- An alcoholic support group could be organized within the district, or some type of incentive system could be developed for those employees who would join Alcoholics Anonymous.
- A weight loss clinic could be organized, and all fees associated with it could be paid by the district.
- A before-school hours, after-school hours, and weekend

exercise program, and athletic leagues could be offered
employees free of charge; and exercise bicycles and other
exercise equipment could be placed in employee lounge
areas for those persons who wished to exercise during free
periods or during the lunch period.

The rapidly rising and projected costs of health benefits has encouraged more districts to approach the preventative technique,
involving a wellness program. The cafeteria plan of benefits, in
which employees can select a mix of cash and non-cash benefits,
has gained in popularity since its inception by Congress in 1978
(further enhanced by the tax incentives clarifications of 1984).
The flexibility offered by such plans more appropriately addresses the employee needs created by the changing demographics of increased female representation in the workforce and
the acute need for child care. Dependent care coverage is a benefit
selected second only to medical coverage [12]. The application of
traditional health cost containment strategies in connection with
cafeteria plans, such as the raising of employee coverage deducti-
bles, the increase of co-payments, and the encouragement of the
selection of less expensive care can be perceived by employees as
punitive. Such strategies must be combined with the undertaking of risk reduction and health promotion benefits, both for the
direct advantage to the district and for the promotion of employee
morale.

If HRD covers all aspects of the development of human resources, then the improvement (when needed) of the physical and
mental health of employees certainly becomes an integral part of
a comprehensive approach to HRD. Mentioning mental health
brings us to a discussion of another important HRD program—
that of *Employee Assistance.*

Employee Assistance

Employee assistance activities are those broad-intervention
programs related to assisting employees who are under heavy
stress or who are suffering from emotional conditions. In general,
school districts who have an employee assistance program in
place provide a contact person to whom any employee can speak,
with total confidentiality guaranteed. This contact person's re-

sponsibility is to discover the conditions that are distressing the employee, and getting a referral established with an appropriate clinic, psychologist, psychiatrist, or other mental health specialist. Sometimes, referrals are also made to drug, alcohol, or suicide clinics. The basic purpose of employee assistance programs is to get assistance for employees in a manner that is confidential, usually conducted off-site, and provided in a manner that does not become part of their work record [13].

Typical situations involve a recent divorce, a drug addiction, a recent death of a loved one, discovery of a serious health condition, or a feeling of loneliness and failure within the employee's mind. In each of these cases, employees are made to feel that professional, accessible help will be provided them by the school district, and that their situation or condition will be kept totally confidential. As a first line of defense, co-workers, managers, and supervisors should be educated to detect and encourage referrals [14].

Even though both wellness and employee assistance activities should be an integral part of a comprehensive HRD program; it should be made clear that, while helping the employee to develop a healthier mental or physical state is the focus of these programs, the day-to-day quality of instruction to students must not be sacrificed. In cases where the individual employee is in such a poor physical or mental state that the quality of service to students is endangered, that individual should be provided with a temporary paid leave of absence until the state of physical or mental health is such as to allow return to the employee's normal responsibilities. Finally, in cases where it is impossible to provide paid leave, the HRD officials should attempt to provide a job placement (working on curriculum guides, serving as an assistant to another teacher, cataloging books, or other non-student contact assignments) that will temporarily keep the employee employed and allow time for healing. "Central to the philosophy under the EAP's is the belief that although the organization has no right to interfere in the private lives of its workers, it does have a right to impose certain standards of work performance and to establish sanctions when these are not met" [15].

Even though the school district has a *wellness* program and an *employee assistance* program, it still has an even broader responsibility for providing staff development activities on a continuing basis for all employees.

Staff Development

Staff development activities include those activities which impart new knowledges, develop new skills, or are related to improvement of the ability of the employee to improve her/his job delivery quality. When planning staff development activities, those HRD persons responsible must keep in mind the research related to teaching adults (andragogy) and how that differs from planning for the teaching of elementary and secondary students.

Researchers and writers such as Donaldson [16], Laird [17], and Tough [18] all stress consideration of a different set of stipulations when planning staff development activities for adults than those considered when planning to teach elementary and secondary students. It is important when planning staff development activities for adults to remember that:

- Adults already have a vast storehouse of information that can be utilized.
- Adults need to be actively involved in planning and carrying out the staff development activities.
- Adults learn from each other when a *cooperative learning* design is used.
- Adults want staff development activities offered that deal directly with their current work.
- Adults want activity-oriented programs, not lectures.
- Adults, basically, want to be treated as caring adults who wish to learn new activities, delivery methods, and information that will assist them in carrying out their teaching (or other functions) in a more effective, efficient, and higher quality manner [19].

Staff development activities can legitimately arise from three basic sources: (1) the identified needs of the individual employee, (2) the identified needs of a sub-group of employees, or (3) the identified needs of the school district. The key to discovering the needs of each of these levels is to put in place a methodological procedure that discovers "what is" and compares this current state with a "what should be" or "what could be" future state. The discrepancy between the current "what is" state and the desired future state identifies the need (gap) between the two states that is to be addressed by an action-oriented staff development program.

Staff development delivery systems may vary all the way from an intensive training session, utilizing the school district's staff or an outside hired consultant, to one that pairs up an individual employee with another employee "coach" who has expertise in the area of identified employee need. Technological update training, mentoring, shadowing, and simulations, to name a few, are other means of delivering staff development activities.

Let's turn to an example of a staff development activity for each of the situations involving an individual, a sub-group of employees, or the total group of employees.

Staff Development—An Individualized Activity

The school district's graphic artist has never had the opportunity to discover the use of computers for graphic renderings. The graphic artist requested such training, and the HRD Director freed sufficient funds from the budget to allow the graphic artist to attend a one-month's workshop on computer graphics that was held in New York City during the summer. Although this workshop, for which the district paid all related costs, was expensive, the graphic artist is now able to produce an increase of 80 percent in the amount of high quality graphics intended for classroom usage.

Staff Development—A Sub-group Activity

Through review of the accident reports transmitted by the Director of Transportation and through focus group discussions with bus drivers about their staff development needs, it was clear that additional training was required to avoid a future serious accident, to reduce the number of minor accidents, and to make the bus drivers feel more in control during the stormy winter months. The HRD Department arranged to have the police barricade a stretch of highway for one-half day, and the district arranged to have foam placed on that patch of highway to simulate snowy and icy winter conditions. After detailed instruction on how to avoid skids and accidents during poor winter weather conditions, each bus driver was provided numerous opportunities to control a bus during these simulated weather conditions.

Staff Development—A Total Employees' Activity

The school district purchased an updated computer system for use by the employees of the entire district. This new system was to be used by all secretarial personnel, by the dispatcher in the bus garage, by all personnel in the business, instructional and personnel offices, by all building level administrators, by the warehouse supervisor, and by teachers and students for instructional purposes. In order to keep the district current with computer technology, this decision had to be made. The task of the staff development specialist, then, became one of training all employees in the use of this new computerized technology. A series of training activities were established, and they were differentiated by category of employee and type of computer applications to be used in performing the specific jobs of each classification of employee.

In some cases outside expertise was hired to handle highly technical training; in some cases teachers who had used the new computer system previously were hired to offer weekend and after normal school hour workshops for other teachers; and, in other cases, on-line technical assistance was provided on an "as needed" basis for employees in the business office.

Also, the length of the training sessions was varied for each group, and a continuing "on call" referral system was initiated. In this case, as is true of many staff development activities, the task is not completed with a workshop, and a maintenance structure has to be put in place.

Now that we have explored Phase One (pre-selection) and Phase Two (employee development) of Human Resource Development, let's turn our attention to those internal and external variables that impact the form and the activities of a district's HRD model.

EXTERNAL VARIABLES IMPACTING HRD

HRD activities do not take place in a vacuum. Many times they are influenced by variables outside the parameters within which HRD functionaries operate. When Sputnik was launched by Russia in 1957, staff development activities, as well as curriculum development activities, were hastily created in the areas of math and science. With the issuance of the *Nation at Risk* Report during the Reagan administration, a tremendous volume of activity took place (and is still taking place) in an effort to make schools more effective [20]. Many other examples could be iterated, but suffice it to say that HRD is not a function that operates well without attending to external influences. In the open-systems theory of contemporary organizational thought, environmental elements present threats or opportunities for an organization [21], and can be characteristically attributed to the forces represented by the External Impact Variables. The social systems model of a school district combines both the "legal" external constituencies [22] of school districts, such as regulatory agencies and taxpayers, with the more general external environmental factors, such as the open market forces and prevailing social attitudes.

Some of the major external forces that impact HRD activities include: (1) social, (2) political, (3) legal, (4) economic, (5) technological, and (6) attitudinal variables. These variables may influence an entire nation's school districts, as in the case of the after-effects of *A Nation at Risk*, or they can be focused on a single school district or on an individual school. An example could well be a single high school that has a student dropout rate in excess of 50 percent, with a community highly agitated about the dropout situation.

Briefly, let's take one example of each of these variables to determine the potential impact on HRD activities:

- A social (cultural) variable could come into play if a large group of immigrants settled in a specific area (for example, when a great many Cubans settled in Miami). The challenge for HRD staff developers was to develop activities for Anglo and Black teachers related to the culture and language of a large proportion of their new students.
- A political variable comes into play when the federal government makes an extensive effort to do something about a specific situation, such as "Students at Risk". In reaction to this federal initiative, numerous school districts have enacted training programs to assist teachers and other school employees to identify students at risk, and to offer these students help by training staff members to utilize different intervention strategies with these students.

- A legal variable can come into play any time a court mandates an action or a legislative body passes a law mandating certain requirements be met in a school district. For example, many states are now mandating that policies be developed and instruction be provided related to AIDS.
- Economic variables quickly come into play in two ways. Sometimes money is cut from the HRD budget because other expense areas are determined to be more important at that point in time. Also, sometimes federal, state or regional dollars are allocated for staff development in specific areas. In these situations, HRD staff developers put in place programs that utilize these available funds; otherwise, the funds are lost to the school district.
- Technological advances sometimes have a direct influence on the staff development activities offered by the school district. Computer literacy training for staff is one example, and another example is training in the use of robotics for teachers of industrial education related classes.
- Attitudinal variables also sometimes determine staff development offerings. If a group of math teachers identify a *need* related to a new theory, they may request (or almost demand) that staff development programs be offered in that area. Certainly the use of computers caused (and still causes) a demand for staff development activities because of employee attitudes toward their use.

Having discussed external variables that can impact HRD activities, let's turn to internal variables that may impact which activities are offered by those responsible for the HRD activities of the school district.

INTERNAL IMPACT VARIABLES

Although internal political, financial, technological, social and attitudinal variables also function as internal impact variables from time to time, the more important internal impact variables deal with the "feeling tone" within the individual employee and within a group of employees. If employees feel that: (1) they are doing meaningful work, (2) they are recognized for their contributions, (3) they have opportunities for input into decisions affecting them, (4) they have security, (5) they are socially accepted, and (6) they have growth opportunities, they will want to improve their performance and the performance of the entire school district. They will be willing to help others and to assist the school district to improve in whatever way they can contribute to that improvement goal.

These variables derive from researched models of motivation and behavior, which have characteristically outlined needs common in importance to most people. The proto-typical and familiar Maslovian Hierarchy of Needs—physical; safety/security; social (affiliation); esteem (recognition); and self-actualization—is such a model, with several components related to the variable of Security [23]. The Social Acceptance variable is strongly underscored in need theory, such as that of Schachter regarding the individual's search for *affiliation* in order to have beliefs confirmed (a structural phenomenon exemplified by the formation of informal groups in the workplace). The Recognition variable is implied in the work of Gellerman on *prestige*—the "recognition and respect accorded them by others" [24]. In the Adlerian concept of *power* as manipulative ability, the variables of Input Opportunities, Advancement Opportunities and Responsibility can be seen [25]. White's "action mainspring" of *competence*, implying control over both physical and social environmental factors, and McClelland's research on *achievement* as a distinct human motive support the variables of both Meaningful Work and Growth [26]. McGregor's Theory Y assumptions concerning the potential for workers to be mature and self-motivated and Argyris' work on the broadening of individual responsibility support the variables of both Meaningful Work and Input Opportunities [27]. Herzberg's *hygiene and motivation* needs are represented in the internal impact variables of the Human Resource Development Model, with an emphasis on the motivation of Meaningful Work, Recognition, Input Opportunities, and Growth. The variables of Social Acceptance and Security correspond more closely to Herzberg's *hygiene/maintenance* needs [28].

With regard to stress factors, three separate characteristics contribute to a person's ability to cope with stress—tolerance for ambiguity, locus of control, and self-esteem [29]. People who can cope with a lack of definition (tolerate ambiguity) believe that they are responsible for what happens to them (in locus of control), and who have high self-esteem are "hardy" individuals and not candidates for burnout. The admittedly stressful school environment can contribute to employee stress levels by exacerbating the given stressors (parental/patron pressures, state and federal regulations, societal demands and attitudes, etc.) with unsupported demands for policy compliance or academic achievement: Districts can offer a variety of Employee Assistance Programs that include preventive stress planning, diagnosis for employee vulnerability, and management training for stress reduction [30]. The visible and constant presence of stress intervention, in whatever form, should contribute to the overall district culture, and should be appropriately promoted and publicized [31].

Visibly demonstrating the attitude supporting these employee considerations, if the administrators of the district, the board of education members and those persons responsible for HRD activities believe that people are: (1) good; (2) well-intentioned; (3) interested in improving themselves, others and the school district; (4) willing to work to achieve the goal of continuing improvement; and (5) willing to put time and effort into improvement activities, the "mind-set" that is required to put forth a positive, comprehensive and high-quality staff development program is present. When the employees have positive feelings about themselves, others and the school district, and when administrators and trainers feel positive about employees, it is easy to focus upon a mutual goal of self and group improvement. When these attitudes exist, staff development is ensured.

Up to this point we have discussed Phase One (pre-selection) activities, Phase Two (employee development) activities, external variables that impact HRD, and internal variables that impact HRD. Let's end this discussion by stressing the requirement for HRD functionaries to approach their tasks with a strategic plan in hand that combines all of these matters.

SUMMARY

Human Resource Development (HRD) involves all activities within the educational organization or school district that have the potential of having a positive (desired) effect or a negative effect on the people who work within the educational organization. There are two phases to the total HRD process. Phase One is the pre-selection stage, and Phase Two is the Employee Development Phase.

The Employee Development Phase includes: (1) wellness activities, (2) employee assistance activities, and (3) staff development activities. Staff development activities can include updating employee knowledge, coaching or mentoring activities, updating technological usage, and updating delivery techniques.

All HRD programs will, from time to time, be influenced by external impact variables that are social, political, legal, economic, technological or attitudinal in nature. In addition, HRD programs are many times influenced by internal variables such as meaningful work, recognition of employees, opportunities for input, security, social acceptance, and growth opportunities.

GUIDELINES

1. In developing a Human Resource Development program, it is important to include within the total program a structure which includes: wellness activities, employee assistance activities, and staff development activities.

2. It is crucial that HRD programs be built upon identified *needs*. Needs are the gaps that exist between "what is" and "what could be" or "what should be".

3. It is important that the *needs* identified include the three levels of: individual employees, specific groups of employees, and the total employee group.

4. HRD programs are ever-changing as *needs* change over time. They can change because of differences in the types of qualitative level of employees hired, the internal variables that can influence the HRD activities conducted, or the external variables that can impact the HRD offerings. The persons responsible for devising, conducting, and monitoring HRD programs must be mindful of the changes that take place over time, and they must realize the causes that direct these changes.

EXERCISES

1. When viewing your educational organization or school district, analyze your current employees' demographics, skills, knowledges, and attitudes. This is the first step in identifying your Hu-

man Resource Development *needs*. A need is the gap between "what is" and "what should be" or "what could be". This baseline data analysis will provide you with a "what is" definition related to the employees' skills, knowledges, and attitudes that currently exist.

2. Develop a method of defining the "what should be" or "what could be" desired future state. This can be achieved by involving the various categories of employees in assisting you to identify the future desired states related to individual employees, specific sub-groups of employees and the total employee group. Once the "what should be" or "what could be" is identified, it leads to the development of HRD activities to meet the identified gaps between "what is" and "what should be" or "what could be". It also allows the development of guidelines for the hiring of new employees who possess the skills, knowledges and attitudes that have been identified as those that are desired.

3. Identify the specific internal variables that will affect your HRD plans, and devise strategies to accommodate these variables.

4. Identify the specific external variables that will affect your HRD plans, and devise strategies to accommodate these variables.

5. Develop an overall strategy for delivering the HRD programs required to meet the *needs* that have been identified. Develop action plans and tactics to implement your strategies.

SELECTED REFERENCES

1. Beer, M. et al., 1985. *Human Resource Management*. New York, NY: Macmillan, p. 1.
2. Beer, M. et al., *Human Resource Management*, p. 4, italics in original.
3. Rebore, R. W. 1982. *Personnel Administration in Education*. Second edition. Englewood Cliffs, NJ: Prentice-Hall, p. 251.
4. Rebore, R. W. *Personnel Administration*, p. 74.
5. Carnegie Forum on Education and the Economy. 1986. *Report on Teaching as a Profession*. New York, NY: Carnegie Forum on Education and the Economy, pp. 26–32.
6. Rebore, R. W. *Personnel Administration*, p. 103.
7. Rebore, R. W. *Personnel Administration*, p. 104.
8. Rebore, R. W. *Personnel Administration*, p. 103.
9. Abramson, L. 1988. "Boost to the Bottom Line", *Personnel Administrator*, 33(7):36–39.

10. Abramson, L. "Boost", p. 37.

11. Beer, et al., *Human Resource Management*, pp. 581–582.

12. Tanker, P. A. 1987. "Why Flexible Benefits Are So Appealing", *Management World*, 16(2):17–18.

13. Tanker, P. A., "Flexible Benefits", p. 17.

14. Stackel, L. 1987. "EAP's in the Work Place", *Employment Relations Today*, 14(3):289–291.

15. Appelbaum, S. H. and B. T. Shapiro. 1989. "The ABCs of EAPs", *Personnel*, 66(7):39–46.

16. Donaldson, L. and E. E. Scannell. 1978. *Human Resource Development*, Reading, MA: Addison-Wesley, pp. 3–8.

17. Laird, D. 1978. *Approaches to Training and Development*. Reading, MA: Addison Wesley, pp. 122–125.

18. Moore, J. R. 1988. "Guidelines Concerning Adult Learning", *Journal of Staff Development*, 8(3):2–5.

19. Carnegie Forum on Education and the Economy, *Report on Teaching as a Profession*, pp. 77–78.

20. Carnegie Forum on Education and the Economy. 1983. *A Nation at Risk.* New York, NY: Carnegie Forum on Education and the Economy.

21. Hoy, W. K. and C. G. Miskel. 1987. *Educational Administration.* Third edition. New York, NY: Random House, pp. 91–93.

22. Hoy, W. K. and C. G. Miskel, *Educational Administration*, p. 88.

23. Hoy, W. K. and C. G. Miskel, *Educational Administration*, p. 179.

24. Hersey, P. and K. Blanchard. 1982. *Management of Organizational Behavior.* Fourth edition. Englewood Cliffs, NJ: Prentice-Hall, pp. 35–36.

25. Hersey, P. and K. Blanchard, *Management*, pp. 36–37.

26. Hersey, P. and K. Blanchard, *Management*, pp. 37–38.

27. Hersey, P. and K. Blanchard, *Management*, pp. 48–55.

28. Hersey, P. and K. Blanchard, *Management*, pp. 56–58.

29. Matteson, M. T. and J. M. Ivancevich. 1977. *Controlling Work Stress.* Englewood Cliffs, NJ: Prentice Hall.

30. Hopper, L. 1988. "Unstressing Work: What Smart Organizations Do", *Public Management*, 70(11):2–4.

31. Sloan, R. P. and J. P. Gruman. 1988. "Does Wellness in the Workplace Work?" *Personnel Administrator*, 33(7):42–48.

CHAPTER 2

The Framework for Organizational Development

ORGANIZATIONAL DEVELOPMENT AS a historical concept has roots in the scientific management and organizational theories that began in the first three decades of the century, reflecting an increasing focus on the human functions of organizations. The self-analytic (T-group) experiences began in the 1950's, followed by emergent theories about human motivation—production vs. people—(McGregor, 1961; Likert, 1961; and Argyris, 1964). All were aimed at the functional improvement of organizations [1].

Organizational Development involves the maintenance and improvement of the total school district and all of its parts (individual schools and departments) by: (1) monitoring the current "health" [2] of the organization, (2) scanning the external and internal environments to determine trends and to project these trends into the future, (3) determining the future vision of the organization that is desired, (4) identifying the needs (gaps between "what is" and "what should be" or "what could be"), and (5) developing intervention strategies that will assist the educational leaders in achieving the "what should be" or "what could be" future organizational state desired. Organizational Development (OD) involves continuous planning, which is designed to achieve the entire system's ability for data collection, self-study and improvement of the entire educational organization or school district. This description relates to the concept of diagnosis, action, and maintenance, which are the basic components of Organizational Development [3]. All important decision makers have a role in Organizational Development activities. The decision makers certainly include the policy-making board of education; the superintendent of schools; the building principals; and the central office administrators, supervisors, employee representatives, consultants, and all categories of employees. Although normally not included in the list of responsible leaders, it is crucial to determine the role of employee union leaders and those employees who lead without a formal title (included in this group could be a master teacher, a beloved bus driver, a long term employee, and previous union officials or other untitled employees of influence).

Regardless of the person, persons or groups involved in OD responsibilities (officially or non-officially) there are certain activities that must be addressed when planning strategies to improve an unhealthy organization or when planning to maintain a healthy organization. These activities may vary depending on the stage of development of the school district (youthful through maturity), depending upon the external and internal variables that are impacting the organization and/or its sub-parts, and depending upon the stage of development and attitudes of individual employees and groups of employees.

An Organizational Development (OD) Model (see Figure 2.1) provides a schematic detail of the major activities and variables that have to be considered when dealing with the OD requirements of a school district and its sub-parts. The OD model will also identify the major external and internal intervening variables that impact the ultimate form taken by those responsible for the level of organizational "health" of the school district and its sub-parts.

Before elaborating on the various stages of the Organizational Development Model, it is important to stress that OD is a "macro" approach, designed to change the entire educational organization in the directions desired to better accommodate an envisioned future state. A macro design involves "the overall structure and outline, sequence of parts, and general forms through which activities flow" [4]. This, obviously, cannot be achieved without attention to the identified needs of the employees within the educational organization or school district. Attention to employee needs may be considered attending to "micro" development needs; the micro design of organizational development involves particular structural elements, such as events and activities that produce such events [5]. Attending to the total organization's needs may be considered attending to the "macro" development needs [6]. Macro and micro needs are highly inter-

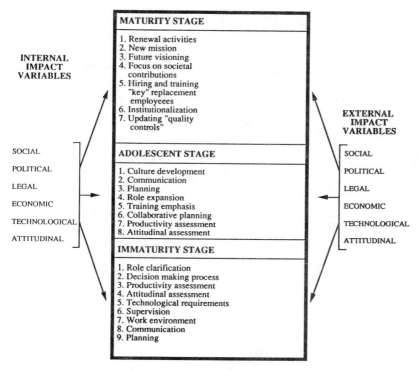

INTERNAL
IMPACT
VARIABLES

EXTERNAL
IMPACT
VARIABLES

MATURITY STAGE

1. Renewal activities
2. New mission
3. Future visioning
4. Focus on societal
   contributions
5. Hiring and training
   "key" replacement
   employeees
6. Institutionalization
7. Updating "quality
   controls"

ADOLESCENT STAGE

1. Culture development
2. Communication
3. Planning
4. Role expansion
5. Training emphasis
6. Collaborative planning
7. Productivity assessment
8. Attitudinal assessment

IMMATURITY STAGE

1. Role clarification
2. Decision making process
3. Productivity assessment
4. Attitudinal assessment
5. Technological requirements
6. Supervision
7. Work environment
8. Communication
9. Planning

SOCIAL

POLITICAL

LEGAL

ECONOMIC

TECHNOLOGICAL

ATTITUDINAL

SOCIAL

POLITICAL

LEGAL

ECONOMIC

TECHNOLOGICAL

ATTITUDINAL

Figure 2.1 An organizational development model.

related and overlapping. Both are needed to achieve the highest
levels of organizational performance and employee satisfaction.
Within the high-performing organization is a "deep commitment
to employees' personal well-being and growth" [6].

As employees change, the organization must attend to these
changes and modify its structures and processes to accommodate
the changes. On the other hand, as the total educational organization or school district changes because of legislation, community attitudes, union master contracts, technological advance-
ments, or a myriad of other impacting variables, the employees
may have to change in order to operationalize the process. Given
the traditional bureaucratic inertia of school systems, having a
process in place that is a vehicle for change works to overcome
the usual entrenched resistance. Organizations must be helped to
detect the need for change at early stages, rather than delaying

until the impacting external variables make it an overwhelming need [7]. A management team must be proactive with respect to environmental response. OD as a process has the hallmark of being both dynamic and constantly changing in structure [8]. Human Resource Development (HRD) programs must be developed to cause these required changes to take place in employee skills, knowledges, or attitudes.

Figure 2.2 demonstrates the interaction and overlap between HRD and OD activities.

Once it is clear to the decision makers of an educational or school district organization that HRD and OD are interactive, they can plan interventions which will improve both the total organization and the employees within the organization. Let's return now to a discussion of the various stages of the Organizational Development Model. The discussion will focus on the developmental stages in an organization's maturity. Albrecht has described the "passages" in an organization's life as determined by long-term growth [9]. Other dimensions, more applicable to a school district, are included.

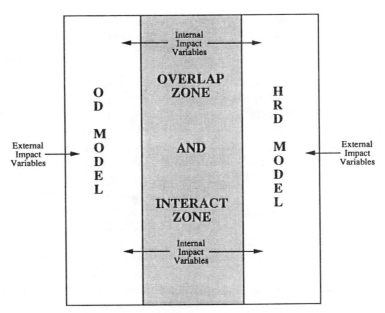

Figure 2.2 Interaction and overlap between OD and HRD.

IMMATURITY STAGE

This stage of Organizational Development (OD) is most crucial when dealing with a newly formed educational organization, or when dealing with one that has a significant number of new employees. It sometimes is also the stage that must be attended to when a new board of education, superintendent, principal or some other leadership person enters an existing organization with the sole purpose of being a change agent.

The Immaturity Stage involves a plan to develop the norms, culture, structures, and procedures of the total educational organization or school district by involving leaders, employees, and (perhaps) consultants in data collection, analysis, feedback, problem solving, action planning, and training activities. At this stage it is important to assess: (1) employee attitudes, (2) technological requirements, (3) the physical work environment, (4) communication requirements, and (5) supervisory requirements. In addition, it is important to determine the structures required to: (6) clarify roles, (7) determine productivity requirements, (8) make decisions in a timely and high-quality manner, and (9) conduct the operational and strategic planning necessary to maintain a productive and healthy organization. Let's take a closer look at each of Immaturity Stage's requirements at this point.

Role Clarification

Role clarification is absolutely necessary for any new organization or for one that is undergoing massive change. Role clarification deals with the question of who has various degrees of autonomy and decision-making authority and responsibility in a wide variety of decision-making situations. If roles are not clear, the organization will be unable to make effective decisions in a timely manner, and the productivity of the organization will be minimal. In all probability the climate and culture of the organization will be negative and can be described best as confusing and one of low employee morale.

A variety of OD interventions can address this problem. Some of the techniques that can be utilized are: (1) Conduct a functional analysis to determine which functions must be performed by the total organization, and then determine at which level(s) of the organization (board of education, superintendent of schools, central administration, building principal, classroom teacher, or other category of classified employee) is best able to perform the tasks within each function. Examples of functions are instruction, business, administration, and public relations; and numerous tasks exist within each function identified; (2) Develop policies that indicate the various responsibilities and authorities allocated to each employee group; and (3) Develop job descriptions that indicate the specific task responsibilities of each employee.

Completion of these three activities does not automatically assure that role clarification has taken place. It would be wise to periodically monitor the roles and activities to determine whether or not clarity of roles exists. Also, it is important to determine if there is negative overlap in roles, and if there is confusion about who has the authority to have the ultimate decision when two or more instructional units or two or more decision makers are involved in the same function and disagree on a decision. To delve deeper into this topic, let's move on to a discussion of the decision-making process.

Decision-making Processes

Decision-making processes must operate smoothly and in a manner that is effective, of high quality, and timely, and the decision must be completed within the resources allocated. To study whether or not the decision-making processes within the school district or educational organization are operating well, we have three very helpful techniques available to us. The first technique is a *time ladder*, the second is a *matrix analysis*, and the third is a *focus group discussion*.

The *time ladder* involves employees jotting down their activities by small time intervals over a period of numerous days. These *ladders* can then be analyzed to determine where the employee is spending time, and what tasks or functions are involved in her/his work day and work week. Ladders can also be used to determine whether or not employees are spending the correct percent of time on the high priority tasks, and whether or not they are performing tasks that overlap excessively or that might better be performed by other employees. An illustrative *time ladder format* is displayed next.

Time Ladder Format

Directions: Please jot down, according to the coding below, the activities or tasks you perform during each 15 minute segment of your work day. Fill in a separate sheet for each day of the next two weeks.

Name: _____   Day & Date: _____

_____

Activities or Tasks I performed

8:00–8:15 A.M. _____

8:16–8:30 _____

8:31–8:45 _____

8:46–9:00 _____

9:01–9:15 _____

9:16–9:30 _____

9:31–9:45 _____

9:46–10:00 _____

10:01–10:15 _____

10:16–10:30 _____

10:31–10:45 _____

10:45–10:46 _____

10:46–11:00 _____

Etc.

(continued)

Two Example Codes: IP = Incoming phone call
                              OM = Meeting called by other
                              OP = Outgoing phone call
                              MM = Meeting called by myself

Once the data from the *time ladders* have been analyzed, they can be used to determine the overall activities, the variance in days of the week, the variance in times of the year, and, more importantly, they can be used to determine whether or not employees are spending their time on tasks and activities related to high priority items that are consistent with their job descriptions. If they are not spending their time on high priority tasks and activities, appropriate changes must be made, and the job descriptions have to be changed to coincide with the changes made. Actually, job descriptions that are general in nature or that are not kept up-to-date are a waste of time and resources. *Living Job Descriptions* should be the rule, and they should be changed whenever there is a change in the tasks and activities assigned to the individual employee.

The analysis of *time ladders* is an important step in determining who has the authority and responsibility to make which decisions within the school district or educational organization. Job descriptions written and rewritten on the basis of data analysis from the *time ladders* will greatly assist in clarifying appropriate decision-making processes.

A second technique that will assist in clarifying appropriate decision-making processes is that of a *matrix analysis*. A matrix analysis is a technique that creates an array consisting of the names of various employees or employee groups on one axis and the major functions to be carried out on a second axis. The matrix can be further detailed by indicating whether the individual employee has: (1) final responsibility, (2) a major decision-making role, (3) a minor decision-making role, or (4) no role in the specific decision indicated. A limited example of a matrix analysis format is displayed here.

Example Matrix Analysis Format

Directions: Place an F with the person or group that you feel has final authority to make the decision, an M for major responsibility, an MI for minor responsibility, or an N for no responsibility.

Decision Area	Person (or Group)				
	Tchr.	Sup't.	Prin.	Bus. Man.	Bd. of Ed.
Student supervision	F	MI	M	N	N
Employee supervision	N	MI	M	MI	N
Budget development	MI	F	M	M	F
Budget control	MI	M	M	F	M
Instruction of students	F	MI	M	N	N
Purchasing	MI	M	M	F	M
Policy development	MI	M	MI	MI	F
Etc.					

Although this example matrix is very limited in scope, it is possible to see where there is overlap in decision making. Identifying the overlaps makes it possible to clarify the ways in which decisions are made in the school district or educational organization, and it allows corrections to be made in decision-making processes if they are not functioning well. Finally, it should be noted that groups, such as employee unions, student councils, citizen advisory groups, non-certified employee organizations, and individuals would be included in a comprehensive *matrix decision-making analysis*. Again, once this analysis is completed, it may be necessary to go back and modify certain employee job descriptions.

With the data from *time ladders* and comprehensive *matrix analyses* in hand, as well as *Living Job Descriptions*, the technique of *focus groups* can be utilized. This technique involves calling together job-alike employee groups or vertical decision teams to discuss specific topics of importance. These focus groups can be presented with the data that has been arrayed, and they can discuss ways of solving, clarifying or improving decision-making processes. They will deal with the decision-making process from the standpoint of decisions being made within their respective job-alike groups, and they will also deal with decisions that their particular group has in conjunction with other groups within the matrix organization of the school district or educational organization.

Vertical decision teams will include such members as teachers, principals, central office administrators and the superintendent (or some other multiple-level appropriate mix of employees) who will focus on discussions of means of making improved decisions between and among various sub-groups within the organization, or they may discuss appropriate means of improving the total decision-making processes of the school district or educational organization and its sub-parts as a whole. The representational nature of the team facilitates districtwide communication and implies cross-strengths and multi-level endorsement of decisions made. These teams are discussed more in detail in Chapter 7 [10].

Communication and Planning Ability

Once we have clarified the roles and determined efficient decision-making processes, we need to address the communication and planning ability of the organization. In the area of planning, the vision and mission of the school district must be clear, and the employees and clients must buy into the vision and mission. A deep sense of mission both sets a direction for all activities and creates a shared sense of identity for individuals within the organization, and this clear sense can enable people to identify with an organization's culture. "Visioning encourages the buy-in process" [11]. Once there is a *buy-in* that leads eventually to the development of culture within a new organization, decisions related to the vision and mission can be developed. Communication during the initial stages of an organization are crucial, particularly in a consistent vertical flow in both directions [12]. They should involve *top-down* and *bottom-up* procedures, and they should be *open* and encourage feedback.

An *MIS (Management Information System)* should be developed to provide appropriate information and feedback opportunity at all employee levels and also to the clients served by the school district or educational organization. The *MIS* should concentrate on those items considered crucial to achievement of the mission of the school district, school building, or other sub-parts of the educational organization.

Once the vision and mission have been determined, roles have been clarified (including supervisory roles) and the decision-making processes have been determined, the organization's decision makers have to determine the technological requirements of the district, and they must find ways to purchase the appropriate technology and to provide training and staff development activities for those who will be using the technology. Since the introduction of technology forces readjustments in the organization, the changes in the relationships that result from individual to individual must be considered [13]. Having accomplished all of this, the working environment has largely been defined, and the culture of the new organization is beginning to take hold.

The Level of Organizational Health

The next OD challenge becomes one of measuring the *level of organizational health* of the school district or educational organization. Although addressed here for a newly formed organization (consolidation of existing school districts, internal restructuring of a school district, annexation, de-annexation, closing schools, opening schools or some other format that causes a new organization to be created or evolve), it is crucial that the school district's decision makers monitor the *level of organizational health* whether the educational organization is in its: (1) Immaturity Stage, (2) Adolescent Stage or (3) Maturity Stage.

Measuring the health of an organization involves collecting information on two very important matters. For an organization to be the best it can be, it must display excellent productivity and it must possess a positive attitude demonstrated by its employees and its clients. Productivity assessment relates to how well the tasks and functions of the organization are conducted as related to: (1) desired outcomes, (2) the resources allocated, and (3) the time allotted for the task or function to be completed. It is crucial that not only are quantitative measures collected, but it is important to collect qualitative data in order to assess the productivity element of a school district or educational organization.

Existence of a positive climate and a positive culture are also crucial if a healthy school district or educational organization is to exist. Mostly, this element can be assessed by direct observation and by attitudinal surveys. At the student level, the classroom and school building climate should display evidence of such matters as: (1) a safe and healthy environment, (2) students display a feeling of trust and caring towards others, (3) teachers and administrators really believe that all students can learn, and they expect high levels of achievement, (4) achievement levels are carefully monitored and are used to adjust instructional materials or instructional delivery methods, (5) the focus within the classroom and the building is clearly on students' instructional and behavioral quality achievements, and (6) students are provided open opportunities for input and feedback. This is an example of the vision and sense of purpose that is operationalized by the alignment of the organization; "the condition wherein people operate as part of an integrated whole because they see that the purpose of the organization is an extension of their individual purposes" [14]. A grasp of this social implication of change is essential if managers are to succeed in implementing the vision that may require change [15].

At the parental, guardian and external client level, the organizational health can be assessed by collecting information that indicates: (1) an aligned agreement and belief in the vision, mission and procedures of the school district, school building and individual classrooms, (2) a belief that quality education is being offered by the school district and its component parts, (3) a trust that students are cared for, welcomed, and given the assistance they need to learn well, and (4) a belief that the adult employees who are entrusted with the teaching and care of the children are very competent and caring individuals. When there is a high consensus of belief that these things exist at the school district, school building and classroom levels, high organizational health marks are assured.

At the employee level, an organization that is determined to have a high degree of organizational health will display the following characteristics: (1) roles and functions are clear, (2) information is accurate and complete, and it flows both from top-down and bottom-up directions, (3) there is ample opportunity for input and feedback, (4) supervision is positive, efficient and helpful, (5) employees are valued and their contributions are officially recognized, (6) they have meaningful work, (7) entrepreneurship is fostered and rewarded, (8) decision making is accurate and rapid and the methods of decision making are clear, (9) the work environment is safe and healthy, and (10) there are many opportunities for individual development and self actualization. These characteristics reflect the alignment described previously and the existence of organizational structure appropriate to the district vision [16]. If the employees exhibit these characteristics and attitudes, coupled with positive marks from the student and client levels, the district and all of its components are winners.

Once the organizational health has been determined to be of very high quality, the task remains of maintaining that high level through the adolescent and maturity stages of the school district or educational organization. As indicated in Figure 2.1, there are internal and external impact variables that must be monitored and addressed and for which planners must scan and adjust in order to maintain the high quality of organizational health. The *internal impact variables* include: (1) social, (2) political, (3) legal, (4) economic, (5) technological, and (6) attitudinal variables. The *external impact variables* also include those that are: (1) social, (2) political, (3) legal, (4) economic, (5) technological, and (6) attitudinal. At this juncture, suffice it to say that any of these variables can affect the level of organizational health of a school district and its component parts. These variables will be discussed in greater detail in Chapters 3 and 4.

Now that the *Immaturity Stage* of the school district or educational organization has been discussed, it is time to turn to the activities and tasks to be addressed during the *Adolescent Stage*. There will be some identical activities to be addressed at both stages, there will be a difference in degree or emphasis in some activities between both stages, and there will be some new areas to be addressed at the *Adolescent Stage* that were not addressed at the *Immaturity Stage* of the school district's or organization's development.

ADOLESCENT STAGE

The *Adolescent Stage* builds upon the activities begun during the school district's organizational stage, but it makes adjustments because of information on outputs monitored during the *Immaturity Stage*. It also adjusts its activities and the data it monitors as the internal and external variables related to social, political, legal, economic, technological and attitudinal factors impact the school district or its sub-parts (schools and departments). Besides attending to all the matters indicated during the *Immaturity Stage* (see Figure 2.1), it adds the areas of (1) culture development, (2) role expansion, (3) training emphasis, and (4) collaborative planning.

As is true during the *Immaturity Stage*, operational and strategic planning will continue, there will have to be adjustments due to technological requirements, and productivity and attitudinal assessments will continue. Also, the internal and external variables have to be closely monitored. These matters will not be discussed here, as they were discussed during the *Immaturity Stage*. However, a brief discussion of an *MIS* (Management Information System) is needed to elaborate upon the types of data that have to be monitored, analyzed, and communicated to the employees and clients of the school district and its sub-units.

During the *Adolescent Stage* of OD (see Figure 2.1), the *Management Information System* will become more comprehensive and will allow targeted and immediate communications, which are differentiated by the various school districts' elements and clients. It will also become an interactive two-way system of information gathering from employees, sub-systems within the school district, and from its external and internal clients; and it will include an information sharing structure geared to the district's sub-units and to its external and internal clients.

The types of information that should be collected, monitored, and analyzed within a comprehensive school district's *MIS* include information about all categories of employees, information about its students, information about internal and external variables, information about and from its clients, and information that tracks the school district's progress towards its vision and mission. Information about employees should include such matters as education, interests, skills, performance, training or staff development needs, and attitudes towards their jobs and towards the *HRD* (Human Resource Development) and *OD* (Organizational Development) programs and activities of the school district and its sub-parts.

Student-related information should include achievement measures, behavioral incidents, and measures of classroom and school building climate as perceived by the students. Client-related information should include the routine collection of compliments and complaints, suggestions from advisory groups and important "key" decision makers within the school district; and the school district and its sub-parts should systematically collect attitudinal data from its external and internal clients. Finally, it is crucial that the internal and external demographic, social, political, legal, economic, technological, and attitudinal variables be monitored and analyzed for impact on the school district and its sub-parts and that the procedures of the district are modified, when necessary, to adjust to the impact of these variables. Let's provide a demographic example: if the composition of the student body of the district is rapidly moving from an almost totally white student body to one that has a high percentage of Asian, Black and Hispanic minorities, the employees should be provided with training and staff development that will assist them in understanding the various cultures and in making the adjustments they would be wise to make in order to allow themselves to more effectively deal with this culturally-mixed student body.

Now that we have elaborated upon the requirement for an expanded *MIS* during the *Adolescent Stage* of school district development, let's investigate the areas which were not discussed during the *Immaturity Stage* discussion. The areas of (1) culture development, (2) role expansion, (3) training emphasis, and (4) collaborative planning become very important during the *Adolescent Stage*.

Culture Development

The development of a positive *organizational culture* is crucial to the organizational health of any school district or any type of organization. Organizational culture is comprised of the district's or organization's heroes (those individuals who have developed reputations for unusual behavior that is to be emulated), the values that are inculcated within the operating structure of the employees, those that the critical mass (if not the total) of employees subscribe to as appropriate and desired, and those policies and standard operating procedures that become the day-to-day guidelines for the operation of the school district and its sub-parts (schools and departments). Two examples will illustrate the type of positive organizational culture towards which any school district and its sub-parts should subscribe.

At the employee level, the two examples suggest the importance of positive *heroes* to the development of a school district's organizational culture. Miss Donohue, our first heroine, is always conducting simple classroom action research to determine which ways are the most effective means of helping her students to learn and achieve at high levels. Currently, she is developing, with the assistance of the district's computer specialist, student drill materials for the computer to provide distributed practice for the students, instead of taking class time to provide multiple practices. She is also checking on the effectiveness of the *Coopera-*

tive Learning innovation (where students of differing abilities are combined into study groups), versus an individualized student instructional delivery system [17]. Principal Sarah Smithsonian also has become one of the district's heroes, as she convinced one of the corporations in the school district to provide her school with consultants, lecturers, mentors for students, and school equipment. The corporate officers actually attend student presentations, and they assist Ms. Smithsonian and her staff with operational and strategic planning.

The *values* that exist within the school district and to which the employees subscribe are also very important in determining the organizational health of the school district and its sub-parts. A few values that would assist a school district in attaining a very positive organizational health quotient could include: (1) every employee wishes to continually improve, (2) employees are committed to assisting one another and the school district organization, (3) employees feel free to offer suggestions to improve the operation of the school district and its sub-parts, and they know that their contributions are appreciated and will be recognized by their peers and by the school district's administrators, and (4) supervisors are seen as *helpers*, and realize that one of the prime functions of supervision is to locate resources to assist others to better perform their assigned responsibilities.

Policies and SOP's (Standard Operating Procedures) are also important factors in establishing a positive school district organizational culture. Employee related policies that clearly state that employee welfare is important (salary and fringe benefits), that employee growth opportunities are important (sabbatical leaves, staff development, and district-paid training opportunities), that employee supervision is geared to a helping relationship, and that employee input is desired. Employee/administrator planning committees and site-based management structures are all very important contributors towards a high quality of organizational health and organizational development. Standard Operating Procedures that are evidenced in vertical planning teams (consisting of all employee and managerial/administrator levels), that are evidenced in a large degree of site-based and classroom-based decision making, and that are evidenced by employee involvement in personnel, instructional, and budgetary decisions are also significant indicators of a strong positive organizational culture.

Role Expansion

The development of a strong organizational culture many times requires an expansion of the roles played by various categories of employees during the *Immaturity Stage*. *Role expansion* may include the involvement of teachers and classified employees in more detailed planning and decision making related to their specific tasks, their school buildings' operation, and the operation of the entire school district. Role expansion may also include a formalization of *collaborative planning* structures within the matrix organization of the school district. That is, since the school district has many overlapping elements, it is probably unwise to operate as if it were a hierarchical organization, where all decisions are made from the top down.

Collaborative Planning

Collaborative planning structures that could be included as standard operating procedures within a school district and its sub-parts might well include: (1) *Vertical Teams*, where employees from various levels of the district's decision-making structure work together to communicate, solve problems, or plan [18] or (2) *Quality Circles*, where job-alike employees groups, or representatives of job-alike groups, identify problems or program needs, prioritize them, and then plan action programs to solve the problems or achieve the programs desired. Ultimately, they present their recommendations to the appropriate decision maker for approval.

Training Emphasis

As a school district moves into a more comprehensive and sophisticated operation during the *Adolescent Stage*, the need for continuous training and staff development increases in importance. A *training emphasis* should be an organizational focus and commitment. For only as employees improve their knowledge and skills with the greater complexity that takes place during the adolescent development of the school district and its sub-parts, can the quality of performance improve. The school district that intends to maintain a high quality of organizational health must have a planned structure for continuous training and staff development for its employees, and the school district must also provide the financial and human resources required to continuously carry on this important function.

MATURITY STAGE

Since we have discussed the important foci of attention during the *Immaturity and Adolescent Stages of OD (Organizational Development)*, we can now turn to those items that demand attention during the *Maturity Stage* of a school district's and its sub-parts' development. Since it has already been stressed that the school district must collect data, monitor, determine the impact, and make adjustments related to the internal and external impact variables, and since many important foci have already been discussed during the previous two stages of school district development, these matters will not be reviewed (see Figure 2.1). However, there are added foci during the *Maturity Stage*. The areas requiring detailed attention during this stage are: (1) renewal activities, (2) development of new mission(s), (3) future visioning, (4) focus on societal contributions, (5) hiring and training "key" replacement employees, (6) institutional of organizational culture, and (7) updating quality controls. Each of these areas will now be discussed.

Renewal Activities

Renewal activities must take place as an organization and the employees within an organization either progress or regress; they cannot remain in a state of status quo as a school district operates as an *open system*—one that is continually in a state of interaction with its environment and one that is always impacted by change [19]. Employees, even those who are long-term, must renew themselves as technological, social, professional, attitudinal, and other changes impact them. The school district and its sub-parts must also renew themselves by updating their structures, strategies, and tactics to maintain a high level of organizational health as their environment and performance requirements are modified over time.

Development of New Missions

New missions may have to be developed as the missions of the school district and its sub-parts that were developed during its *Immaturity and Adolescent Stages* become outdated or require modification in order to be in tune with changes in the environment. Such matters as increased mandates from state legislative bodies or state departments of education, major shifts in the demographic patterns of the communities served by the school district, calls for accountability, changed relationships with an employee union or other employee groups, or changes in the type of student body or the home structure within which the students live may cause the school district and its constituent parts to develop new missions. The district's *future vision* will also have to be modified. School district decision makers who develop a vision and mission and who do not realize that as matters change, the vision and mission may have to also be modified, miss a very crucial decision-making requirement. Adjustments to mission and vision have to take place as the environment within which the school district and its sub-parts operate requires adjustment by the school district and its sub-parts.

As a school district achieves its *Maturity Stage*, it should also be able to focus on its role in the broader societal context, as a school district is not an island within itself; it is only one player in the societal life of a community. During the *Immaturity Stage*, the school district and its sub-parts must, of necessity, attend to establishing its internal (micro) structures that will allow it to operate on a day-to-day basis. During the *Adolescent Stage*, the school district's employees and key decision makers concentrate on developing a smooth and productive operating structure that combines the efforts of all the employees, the sub-units, and the central structure into a positive holistic system. Attention during this stage is on the total district organization's (macro) structure.

During the school district's *Maturity Stage*, while attending to the micro and macro requirements of the school district, its decision makers should be able to attend to the societal (mega) needs for which the district can take some responsibility. Examples of a school district's areas of mega possibilities include: (1) cooperating with health agencies to offer wellness activities for the citizens of the community, (2) joining with business, industry and civic groups to assist in the economic development of the area, (3) joining with recreation departments in offering use of the school district's building and sites for after school and vacation time community recreation opportunities, (4) opening the school district's running tracks, pools and other facilities to the citizens when they are not in use by the day time students, (5) offering community education programs in conjunction with universities, colleges or other educational organizations in the community, (6) teaching students about community service by requiring every senior high student to earn one hour of course credit by performing a community service for a few hours each week for one semester, (7) working with business and industrial groups to develop a retraining and job placement service for their employees, or (8) any other activity that puts the district in the mainstream of societal program requirements.

Hiring and Retraining

Another crucial activity during the *Maturity Stage* of a school district's development is that of hiring and training "key" replacement employees. Any school district's, or, for that matter, any organization's, quality depends totally on the quality of its employees. Those "key" employees who were hired and/or trained during the *Immaturity and Adolescent Stages* of the school district's development will probably retire or leave for larger challenges during the school district's *Maturity Stage*. It is crucial that the school district's *HRD* (Human Resource Development) decision makers maintain an employee profile matrix that includes the skills required to perform "key" functions. These decision makers also must prognosticate the possibilities of losing "key" employees due to job changes or retirements, and they must set up a structure that will train replacement personnel and/or permit the hiring of new employees with the knowledge and skill to step in and take over the responsibilities of these "key" employees. If these provisions are not made, the effectiveness and efficiency—thus, the organizational health—of the school district and its sub-parts will rapidly deteriorate during its *Maturity Stage*.

Institutionalization of Organizational Culture

Earlier in its organizational life, a climate and culture developed within the school district. If the culture (its heroes, values, policies, and standard operating procedures) is of high quality and if the components promote the high quality of culture that makes the school district and its constituent parts a very healthy organization, attention must be paid to institutionalizing that culture as replacement employees come aboard at all levels of the school district. Such values or beliefs as: (1) everyone can improve, (2) clients should be treated courteously, (3) employees should assist one another and the school district, (4) students are the "raison d' etre", and they should be cared for, challenged and respected, (5) employees should feel that *all students can learn,* (6) student learning is the prime focus, and (7) improvement of student achievement, employee performance and school district results are a commitment of all employees, are the guiding cultural foundations of a healthy school district.

Updating Quality Controls

Finally, a healthy school district organization will update its quality controls during its *Maturity Stage* of development. Such techniques as adding mastery criteria to student performance that can be measured by CRT's (Criterion Referenced Tests) to those norm referenced tests already utilized to measure the quality of student achievement are valuable. Employee quality control updates might well include developing job descriptions and employee assessment systems that spell out the criteria and the descriptors or indicators within which to measure the performance compared to a predetermined standard for each criterion. This should be done for each employee, and concentration should be placed upon those tasks that are considered *critical* to quality performance.

At the building and district levels, specific strategic objectives should be developed, and data should be collected and analyzed to determine the degree to which the objectives are achieved. Of course, the objectives decided upon should be directly related to the mission and vision established for the district and its subparts. Examples of specific objectives can be illustrated by the following:

- Within the next five years (by June 30, 19–), the student graduation rate will increase from its current 56 percent to 93 percent.
- By June 30, 19–, the number of fifth grade students who

are reading at or above grade level, as measured by scores on the XYZ Reading Test, will increase by 7 percent over the current level of 72 percent. Within five years, 98 percent of the fifth grade students will be reading at or above grade level.

- By June 30, 19–, every teacher will utilize technology in the classroom as an aid to her/his teaching and as a reinforcement of student learning (this to be verified by direct observation).

Quality control is the key to keeping an excellent school district, excellent school building, excellent instructional departments and excellent employees on a winning and highly productive track. The Maturity Stage is substantially different from the Immaturity and Adolescent Stages of a school district's development. It is different in that it is a continuing stage, and therefore it must undergo continuous OD surveillance. Maintenance and change structures must be devised as part of the day-to-day data collection, monitoring, analysis, and decision-making structures of a school district and its sub-parts if the pupils, employees, and the district organization are to continue to be all they can be. The school district's decision makers must develop intervention strategies that will maintain and, when possible, improve the school district's health quotient [20]. Altogether, like the client (district)–consultant relationship described by White and Wooten regarding OD change agentry [21], the Maturity Stage is characterized by task clarity and specificity, and by role clarity and flexibility.

SUMMARY

Three stages of *OD* (Organizational Development) were discussed. These stages parallel the developmental stages of a person, in that an organization evolves through an (1) Immaturity Stage to an (2) Adolescent Stage to a (3) Maturity Stage. Each stage has a specific list of focal activities or responsibilities to which decision makers must attend if the district is to become and remain a healthy organization (see Figure 2.1 for details).

The responsibility of the school district's decision makers to devise intervention strategies and implementation tactics to cause these foci to be successfully addressed was emphasized.

Specific example strategies, tactics, and action programs were presented. Attention to internal and external impacting variables was stressed, and the need for a comprehensive data gathering, monitoring, analysis, and collaborative decision-making structure was considered essential.

GUIDELINES

1. In considering the stages of organizational development, it is important to stress the "macro" approach and the attention necessarily given to "micro needs".
2. HRD programs and activities are intended to carry out changes required by OD; the two dynamically overlap and interact.
3. During the Immaturity Stage, vision and mission identification, role clarification, the determination of efficient decision-making processes, and the measuring of organizational health are critical steps.
4. During the Adolescent Stage, the Management Information System must become refined to gather information from all district levels in order to monitor impacting variables. This stage also involves the development of a positive organizational culture, which should include the identification of heroes, values, policies and standard operating procedures, and the development of role expansion.
5. During the Maturity Stage renewal activities must take place and any required new missions be developed; there must be a focus on the district's broader societal role and mega needs. The HRD function must consider the "key" employee skills and carefully attend to the personnel profile of employee retention and retirement. Additionally, the institutionalization of the developed climate and culture and the updating of quality controls are required during this stage.

EXERCISES

1. Given the indicators for each stage of organizational maturity, determine which stage best describes your district's present level.
2. If your district is at the Immaturity Stage, conduct a functional

matrix analysis to begin the process of Role Clarification, and to begin the monitoring of roles and activities by requesting several key staff members to perform a time ladder record.

3. Create a vertical decision team as an initial focus group effort, (including sufficient key players representing each level), which will become a model for other focus groups.

4. If your district is at the Adolescent Stage, employ a vertical team or Quality Circle format to address a particular district problem in order to formalize the beginning of the standard collaborative planning structure.

5. If your district is at the Maturity Stage, employ a collaborative planning structure such as a vertical team or Quality Circle to consider the current mega needs of the organization.

SELECTED REFERENCES

1. Schmuck, R. A. and M. B. Miles, eds. 1971. *Organization Development in Schools.* Palo Alto, CA: National Press Books, pp. 4–5.

2. Schmuck, R. A. and M. B. Miles. *Organization Development*, pp. 1–2.

3. French, W. L. and C. H. Bell, Jr. 1973. *Organization Development.* Englewood Cliffs, NJ: Prentice-Hall, p. 33.

4. Schmuck, R. A. et al. 1977. *The Second Handbook of Organization Development in Schools.* Palo Alto, CA: Mayfield Publishing Company, p. 370.

5. Schmuck, R. A. et al. *Second Handbook*, p. 419.

6. Kiefer, C. and P. Stroh. 1983. "A New Paradigm for Organizational Development", *Training and Development Journal*, 37(4): 2735.

7. Hampton, D. R., C. E. Summer, and R. A. Webber. 1987. *Organizational Behavior and the Practice of Management.* Glenview, IL: Scott, Foresman and Company, p. 87.

8. French, W. A. and C. H. Bell, Jr. 1973. *Organization Development*, pp. 45–46.

9. Albrecht, K. 1983. *Organization Development.* Englewood Cliffs, NJ: Prentice-Hall, p. 9.

10. Metz, E. J. "The Verteam Circle", *Training and Development Journal*, 35(12): 79–85. (1981).

11. Kiefer, C. and P. Stroh, "A New Paradigm", p. 32.

12. Hampton, D. R., C. E. Summer, and R. A. Webber. *Organizational Behavior*, p. 500.

13. Hampton, D. R., C. E. Summer, and R. A. Webber. *Organizational Behavior*, pp. 494–495.

14. Kiefer, C. and P. Stroh. "A New Paradigm", p. 32.

15. Hampton, D. R., C. E. Summer, and R. A. Webber. *Organizational Behavior*, pp. 494–495.

16. Kiefer, C. and P. Stroh. "A New Paradigm", pp. 32–33.

17. Joyce, B., B. Showers, and C. Rolheiser-Bennet. 1987. "Staff Development and Student Learning: A Synthesis of Research on Models of Teaching", *Educational Leadership*, 45(2): 11–23.

18. Metz, E. J. 'The Verteam Circle", pp. 82–83.

19. Hoy, W. K. and C. G. Miskel. 1987. *Educational Administration*. Third edition. New York, NY: Random House, pp. 20–21.

20. Schmuck, R. A. and P. J. Runkel. 19888. *The Handbook of Organization Development in Schools*. Third edition. Prospect Heights, IL: Waveland Press, Inc., pp. 10–11.

21. White, L. P. and K. C. Wooten, 1986. *Professional Ethics and Practice in Organizational Development*. New York, NY: Praeger Publishers, pp. 100–105.

CHAPTER 3

Determining the Human Resource Needs and the Organizational Development Needs

IN ORDER THAT a school district and its constituent parts (school buildings and departments) remain as a healthy, first-class school district, the leaders of the school district must participate in strategic and operational planning on a continuous basis. *Strategic planning* can be defined as *long term planning* which contains a *vision* of "what should be". *Operational planning* can be defined as *short term planning* of an action nature which is designed to operate the district at an optimum level of performance for the present and for the next year [1].

Figure 3.1 demonstrates both of these types of planning as part of a systems model. This chapter will discuss strategic planning, and Chapter 4 will be devoted to the planning structures of operational planning. If the district is to remain healthy, both types of planning for HRD (Human Resource Development) and OD (Organizational Development) must be integrated into a systematic and holistic approach to improvement and maintenance of the school district and its constituent parts; and this healthy state can only be maintained if great attention is placed upon the human resources that make the school district function at an optimum level of performance.

Let's explore in depth the various elements that comprise a systematic and holistic approach to strategic planning for HRD (Human Resource Development) and OD (Organizational Development). The components include: (1) macro (OD) and micro (HRD) foci, (2) a beliefs system, (3) an external scanning mechanism, (4) an internal scanning mechanism, (5) identification of the CSF's (Critical Success Factors), (6) creation of a vision, (7) identification of a mission, (8) a SWOT (strengths, weaknesses, opportunities and threats) analysis, (9) identification of strategic goals, (10) identification of objectives for each

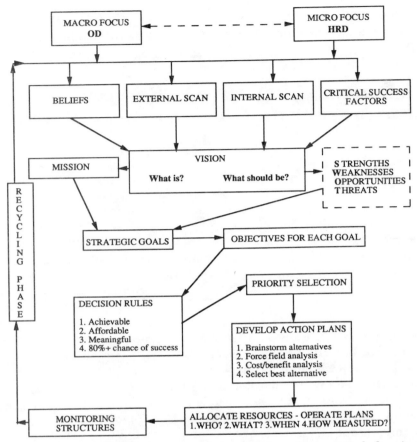

Figure 3.1 A systems holistic approach to strategic and operational planning for HRD and OD.

goal, and (11) decision rules to assist in selecting priorities [2]. Chapter 4 will explore the matters of: (1) developing action plans by brainstorming, force field analysis, cost benefit analysis and selection of the best alternative, (2) allocating resources, (3) operating the action plans, (4) developing monitoring structures, and (5) recycling the entire systems approach.

MACRO (OD) AND MICRO (HRD) FOCI

A school district that focuses on the entire operation is utilizing a *macro* focus as its approach to improvement. This macro focus, when applied to OD (Organization Development), has the decision makers planning a sustained effort at total school district self-study and improvement, one that also empowers the organization with the capacity to maintain problem-solving abilities [3]. This is done by focusing on changes in norms, culture, structures, and processes, using intervention strategies to improve the organization and, subsequently, its sub-parts (buildings and departments) [4]. OD involves the school district's employees themselves in active assessment, diagnosis, and strategic planning efforts that transform the school district into one approaching the desired "what should be" state. Sometimes an outside OD consultant is also hired to work with the school district's employees as they go about the functions of assessment, diagnosis, and strategic planning for the desired changes.

A school district that primarily focuses on the individual employee or the sub-groups within the school district, rather than the school district as a whole, is utilizing a micro focus strategy. Microdesigning refers to the particular elements and events within the structure, and the activities that make up such events. "Although all those activities are interrelated, microdesigning is more concerned with the *logistical, substantive*, and *methodological* details of the consultation" [5]. When the thrust of this micro focus is improvement of the employees of the school district, the district's decision makers are clearly operating on an HRD (Human Resource Development) wavelength. That is, the assessment, diagnosis and strategic planning to achieve the "what should be" state is clearly geared to the betterment of individual employees and to the collective group of employees [6]. This micro focus on HRD also involves the employees in the assessment, diagnosis, and strategic planning functions. The employees may well participate in training and staff development activities, problem solving, or any activities that improve the individual or the employee group, and that also improve the environment within which they work.

The desired approach to school district improvement and to improvement of the employees of the school district is to combine the macro and micro foci, as well as to combine the OD and HRD foci, in a systematic and holistic manner that recognizes that the parts make up the whole, and that the whole is only as good as the sum of its parts [7]. In other words, to have a first-class school district, one must have first-class employees who are concerned about the quality of their individual and collective performance, and who are also concerned about the quality of the school district as a whole. This integrated approach, which combines both the macro and micro foci and the OD and HRD foci, is the basic underlying theme of this entire volume. It is the preferred approach to school improvement.

Once we have decided upon a combined and integrated approach to OD and HRD, we can develop a belief system upon which to build our later activities. Beliefs that assist in this process can be simply outlined by reviewing the beliefs agreed to by the decision makers in the Hypothetical School District.

Hypothetical School District's OD and HRD Beliefs

- We believe that the school district's outputs and outcomes will only improve by improving the quality of performance of the employees of the school district.
- We believe that technological, legal, political, demographic and attitudinal variables, external to the district and internal to the district, must be closely monitored; and sometimes these variables will necessitate changes in the structures, programs, and processes of the school district.
- We believe all employees of the district must join in the belief that *all students can learn*, as this should be the foundational bedrock upon which all of the school district's activities should focus.
- We believe that all employees wish to improve themselves, wish to help improve other employees, and wish to improve all aspects of the total school district.
- We believe that all employees desire to be involved in this improvement process, and that they can greatly assist in the assessment, diagnosis and strategic planning activities that are necessary to cause the school district and its constituent parts to achieve its "what should be" future state.
- We believe that by isolating clearly defined needs (gaps between "what is" and "what should be" or "what could be"), OD interventions can be devised and HRD activities can be initiated which will assist the school district, its constituent parts (schools and departments), and the employees to achieve their "what should be" future states.

- We believe that all employees have to buy into the future visions and the missions of the school district; and that these visions and missions are such that they meet, or are not in conflict with, the missions of the individual employees.
- We believe that the district must have clear strategic goals and objectives that are measurable, and that these goals and objectives are subscribed to by the employees and the other stakeholders of the district.
- We believe that the success level of the district's improvement strategy can and will be measured by the ability to achieve the results as outlined in the specific goals and objectives subscribed to by the district's decision makers (employees and other stakeholders).
- We believe that employees will voluntarily and actively involve themselves in training, staff development, assessment, diagnosis, and planning activities that are designed to improve the total district, and that are designed to improve the employees as well. Thus, both the OD (Organizational Development) and the HRD (Human Resource Development) functions are unified for the betterment of both the employees and the entire school district.

Now that we have reviewed the stated beliefs of Hypothetical School District, let's turn to some of the external and/or internal political, instructional, legal, demographic, economic, social, technological, and attitudinal variables that might have an impact on the OD and HRD activities of the district [8]. Although these variables have been consistently monitored, the trends that have been identified over time and the potential impact on the school district and its employees are the focus of the future planning activities that will take place within Hypothetical School District.

Hypothetical School District's Potential Internal and External Impact Variables

Instructional scanning indicates that there is a definite national trend towards developing an early identification system and specifically designed instructional delivery systems for "students-at-risk". Internally, there is a trend towards developing a "whole language" delivery system rather than dealing with the teaching of reading, English, spelling, listening and writing as separate subject areas. Also, there is a trend developing in the school district for teachers to use "cooperative learning groups" (assigning students of varying abilities to study in work groups) as a learning delivery methodology [9]. The impact of these matters on the district's instructional activities is clear—much staff development must take place, and budget allocations must be made to cover employee training and equipment and supplies required to facilitate the district-wide introduction of these programs. In addition, a monitoring system must be put in place to assess the results of these new approaches on student learning and on teachers' abilities to improve their performances. This can be considered part of the recommended self-renewal process, enabling a district to adapt to such current changes in its environment "while still maintaining an effective educational program" [10].

Attitudinal scanning indicates that there is a generally favorable attitude in the community about the students, employees, and programs of the school district. A bi-annual survey is put in place, and specific suggestions about what is desired by the community are tracked and become part of the action planning of the school district. Internally, scanning indicates a trend of the high school students feeling that they have little or no input into decisions that directly relate to their education. Because of this trend, the school district planners have initiated a joint student/faculty planning committee to devise methods of allowing students meaningful input activities into areas that directly involve their education. Finally, there is an increasing trend demonstrated by employees involving their belief that continuing training and/or staff development activities are necessary; and also a feeling that they have no say in the allocation of resources for employee training and/or staff development activities. The district's decision makers are considering a procedure whereby all long term training and/or staff development activities, and the resources necessary to implement them, will be determined by a staff development committee comprised mostly of district employees [11].

Technological scanning indicates a clearcut trend towards requiring the introduction of very expensive technology into the school district's instructional and managerial operations. Such technology as interactive video, robotics, and advanced computer technologies provide a planning challenge in terms of instruction, management, employee training, and financial resources. All of these will have a long term impact on the school district and the humans who are served or who interact with the school district, and very careful and detailed strategic plans have to be developed to successfully meet the needs identified by these trending data [12].

Social trends clearly indicate a diminution of the traditional family structure in favor of a variety of home environments for the students of the district. Single parent families, groups of relatives in a single home environment, home environments where parents have not followed the tradition of a formal marriage, homosexual family situations where children are being reared—this increasing variety of home environments indicates a need for innovative long term adjustments by the school district's decision makers [13].

Economic trends indicate a lessening of the percent of financial support by the federal and state governmental units, with the resulting requirement of increasing local taxes to maintain the quality of the school district's offerings. Locally, the percentage of land utilization in the school district indicates a higher percentage of increase by business and small industries with a lessening percentage of local home ownership. The projection of income from local property taxes over a five year future period displays the type of income that can be generated with various levels of taxes. These projections, when coupled with expenditure projections required to operate the school district in a high quality manner, provide the data necessary to devise strategic plans in the economic impact area [14].

Demographic trends indicate an aging population in the school district, and a potential decrease in students of 40 percent over the next ten years. Also, it is determined that the high school student dropout rate will increase to 52 percent over the next ten years if intervention strategies are not successfully developed. The impact on favorable votes on any tax increases and the impact on the productivity, health, and happiness of the district's students and products are very serious variables for which successful strategic intervention plans must be developed [15].

Legal trends indicate that an increasing number of mandates will impact the school district as state legislators and the state department of education attempt to force more effective schools through mandated employee certification programs, through specific mandates for updated employee training, and through specific instructional programs mandates [16].

Political trending indicates that politicians will continue to use the schools as the tool to cure all the ills they see in society (job skills to compete with other nations, drug education, and any other ill that they determine must be addressed). In addition to this overall trend, another trend indicates that various political players (governors, legislators, and state and federal level education officials) are all trying to use "one upmanship" on each other as the "educational politician" who improved the schools. Much of this political activity is created by behind-the-scenes pressure of business and industrial groups [17].

Each of the variables mentioned has to be carefully monitored by the school district's decision makers, and strategic and operational plans must be developed to adjust to or direct the impact of those variables wherever the school district can successfully intervene. Only by monitoring, by strategic and operational planning, and by skilled interventions can a school district's decision makers approach the "what should be" desired future school district state [18].

Once a belief system exists and external and internal variables are scanned for trends and impact potentials, it is important that one additional piece of information be collected before the school district can decide on its vision. The last missing prerequisite information is that of the CSF's (Critical Success Factors) which are the high priority outcomes (results) expected to be produced by the school district [19]. Let's now turn to the CSF's which were decided upon by the employees and other stakeholders of the Hypothetical School District.

By identifying the school district's Critical Success Factors prior to developing the district's strategic and operational plans, two important matters are accomplished: (1) by identification of the few CSF's, the information utilized for monitoring and planning is simplified; and although other information is shared, the information related to the CSF's is that most attended to by the school district's decision makers, and (2) by identifying the few CSF's, major priority decision structures are identified prior to conducting detailed planning activities related to strategic and operational planning.

Hypothetical School District's CSF's (Critical Success Factors)

- All students in Hypothetical School District will be provided with a safe, healthy and positive learning environment.
- All students of Hypothetical School District are expected to graduate, and it is expected that they will graduate with sufficient knowledge and skill to be productive members of society. Productive societal members are those who produce more than they consume.
- All students shall be expected to learn well, and all teachers and other employees shall expect students to demonstrate that learning.
- All employees shall possess the desire to improve their performance; and to assist in improving the performance of students, other employees, and the school district.
- Sufficient resources shall be allocated to initiate and maintain the high quality programs that the district desires to achieve in its "what should be" future vision.
- Community members, employees and students all feel an ownership sense of pride in the school district, and they all have a desire to assist in the strategic planning efforts to improve the school district.

Now that the decision makers of Hypothetical School District have agreed upon the six CSF's that shall guide their major communication and strategic planning efforts, a vision of "what should be" or "what could be" in the future can be devised because the prerequisite information of "what is", as determined by the belief system and the external and internal scanning data, is available to help the strategic planners from "what is" to "what should be" or to "what could be". Utilizing these data, the decision makers of Hypothetical School District have arrived at the following future vision for the school district [20].

Vision Components of Hypothetical School District

Hypothetical School District's stakeholders envision the school district's future as one in which: (1) all students will learn at a high qualitative level; (2) all employees will insist on a high level of achievement from their students, from themselves, from other employees and from the entire school district's operations; (3) the community buys into the vision, and the community is supportive of the efforts of the students, employees and the school district; (4) a learning environment is created and maintained that is safe, healthy and positive; (5) all employees desire to update their knowledge and skills by attendance at training and/or staff development activities sponsored by the school district or by other organizations; and (6) sufficient resources are available from the various collective sources to allow the school district's decision makers to attain the "what should be" future state.

Once the components of the vision are decided, the stakeholders can develop a specific mission statement to guide its strategic and operational planning efforts. The mission agreed upon by the stakeholders of Hypothetical School District includes many of the crucial elements spelled out during the envisioning process.

Hypothetical School District's Mission Statement

The mission of Hypothetical School District is to graduate productive citizens (persons who produce more than they consume) as the end product of educating *all students* in a safe, healthy and positive environment that is nurtured by employees who believe all students can learn, who monitor student progress for the purpose of adjusting instructional content and delivery methodologies, and who set and demand high achievement standards while demonstrating a trust and caring for each and every student who attends Hypothetical School District's schools.

Once the vision and mission statements are agreed upon, the stakeholders must turn their attention to the ability of the district, under its current conditions, to meet the desired "what should be" or "what could be" future state. The technique chosen by the stakeholders of Hypothetical School District to conduct this analysis is one entitled SWOT (Strengths, Weaknesses, Opportunities, and Threats). Although many SWOT users only analyze the internal organization's strengths and weaknesses, while analyzing only the external environment for opportunities and threats, it is recommended that all four categories be utilized to examine both the internal and external environments [21]. The SWOT analysis conducted by the stakeholders of the Hypothetical School District revealed some very interesting findings.

Hypothetical School District's SWOT (Strengths, Weaknesses, Opportunities and Threats) Analysis

As related to its internal SWOT analysis, the stakeholders determined that the following situations were present.

Internal Strengths Include

- a combined OD and HRD department as part of the formal structure of the school district
- a generous budget allocation for employee training and/or staff development
- an existing culture that involves representatives of all stakeholder groups in the formal strategic and operational planning activities of the school district
- an environment that is safe, healthy, and positive
- a well-educated and caring group of employees
- a history of successful intervention strategies
- a clear vision of "what should be" in the future
- a clear, directional mission statement that was developed by representatives of all stakeholder groups, a mission for which all stakeholders hold ownership

Internal Weaknesses Include

- a lack of sufficient planning to replace "key" employees who will retire or leave the school district's service over the next few years
- a lack of a long term training and staff development strategy that maximizes the predicted future human and financial resources
- a lack of intervention strategies to meet the predicted increase in "at risk" students

- a lack of intervention strategies to eliminate the extremely high predicted student dropout rate
- an insufficient understanding of and utilization of technology applications to the instruction and management operations of the school district

Internal Opportunities Include

- untapped employee resources that are more than willing to assist the school district to achieve its future vision
- many students who wish to assist in improving the instructional programs

Internal Threats Include

- numerous students who intend to drop out of school as soon as they are of legal age
- potential union leadership interventions that may restrict the ability of employees to participate in many of the activities directed at improving the school district, and for which employees may receive little or no extra pay

Having determined the internal strengths, weaknesses, opportunities, and threats, the stakeholders turned to determining the external strengths, weaknesses, opportunities, and threats. The stakeholders found that numerous external SWOT's were present in the environment that would have to be taken into account when laying plans to achieve the future desired vision of "what should be" or "what could be" for the Hypothetical School District.

External Strengths Include

- an increasingly favorable local tax base
- a positive community attitude towards the students, employees and the school district's programs
- an understanding of what the school district is trying to accomplish, and support for its planning attempts designed to improve the school district's operations

External Weaknesses Include

- a growing competition from other governmental organizations and civic taxpayer groups for the monies currently being allocated for educational purposes
- an aging population that is exhibiting some concern for its financial security in the future, which may have a negative effect on future tax increases if they become necessary to support the qualitative level desired for the school district

External Opportunities Include

- Many of the retired citizens have indicated a willingness to serve as tutors for students. They would, of course, do this under the direction of a teacher; and they would, of course, do this according to the plans developed by the teacher.
- Some of the major businesses and industries in the area have decided to assist the school district in upgrading its technological resources, and to permit some of their training staffs to assist in the training of the school employees. The CEO's (Chief Executive Officers) have decided who will put the new technology to use for instructional and/or management purposes.

External Threats Include

- the origination of a small "citizens against increased taxes" group in the community
- a concern that the school district's largest industrial employer is considering shutting down its operations within the district to move to another location, which would have a devastating impact on the funds available for the operation of the school district

Once the district's stakeholders have decided on the vision of "what should be" or "what could be" the future state of the school district and they have analyzed the strengths, weaknesses, opportunities, and threats that exist in its internal and external environments, they are ready to develop strategic goals and objectives which are designed to achieve the "what should be" or "what could be" desired future vision for the Hypothetical School District. Even though there would be a myriad of goals and objectives, only a few examples of those that relate to OD (Organization Development) and HRD (Human Resource Development) will be detailed.

Three Examples of OD and HRD Strategic Goals of Hypothetical School District

Goal #1: To maintain a group of employees who will possess the knowledge, skills and attitudes necessary to achieve the future "what should be" or "what could be" vision of Hypothetical School District.

Goal #2: To devise intervention strategies that will lead to OD structures that will achieve the long term programs required to address the identified needs of "students at risk" and students who are potential dropouts.

Goal #3: To continually upgrade the school district's technological resources to permit the maximum usage of technology for instructional and management purposes.

Once the strategic goals have been identified, specific measurable objectives can be identified for each of the goals. Although each goal may have many objectives subsumed under it, this discussion will be limited to two potential objectives for each of the three goals identified earlier [22].

Example of Goal-Related Strategic Objectives for Hypothetical School District

Objectives Related to Goal #1

Objective #1: Within five years to have a complete system of HRD in operation that will continuously update all categories of employees through school district sponsored training and staff development activities. It will use the employees' talents for planning the program, and it will use employees who possess specific knowledge and/or skills as system-wide trainers. Measurement will be observation; the testing of skills and knowledge possessed by employees as related to the knowledge and skill levels desired and required for the future operation of the district.

Objective #2: Within three years the district will have a complete employee skills, knowledge and attitudinal data bank in place that will permit the identification of specific future employee needs, will allow the screening of potential candidates, and will allow sufficient enticements to permit the hiring of replacement employees for "key" employee leadership positions. Measurement will be the existence of a comprehensive HRD data bank and the retrieval of information as to the knowledge, skills, and attitudes of new employees hired to replace "key" employee leaders who have retired or left the district for promotions or other reasons.

Objectives Related to Goal #2

Objective #1: Within five years the dropout rate of students shall be reduced by 80 percent over the historical trend, and the dropout rate will be zero within ten years. Data collected over these time periods will prove that the intervention strategies devised by the employees will cause the desired results to be evidenced.

Objective #2: Within two years the various categories of "students at risk" will be clearly identified and intervention programs will be put in place at the elementary level. Within five years, intervention programs will be put in place for all "at risk" secondary students, and by six years evidence will be collected to prove that the intervention programs are having the specific desired results for a minimum of 80 percent of all categories of students who are identified as "students at risk".

Objectives Related to Goal #3

Objective #1: Within two years, with the help of consultants from technological firms within the school district, with hired consultants and with a planning committee of employees, a plan shall be in existence that describes: (1) the technology needed, (2) the instructional and management uses of that technology and (3) the training and staff development programs required to get the employees at a skill level that will permit them to use the technology for student instruction and for management purposes.

Within three years, all technology will be purchased and all employee training and staff development activities will be completed. Within four years, direct observation will prove that all employees are capably using the technology for instructional and management purposes. Within five years, quality control data will be collected to prove the cost/effectiveness and cost/benefits gained by use of the technology to be positive.

Objective #2: By five years, an evaluation, budgetary and training structure will be firmly in place to maintain updated technology for all instructional and management purposes within the district. Measurement will be the existence of this comprehensive system related to technological utilization in the Hypothetical School District.

As is true of many organizations, there may be multiple strategic goals that are desired; and there may be numerous objectives related to each of these goals. Since the human and financial resources of any school district or any organization are always limited, some system of prioritizing those goals and objectives that should receive initial attention must be devised [23]. The stakeholders of the Hypothetical School District devised a very simple set of decision rules to assist in determining the highest priorities of the school district as it started its long term journey to achieve its future vision of "what should be" or "what could be" [24].

Hypothetical School District's Decision Rules

Is the goal or objective meaningful? Without any ill intent, and often without any realization of what is happening, many decision makers in many organizations do a great job of achieving items that are not meaningful as related to the organizational vision, mission or desired results.

Is the goal or objective affordable? Oftentimes organizations attempt goals or objectives that are not affordable in terms of available human or financial resources. In these cases, the entire organization's operations may suffer because of the nonproductive waste of available resources diverted to attempting to reach the "pie-in-the-sky".

Is the goal or objective doable? That is, even though it may be meaningful and the resources are available, it may not be doable in terms of time constraints, political constraints, legal constraints, or because of the existence of some other intervening variable beyond the control of the local school district's decision makers.

Does the goal or objective stand an 80 percent chance of being successfully achieved? This high success probability should be utilized when the employees and other stakeholders are attempting to achieve initial results. Once they have experienced success, the probability of success can be lowered progressively to 70 percent, 60 percent, 50 percent or less than 50 percent. Success builds upon success, and partial achievement of success down the timeline is sufficient to keep the motivation of employees at a high level. It is also sufficient to cause them to modify the interventions and try again to achieve the entire goal or objective.

Before summarizing, let's examine ten ways to ensure success when doing strategic planning, and let's also examine ten traps to avoid when doing strategic planning.

Ten Ways to Ensure Strategic Planning Success

(1) Involve all significant stakeholders in the strategic planning activities. This will assure ownership.

(2) Don't rush it. The initial planning may well take one or two years.

(3) Think of strategic planning as an ongoing process. It is not an activity that comes to an end once the original strategic plan is developed.

(4) Develop your desired outcomes (results) as statements of goals and objectives *before* you attempt to develop action plans.

(5) Devise your monitoring structures *before* you develop your strategies and tactics.

(6) Attend to your internal and external scanning trends, and use them to project future states. Then, use these projections to make required modifications in your existing strategic plan.

(7) Sell others on the district's future vision of "what should be", as the more people who you get to "buy in", the more likely that future vision will be achieved.

(*8*) Remember that your plan must be managed. It cannot be merely developed and left to chance.

(*9*) Realize that yearly operational action plans must be developed in order to implement your strategic plan.

(*10*) Finally, again remember that the key to success is *involvement! involvement! involvement! and involvement!*

Ten Traps to Avoid When Doing Strategic Planning

(*1*) Neglect involving representatives of all important stakeholder groups.

(*2*) Neglect allowing sufficient time to develop your strategic plan. Remember that this is a long term continuing process, not just a one time activity.

(*3*) Neglect allocating sufficient and financial resources to do it correctly.

(*4*) Neglect using knowledgeable internal and/or external strategic planners to assist the district.

(*5*) Neglect developing a future vision of "what should be" or "what could be".

(*6*) Neglect scanning the external and internal environments to determine trends that will impact the district and its strategic plan.

(*7*) Neglect arriving at a statement of beliefs, or to do an external and internal SWOT (Strengths, Weaknesses, Opportunities and Threats) analysis before devising action plans to implement the district's strategic plan.

(*8*) Neglect developing a mission statement or monitoring structures.

(*9*) Neglect taking sufficient time to get a critical mass of stakeholders to develop ownership of the goals, objectives and strategic plan.

(*10*) Forgetting that the key to success is *involvement! involvement! involvement! and involvement!* [25].

SUMMARY

By utilizing the fictitious Hypothetical School District, we have demonstrated the steps that a school district's stakeholders would use to develop strategic plans related to the OD (Organization Development) and the HRD (Human Resource Development) functions of a local school district. This chapter emphasized the need for a systematic and interactive planning approach related to OD and HRD. It also took the reader through the planning steps of (1) developing a beliefs system, (2) conducting an external environmental scan, (3) conducting an internal environmental scan, (4) identifying the CSF's (Critical Success Factors) of the school district, (5) envisioning a future "what should be" or a "what could be" state for the school district, (6) developing a mission statement, (7) conducting a SWOT (Strengths, Weaknesses, Opportunities and Threats) analysis relating to both the internal and external environments of the school district, (8) identifying strategic goals, (9) identifying specific, measurable objectives related to each strategic goal and (10) developing a set of decision rules to be used to prioritize the numerous goals and objectives identified when they cannot all be addressed immediately.

Chapter 4, which follows, will pick up the strategic goals and objectives; and it will elaborate upon the action plans that are necessary to develop short term operational plans that will initiate the year-to-year journeys necessary to ultimately achieve the future visions of "what should be" or "what could be" for the Hypothetical School District. Chapter 4 will discuss: (1) action planning, which includes the activities of brainstorming, force field analyses, cost benefit analyses and selection of the best alternative; (2) implementation tactics; (3) resource allocations; (4) operation of the action plans used; (5) development of monitoring structures; and (5) recycling the entire systems approach to interface with the strategic planning operations.

GUIDELINES

1. In determining HRD and OD needs, a district must consider both strategic and operational planning.
2. When focusing on the entire operation of a district, use a *macro* and a *micro* focus; the total school district perspective and the individual employee perspective.
3. A belief system must be developed upon which to build activities.
4. Trends deriving from external and/or internal variables impacting the OD and HRD activities must be identified and assessed as to the possibility of successful school district intervention.

5. The Critical Success Factors (CSF's) must be decided upon by the district's employees and by other stakeholders.
6. The vision of "what should be" or "what could be" in the district's future must be devised and a specific mission statement developed.
7. A Strengths, Weaknesses, Opportunities, and Threats (SWOT) analysis should be conducted to assess the ability of the district to meet the desired future state.
8. Strategic goals and objectives must be designed to achieve the desired future vision for the district, and these should be prioritized using predetermined decision rules.

EXERCISES

1. Develop an OD and HRD beliefs system for your district.
2. List trends derived from the instructional, attitudinal, technological, social, economic, demographic, legal, or political information available, and identify which may impact your district. Also, assess your district's potential for successful intervention related to these trends.
3. Identify a few Critical Success Factors (CSF's) for your district, in order to have information to attend to and to identify major priority decision structures.
4. Describe a future vision of "what should be" or "what could be" for your school district.
5. Conduct a SWOT (Strengths, Weaknesses, Opportunities, and Threats) analysis for your district, and use the information gained to design three district goals and the objectives related to each goal.

SELECTED REFERENCES

1. Kaufman, R. and J. Herman. 1991. *Strategic Planning in Education.* Lancaster, PA: Technomic Publishing Co., Inc.
2. Herman, J. 1989. "School District Strategic Planning (Part I)", *School Business Affairs*, 55(2): 10–14.
3. Kaufman, R. and J. Hyerman. 1989. "Planning That Fits Every District", *School Administer*, 8(46): 17–19.

4. Schmuck, R. A. and P. J. Runkel. 1988. *The Handbook of Organization Development in Schools.* Third edition. Prospect Heights, IL: Waveland Press, Inc., p. 34.

5. Schmuck, R. A. and P. J. Runkel. 1988. *Handbook,* p. 329. italics in original.

6. Schmuck, R. A. and P. J. Runkel. 1988. *Handbook,* p. 330.

7. Schmuck, R. A. and P. J. Runkel. 1988. *Handbook,* p. 369.

8. Burke, W. W. 1987. *Organization Development* Reading, MA: Addison-Wesley Publishing Co., p. 39.

9. Sparks, G. M. 1983. "Synthesis of Research on Staff Development for Effective Teaching", *Educational Leadership,* 43: 46–53.

10. Schmuck, R. A. and M. B. Miles. 1971. *Organization Development in Schools.* Palo Alto, CA: National Press Books, p. 219.

11. Herman, J. 1989. "A Vision for the Future: Site-Based Strategic Planning", *NASSP Bulletin,* 73(518): 23–27.

12. Kaufman, R. and J. Herman. 1991. *Strategic Planning.*

13. Herman, J. 1989. "Site-Based Management: Creating a Vision and Mission Statement", *NASSP Bulletin,* 73(519): 79–83.

14. Herman, J. 1989. "External and Internal Scanning: Identifying Variables That Affect Your School", *NASSP Bulletin,* 73(520): 48–52.

15. Herman, J. "External and Internal Scanning", p. 50.

16. Herman, J. "External and Internal Scanning", pp. 516–52.

17. Herman, J. "A Vision for the Future", p. 25.

18. Kaufman, R. and J. Herman. 1991. *Strategic Planning.*

19. Herman, J. "Strategic Planning (Part I)", p. 13.

20. Herman, J. "Site-Based Management", p. 82.

21. Kaufman, R. and J. Herman. "Planning That Fits", p. 18.

22. Kaufman, R. and J. Herman. 1991. *Strategic Planning.*

23. Kaufman, R. and J. Herman. 1991. *Strategic Planning.*

24. Kaufman, R. and J. Herman. "Planning That Fits", p. 18.

25. Herman, J. "Strategic Planning (Part I)", p. 14.

CHAPTER 4

Developing Action Programs to Meet Identified Needs

STRATEGIC GOALS AND objectives represent the results that are desired by the planners. These results are not achieved by magic; rather, they are achieved by a series of very specific actions, activities and events planned on a year-to-year basis. Only by this careful planning of short term actions can the ultimate strategic goals and objectives be achieved; and only by integrating the operational short term action plans with the long term strategic plans can the future *vision* of "what should be" or "what could be" come to fruition.

Chapter 3 discussed the elements of strategic planning. This chapter is devoted to a discussion of *operational action planning*. Operational planning involves: (1) developing action plans by utilizing the techniques of brainstorming, force field analysis, cost benefit analysis and, then, selecting the best alternative, (2) devising tactics and allocating resources that permit the use of the agreed upon tactics, (3) operating the action plans, (4) developing monitoring structures and (5) recycling the entire systems approach in a manner that integrates the operational planning with the strategic plans [1]. Although Figure 3.1 displays the entire holistic system, Figure 4.1 illustrates the operational planning aspects discussed in this chapter.

Once the strategic objectives have been agreed upon by the stakeholders during the strategic planning activities, the employees and the district decision makers can begin developing action plans that will achieve those strategic objectives. It should be stressed that involvement of a variety of stakeholders (parent, community members, students and others) in the strategic planning activities of developing beliefs, identifying CSF's (Critical Success Factors), doing external and internal scans, developing

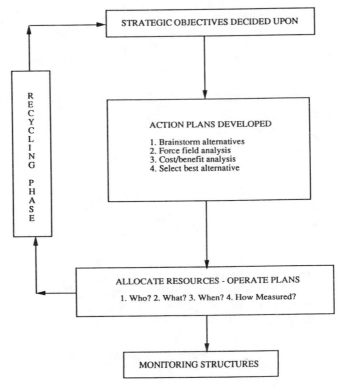

Figure 4.1 *A model of OD and HRD operational planning.*

visions and missions, conducting a SWOT (Strengths, Weaknesses, Opportunities and Threats) analysis, establishing strategic goals, and establishing strategic objectives is a desirable technique [2]. However, when the task at hand is one of developing operational action plans designed to achieve the strategic goals and objectives, the activities related to this operational planning should remain solely in the hands of the school district's employees and decision makers.

The initial step in operational planning is that of implementing the strategic goals and objectives previously agreed upon by devising action plans that are designed to accomplish those goals and objectives. An action plan can be developed through such processes as specific activities or events, analytical or problem-solving approaches, or a series of smaller or shorter term objectives [3]. Initiating action planning involves four distinct activities: (1) brainstorming alternative solutions or courses of action, (2) conducting a force field analysis for each alternative being considered, (3) doing a cost/benefit analysis for each alternative being considered and (4) selecting the best alternative solution [4]. Let's explore these four activities in more depth.

Let's assume a *strategic goal* that relates to both OD and HRD and that states:

> A comprehensive staff development and training operation will be developed and it will become an integral structure within Hypothetical School District.

You will note that it applies to OD because the intervention strategy of including a comprehensive staff development and training operation dramatically changes the entire structure of the organization [5]. All school districts are matrix organizations, and this new intervention structure will cause changes in the functions performed by many of the other matrix structures within the school district. It also applies to HRD because the focus of this intervention is that of providing training and staff development activities for all employees in order that they may improve their performance.

Now that we have an example strategic goal, let's develop a single objective related to this goal. Of course, in reality, there would probably be numerous objectives tied to this goal.

The objective related to this goal was agreed upon by the stakeholders of Hypothetical School District as follows:

> Within five years Hypothetical School District will have in place a comprehensive training and staff development program in operation for all employees of the school district; the effectiveness of it will be determined by measurement of: (1) improved interpersonal relations among employees and between employees and students, (2) improved classroom effectiveness as measured by personnel appraisals and (3) improved learner accomplishments as measured by students' grades and test results.

Once the goal and objective is clear, the employees and the school district's decision makers can initiate action plans that are designed to meet the goal and objective. We began this action planning process by developing alternative means (tactics) to achieve the objective and goal. This initial step involves brainstorming alternatives.

Brainstorming alternatives is an activity wherein all the planners mention as many ideas as possible over a relatively short time frame [6]. During the brainstorming there is no discussion of the ideas mentioned, nor is there any value placed on any of the ideas. Brainstorming is best conducted with a recorder jotting down all ideas for further review purposes once the brainstorming is completed according to the formal brainstorming rules.

BRAINSTORMING RULES

- All suggestions are welcomed.
- There is no discussion of the suggestions.
- Innovative ideas are encouraged.
- The practicality of the idea is not questioned.
- There is no elaboration or explanation of the idea at this point.
- Piggybacking (adding) on to a prior idea is legitimate.
- Participants shall display no verbal or non-verbal agreement or disagreement with any idea proffered.
- All suggestions are considered as valuable contributions.

Utilizing the official brainstorming rules, the planners of Hypothetical School District arrived at 100 suggested means of achieving the strategic objective and goal. Some of their ideas were:

- Provide each employee with a sum of money to be spent on training or staff development activities however and wherever she/he wished.
- Contract with Consultation Intermediate School District to provide for all the training and staff development needs of the employees of Hypothetical School District.
- Determine which of the district's existing employees have specific knowledges and skills that could be utilized to train other employees, and provide employee released time to accomplish the training and staff development activities.
- Videotape persons exhibiting exemplary skills, and provide the videotape to all employees who should acquire those specific skills.
- Develop computerized training packages that can be used by employees during any time period that they have available during the work day or after the work day.
- Use students to train teachers in terms of the students'

needs for feedback, distributed practice, reinforcement, and checking for understanding.
- Have a master custodian demonstrate the appropriate use of the new high tech cleaning equipment and the monitoring and setting of controls related to the computerized heating and ventilating system.
- Have a master teacher train teacher aides to do a lesson task analysis to be used with students whom they tutor under the guidance of the teacher.
- Have a master bus driver work with all new bus drivers to train them in the proper operation and care of the school bus *before* they actually are permitted to transport students.
- Hire employees of equipment suppliers to train the food service staff in the proper operation and maintenance of sophisticated equipment, such as the computerized baking ovens.
- Hire outside professional training and staff development firms to do training on the school district's sites.
- Organize Hypothetical School District's own training and staff development department.
- Allow free employee selection of employee training and staff development activities with the school district agreeing to pay the costs (note that this is similar to a previous suggestion, but it has been piggybacked).
- Develop a training and staff development structure that combines all the suggestions of the group.

Once all of the brainstorming ideas are completed, they can be reviewed. At this point questions can be asked, elaborations can be given, and clarifications can be provided. After all the discussion has taken place, the planners should decide upon which of the hundred or more suggested alternatives they should explore in greater depth. Following a lengthy period of discussion of all the brainstorming suggestions, the planners of Hypothetical School District decided to explore more thoroughly the following suggestions:

(1) Allow free employee selection of their training and staff development activities, and the district will pay the costs associated with their choices.

(2) Hire outside firms or consultants to do the training and staff development activities on the school district's sites.

(3) Organize the school district's own training and staff development department.

Once the ideas to be explored in additional depth have been selected, a listing of the various activities that must be undertaken for each of the ideas should be elaborated upon. An abbreviated example of the various activities (in reality, there would be many additional activities) for each of the three ideas selected for further study by the planners of Hypothetical School District includes those listed below.

AN EXAMPLE OF ACTIVITIES TO BE CONDUCTED FOR THREE MEANS OF PROVIDING TRAINING AND STAFF DEVELOPMENT WITHIN HYPOTHETICAL SCHOOL DISTRICT

Allow free employee selection and pay costs	Hire outside firms to do training on site	Organize the district's own training department
1. Conduct a needs assessment.	1. Develop measurable objectives.	1. Advertise positions, select personnel and organize the department.
2. Develop measurable objectives.	2. Have the firm determine the training menu.	2. Conduct a needs assessment.
3. Arrange for employees' promises/ commitments.	3. Do an employee interest inventory.	3. Develop measurable objectives.
	4. Obtain employees' commitments to attend.	4. Arrange for employees' promises/ commitments.
1. Identify costs.	1. Identify costs.	1. Identify costs.
2. Identify times.	2. Identify times.	2. Identify times.
3. Arrange payment procedures with the provider.	3. Identify locations.	3. Identify locations.
	4. Arrange contract with outside firm.	

Allow free employee selection and pay costs	Hire outside firms to do training on site	Organize the district's own training department
1. Develop attendance monitoring system.	1. Develop attendance monitoring system.	1. Develop attendance monitoring system.
2. Develop quality control assurance methods.	2. Develop quality control assurance methods.	2. Develop quality control assurance methods.
Operate the program.	Operate the program.	Operate the program.
Collect quality assurance data and evaluate program.	Collect quality assurance data and evaluate program.	Collect quality assurance data and evaluate program.
Make decisions to drop program, continue or modify (separately for each employee group).	Make decisions to drop program, continue or modify (separately for each employee group).	Make decisions to drop program, continue or modify (separately for each employee group).

With this initial overview of all three alternatives in hand, the planners can develop a *force field analysis* for each. A *force field analysis* is a technique that causes the planners to determine the potential restraining and supporting elements related to each of the alternatives being investigated [7]. Let's look in on the planners of the Hypothetical School District as they develop these analyses for each of the three solutions they have decided to investigate further.

Suggested Solution #1

Allow free employee selection of training and staff development activities, and the district will pay the costs. The restraining and supporting elements for this solution, as determined by Hypothetical School District's operational planners were:

Restraints

- Some employees will not participate.
- There will be no district control over program quality.
- This procedure will not automatically take care of district and sub-group identified needs.
- The district will have absolutely no control over the providers.
- If the training chosen is conducted during normal work hours, the cost of substitutes may make this very expensive.
- It would be extremely difficult to determine the results and impact of this freedom of choice training.

Supports

- Employee freedom of choice will promote self development.
- The district will not have to establish an internal organizational structure.
- This will be less expensive than establishing an on-going district structure.
- Employee unions will be supportive of this approach since it is employee controlled.

Suggested Solution #2

Hire outside firms and consultants to perform training and staff development activities on the school district's sites. The planners decided upon the following list of restraints and supports:

Restraints

- The fees and expenses of outside consultants are many times too expensive.
- A great deal of employee time would be spent previewing the consultants' presentations in other settings.

Supports

- These consultants are specialists who perform training and staff development activities for a living
- Once excellent consultants are located, they can be used many times.

Restraints

- There are no follow up activities to maintain the training.
- The district's staff would still have to develop quality control specifications for the training or staff development sessions.

Supports

- If employees do not evaluate the training or staff development activity as helpful, the consultant is not employed again.
- The high quality presenters can be employed over long time periods, and they can work with the employees in planning and maintenance activities as well as provide presentations
- Excellent providers can assist in the training of the school district's employees to the point that they can monitor the results and assist in interim training needs.

Suggested Solution #3

Organize the school district's own training department. The school district's operational action planners arrived at a variety of restraints and supports for Suggested Solution #3:

Restraints

- This method will be extremely costly.
- Some jealousies may develop by those employees not selected to do the training.
- The district could offer training and staff development activities related to identified needs at the total district, sub-group and individual employee levels.

Supports

- This approach will provide recognition to many of the district's finest employees.
- The expertise of the trainers would be known because they are co-workers.
- Quality control would be easy to obtain since it is an "in-district" approach.
- Long term training and staff development could be assured, and "one shot" programs would be avoided.

Restraints	Supports

- Some staff members who were well qualified to do training could not afford to be frequently away from their normal duties (a teacher could not be away from her/his students, nor could a principal be away from the building she/he supervises).

Once the planners of Hypothetical School District outline the supporting and restraining factors for each suggested solution, they can go to the challenge of devising the detailed action plan for the alternative of their choice. A simplified version of this approach is displayed in the "Employer Recognition Plan" below, which uses a totally different objective than that previously discussed. The approach illustrated follows the following steps: (1) determine all the detailed tasks to be accomplished without consideration of the chronology for which they will be done; this approach speeds up the planning process; (2) once all tasks are listed, place them in chronological order (for example, when building a house, you don't want the electricians scheduled after the plasterers have enclosed the walls); (3) next, you decide which specific person or persons have the responsibility of completing that task; and (4) you predetermine the date at which each task is to be completed [8].

For our example, let's assume that the objective agreed to by the strategic planners was to devise a recognition program for all of the school district's employees. The district's employees who were selected to develop an operational action plan came up with the detailed action plan outlined as follows.

An Employee Recognition Action Plan

Tasks	Chronology	Who's Responsible	When to Be Completed
Develop recognition programs.	2	Each administrator and building's employees	Oct., 19—

Tasks	Chronology	Who's Responsible	When to Be Completed
Decide upon recognition awards.	3	Each administrator and building's employees	Oct., 19—
Determine the cost of each recognition program and of the total recognition effort.	4	Business manager	Nov., 19—
Arrange for production or purchase of the awards.	6	Business manager and building administrators	Jan., 19—
Decide upon the times and places for granting the awards.	7	Planning committee	Feb., 19—
Determine the interest level of employees in initiating an employee recognition system.	1	Planning committee	Sept., 19—
Determine the source of funds to operate the program.	5	Business manager and superintendent	Nov., 19—
Develop an evaluation system to determine the effectiveness of the program and conduct the evaluation.	9	Planning committee	May yearly
Conduct the awards activities.	8	Employee, planning committee and administrators	April and May yearly
Other tasks.	10+	?	?

A *cost/benefit analysis* should also be conducted for each alternative, and one should definitely be conducted after the alternative selected has been made operational. If the *cost/benefit analysis* is done on all the alternatives being considered, the planners have to predict the ratio of cost to benefit. If, however, it is conducted after the alternative has been put into operation, it can become part of the evaluation structure—both formative evaluation and summative evaluation [9]. This type of analysis is valuable in determining the worth of what you get for what you pay. For example, is an expenditure of 100 additional dollars per potential student school dropout a reasonable expenditure to reduce the dropout rate by 10 percent? Will the expenditure of $1,000 per potential dropout per year provide equivalent or greater benefit than the expenditure if the dropout rate is lowered by 50 percent? These are the types of questions that can be related to the computation of a ratio of benefit to cost. After the force field analysis and the cost/benefit have been completed for each alternative, the selected best solution should be put into operation.

Once the action plan is completed, the operational stage is conducted. During the operation of the action plan, the predetermined *formative evaluation* monitoring structures are utilized. Once the operational action plan has been completed, the predetermined *summative evaluation* structures are used. It is at this point that a decision is made to eliminate the specific operational action plan, continue it as previously planned, or modify it and put the modified action plan into place within the school district. Not only is the operational action plan reviewed, but the results must be related to the strategic plan to see if it is in accordance with the vision, mission, goals and objectives that were put in place during the strategic planning [10].

This *recycling activity* that relates the action planning directly to the strategic planning is crucial to the success of any school district's planning efforts. If one realizes that planning is a continuous process and not an event, it is easily recognized that both the operational action planning and the long term strategic planning must work in tandem [11]. For only as these planning efforts are successfully interwoven can the planners assure a high quality holistic system of OD and HRD activities.

Before leaving this chapter, let's take a look at an actual dramatic district level restructuring that had great implications for the OD and HRD activities required to implement the restructuring that followed a massive OD intervention. The title of Hypothetical School District will again be used in order to mask the real identity of the actual school district that was involved in the restructuring described.

We shall begin this discussion by first describing the district and the structures that were in place prior to the restructuring; we shall next describe the reasons for the massive restructuring; and, finally, we shall present many of the details of how the district was restructured to improve its student services and instructional delivery systems.

DESCRIPTION OF HYPOTHETICAL SCHOOL DISTRICT PRIOR TO RESTRUCTURING

Hypothetical School District is a first-ring suburb of a major city. It has a wide variety of residential socio-economic levels, varying from low-low to middle-upper socio-economic clientele. Most observers, however, would describe the district's residents as being predominantly of the upper-middle socio-economic level.

The school district consists of three high schools (composed of grades 9–12), with each containing approximately 1,400 students. There is also an alternative high school for academically able students who have difficulty adjusting to a normal high school environment. There are three large junior high schools that contain grades 7 and 8, and there are 16 elementary schools that contain grades K–6. The elementary schools vary in size from 280 students to 820 students.

The organizational structure of the district is as follows: (1) there is a nine member elected board of education, (2) there is a superintendent of schools, (3) there is an assistant superintendent for elementary education, who has a staff of curriculum specialists assigned to his charge, (4) there is an assistant superintendent for secondary education, with a staff of curriculum specialists assigned to her charge, (5) there is a director of research who primarily serves as a psychometrist, (6) there is a director of personnel, (7) there is a business manager, (8) each high school has an athletic director, a director of guidance, and four assistant principals, (9) each junior high school has two assistant principals and a director of guidance, (10) the alternative school has a principal, a director of guidance, specially selected teachers who have very small class sizes, and vocational and psychological counseling specialists, and (11) the larger elementary schools have an assistant principal and an elementary guidance counselor.

Approximately 80 percent of the student body finish high school; and, in general, the test results indicate that they achieve, as a group, at about the 57 percent level when compared on national norms. The class sizes are reasonable, with early elementary averaging twenty students, the later elementary twenty-four students, the junior high twenty students, the senior high eighteen students and the alternative school twelve students.

The community has been supportive of the schools, and the citizens have always voted favorably on the yearly budget, although the votes have been getting closer to failing in the past three years. The taxpayers have also voted favorably on a sufficient number of bond issues to keep the physical environments in healthy, safe, and pleasant states.

IF ALL THIS EXISTS, WHY CHANGE THE STRUCTURE?

Although Hypothetical School District possessed a great deal of positive indicators, there were some basic and important reasons for making massive changes in the structure. Obviously these changes would have to be approved by the board of education, and they had to be accepted by the community and staff—at least, a critical mass of employees and citizens would have to permit the changes to take place without major disruption. Up front it was realized that massive restructuring would change the traditional way of doing business, change the culture of the organization, and change many of the activities of both the students and employees [12]. It was anticipated that there would be some "rough spots" to overcome, but it was decided that the restructuring would improve the school district's ability to deliver quality education to the students.

The major reasons for the massive restructuring are listed below:

- *There was little or no vertical articulation* between the elementary and secondary education programs [13]. The situation could be compared to hiring a contractor to build a high quality house foundation and hiring a different contractor to build a high quality house to be placed on that foundation; but providing each contractor with different specifications and dimensions. The result is that although both contractors did excellent quality work, the house would not fit on the foundation.

- *There was unnecessary duplication of staff curriculum specialists.* Both the assistant superintendent for elementary instruction and the assistant superintendent for secondary instruction possessed full time specialists for each subject area.
- *There was no outcome-based monitoring of student achievement* except that of general comparison of test scores at certain grade levels with the national norms for standardized tests that were administered. These were analyzed by the director of research for the district.
- *There was no existing plan for curriculum mapping or for instructional auditing.* Curriculum mapping allows a determination to be made as to whether or not the written curriculum is the *taught* curriculum and is the *tested* curriculum [14]. *Instructional auditing* allows a determination to be made as to whether or not the instructional program that is agreed upon is actually being taught, is being delivered in the manner described in the program, is having the impact that is described in the program write-up, and is documented in records to prove these things have taken place [15].
- *Parents and citizens have little or no involvement* in judging the quality of instruction that takes place within the schools.
- *No plan or budget existed for employee training or staff development activities.* The only expenditures made for this purpose were haphazard ones that paid for employees to occasionally attend a workshop, conference, or a national or state meeting. The employee had no responsibility to share the information gained, nor did the employee have any obligation to use the information in her/his teaching or other employee duties.
- *The building principals and assistant principals were seen as managers*, not as instructional leaders. This fact and the fact that articulation between the elementary and secondary education programs was practically non-existent were the two most serious flaws in the current instructional operation of Hypothetical School District.

THE RESTRUCTURING

The restructuring process took place over a period of two years, and each major restructuring step was reviewed with the staff before it was presented to the board of education for formal approval. Also, each restructuring activity of any significance was presented to the newspapers and other media, and it was emphasized at the board of education meetings which were broadcast to each home in the school district. The elementary and secondary instructional structures were dramatically changed to force a K–12 systems approach to curriculum development, instructional delivery, monitoring, and instructional auditing and assessment. This was accomplished by making the following changes in functions (see Figure 4.2):

(1) The assistant superintendents for secondary education and elementary education were changed to create the following structure: (a) *An assistant superintendent for curriculum and staff development* was created. This assistant was given a staff specialist for each curriculum specialty, all of whom coordinated curriculum development K–12. A district-wide director of guidance and a district-wide director of vocational education were also provided. The excess curriculum specialists had a choice of being trained as staff development specialists or returning to classroom teaching. Ultimately, six full time staff developers were added to this department, $300,000 was budgeted yearly for staff training and development activities and the full time staff developers trained the employees in any skills related to curriculum changes or instructional delivery methodologies. In other words, this

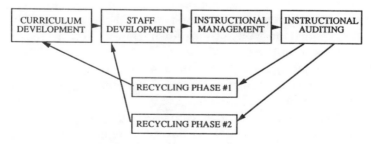

Figure 4.2 Instructional systems model for Hypothetical School District.

department was held responsible for working with teachers and outside consultants to develop curriculum and to train teachers to use the curriculum in the manner intended. (b) *An assistant superintendent for instructional management* was created, and two of the original curriculum specialists were assigned as assistants to this department. The function of this assistant superintendent was to supervise the principals, as all principals reported to this position in a direct line function. The department was responsible for seeing that the curriculum that was developed and the instructional delivery for which the teachers were trained were actually being carried out in the classrooms and in the individual school buildings. (c) A position of *director of instructional auditing and research* was created and this person was provided an assistant. The functions of this department included the working with the staff to develop instructional program descriptions, to develop auditing procedures, to train and supervise auditing teams, to develop criterion-referenced tests for all subjects and all courses, to analyze all test results, to develop program impact reports, and to share this information in a meaningful way that would allow the teachers, curriculum specialists, staff developers, and administrators to make meaningful instructional program adjustments based upon these data analyses.

This restructuring was done without added cost, with the exception of the $300,000 annually allocated for training and staff development activities. This created a *systems approach* to instruction in that it continually recycled from: (1) curriculum development (2) to staff development to implement the curriculum (3) to instructional management (4) to instructional auditing which permitted evaluation (5) to recycling, when necessary, to curriculum development or staff development. This new structure, because everything was approached on a total district K–12 basis, ensured vertical articulation. Horizontal articulation was assured by the curriculum development and instructional auditing procedures that were implemented.

(2) Each of the building principals and their staffs were provided with staff development activities related to instructional leadership. These activities concentrated on

clinical supervision and curriculum development processes [16]. A goal was established that each building administrator would spend a minimum of 50 percent of his time on activities related to instruction. Since there existed a number of assistant principals at each high school, the functions of these administrators were dramatically changed, and the administrators at the elementary and junior high levels were provided with additional assistance from the central office instructional specialists.

At the high school level, each principal was seen as the immediate monitor of the entire instructional operation within her/his school building. She/he also was expected to actively supervise a portion of the teaching staff and to become personally involved with the building's teachers and central specialists in a curriculum specialty area. Each of the assistant principals had three very specific functions to perform: (1) They were paired with a full time guidance counselor and accepted full responsibility for a class of students from the time they entered as freshman through their graduation. They were to attend every student activity, work with the class officers, and even plan the commencement activities. By doing this and pairing them with a guidance counselor, they were expected to know each student and to follow each one throughout her/his high school career. (2) They were to be an integral part of a curriculum planning committee in one area of specialty (math, science, English, social science, the arts, vocational education). They worked directly with the building's teachers and with the district's curriculum specialist in their area of specialty. All of the assistant principals were reassigned in order that all basic subject specialties were covered by the assistant principals and the principal in each high school. (3) They were also to be clinical supervisors for one-fifth of the teachers in the building.

(3) The director of personnel was assigned the function of working with a committee to determine the specific knowledge and skills required for any vacancy that developed in the teaching, administrative or central staff as related to the instructional responsibilities for that vacancy. This committee then proceeded to interview the candidates with questions directly related to the knowledge and skills desired,

visited the current place of employment (when applicable) to gather evidence of the specific skills and knowledge being utilized in practice, and recommended employment of the candidates that "best fit" the district's pre-identified needs.

(4) The business manager was responsible for transferring funds from non-instructional related accounts to provide the $300,000 for staff training and development and to support any other instructional restructuring expenses.

(5) Parents and citizens were included as members of curriculum planning committees, and they were used (after eight hours of training) as members of the district's instructional auditing committees. Instructional audits *are not* evaluations. Rather, they are audits in the same sense that financial audits are conducted to determine whether or not the operation is being conducted as planned. The quality measures come from item analyzed norm referenced test analyses or analyses of the results of criterion referenced (has the student been able to achieve the specific result a minimum of 80 percent of the time?) test item analyses. Perhaps, instructional auditing procedures that utilize parents as part of the auditing teams require additional explanation. The instructional audit procedures include the following:

- The audit is conducted by sampling items and by a discrepancy analysis comparing what is intended to what is in actuality taking place.
- The audit process uses three techniques: (1) existence check (is it in existence as planned?), (2) process trace (does direct observation prove that delivery of instruction is being done as described in the instructional program plan?) and (3) do records exist to prove that what has been described as the program plan and desired impact has actually taken place?
- The resulting conditions of the audit can be: (1) the instructional program is operating as intended, (2) deviations from the instructional plan are noted by direct observation or by a paper trace, or (3) errors or omissions in records exist that make it impossible to determine if the instructional program is operating as intended.

Each group of teachers who teach the same instructional area develop a written program plan that includes the following: (1) the title of the specific instructional program, (2) the target audience (students) for which the program is intended, (3) the student performance outcome expectations, (4) major program instructional delivery procedures, (5) the evaluation strategy to be used by the teachers of the program, (6) the sources of evidence to be used by the teachers for evaluation purposes, and (7) any decision rules that the teachers have developed for deciding required modifications or the future of the program. These written instructional program plans are generally only four to six pages in length, and they are used as the basic document from which the audit is conducted.

The procedural steps for the entire audit procedure are: (1) Teachers are trained by the director of auditing and the assistant director to write program plans if this is necessary with certain groups of teachers. (2) The programs to be audited for the year are selected because all programs cannot be audited at any one time. (3) The program plans are written. (4) The auditing team, which consists of teachers and citizens, is trained to perform an instructional audit. In each case, the chair of the auditing team is a professional educator, and approximately six citizens join the chair as auditing team members. (5) The specific audit plan and procedures to be used are finalized. This includes a decision as to which buildings and classrooms are to be visited and the number of classrooms to be included in the audit sample. (6) The audit is conducted and the results are recorded on the district's instructional audit form. This form includes information related to the date of the audit, the buildings and classrooms visited, the names of all audit team members, the observations of the audit team, the records and evidences reviewed by the audit team and the findings of the audit team and the findings of the audit. (7) The chairperson of the audit team meets with the building principal to review the audit report. (8) The principal reviews the findings with the teaching staff involved in the program. (9) The audit report indicates whether the audit proved the instructional program operated as planned, whether there were deviations or discrepancies from the instructional program plans or whether there were insufficient records kept to determine whether or not the program was being presented as planned. If the principal and his teaching staff agree with the audit and some aspects of the program require improvement, she/he can indicate to the director of auditing whether the building's staff can make those needed improvements or whether central district resources would have to be allocated to assist the building's staff to make the improvements. (10) If the building principal and her/his teaching staff disagree with the audit reports, he/she can provide additional evidence of conformance to the instructional plan, or the audit chairperson and the director of instructional auditing can meet with the principal to negotiate adjustments to the report when necessary. In any case, an additional audit would be scheduled in the immediate future. (11) When necessary, improvement plans are developed and action is initiated to put those improvements in place [17].

The director of research and instructional auditing developed a format for writing high quality criterion-referenced test items for every subject taught in the school district. To accomplish this in an economical manner, a dollar amount per each test item of acceptable quality (determined by the director and/or assistant director) was paid to any teacher who wrote the item. They could be developed at home, during planning periods, during summer months or whenever the individual teacher found the time and wished to supplement her/his income. These items were then combined into a test item bank from which sample items were selected to test the achievement level of individual students and groups of students in each instructional program offered by the Hypothetical School District.

This system model is depicted in Figure 4.2. The continuous recycling is evident from viewing the model.

The example of the restructuring of Hypothetical School District's instructional operations clearly illustrates the effect of OD interventions and the resultant requirement for many HRD activities. The interweaving of the OD and HRD components as a change process shows the balance of HRD corrections and responses required to stabilize the "frame-breaking" change that results from a profound restructuring of a district's organization [18]. Although the Hypothetical School District example is quite a dramatic one, it is not unusual for parts of this restructuring to be taking place today in school districts across this entire nation. One only has to think briefly about the potential impact on school districts and on the employees of the school district who are currently dealing with such matters as: (1) parental choice;

(2) magnet schools; (3) reductions in finances; (4) state mandates; (5) union/management conflicts; (6) whole language programs; (7) effective schools research impacts; (8) clinical supervision methodologies; and (9) equity issues, or numerous other internal or external variables or changes to realize that school districts and their constituent parts, and the employees of the school districts, are currently, and always will be, subject to change. In order to best cope with these changes and direct them in a manner that improves the school district and the employees as well, it is important that each school district develop a comprehensive high quality plan for an integrated OD (Organization Development) and HRD (Human Resource Development) program.

SUMMARY

This chapter outlined operational action planning, and the processes which follow the determination of strategic objectives agreed-upon during the planning activities. Unlike the strategic planning, a variety of stakeholders should not be involved during this process. Action plans designed to carry out the predetermined strategic goals and objectives involve four distinct activities: (1) brainstorming alternative solutions or courses of action, (2) conducting a force field analysis for each alternative being considered, (3) doing a cost/benefit analysis for each alternative being considered and (4) selecting the best alternative solution. The fictitious Hypothetical School District was again used to illustrate the operationalizing of these activities, including the reporting of multiple brainstormed suggestions for achieving strategic objectives and goals; the selection (and display of strategies) of alternatives for further exploration; the force field analysis of those strategies to determine the potential restraining and supporting elements; and the details that go into the chosen action plan. A detailed description of an actual dramatic district level restructuring provided insight into the OD and HRD activities that took place.

Once the action plan is completed and assessed through the summative evaluation structures, the recycling process of the strategic planning model determines the eventual outcome of the action plan—elimination, continuation, or modification and implementation.

GUIDELINES

1. Do not involve a variety of stakeholders in the operational planning process; this is a matter for the district's employees.
2. Employ the four distinct activities designed to accomplish previously agreed upon goals and objectives, which are brainstorming alternative solutions or courses of action; conducting a force field analysis for each alternative being considered; doing a cost/benefit analysis for each alternative being considered; and selecting the best alternative solution.
3. Review all the brainstormed ideas, obtain clarification of them and select several of them for greater exploration, if necessary.
4. Develop a force field analysis for all alternatives to determine the restraining and supporting factors.
5. Develop a cost/benefit analysis when this will prove helpful.
6. Devise a detailed action plan for the alternative of choice.
7. Review the operational plan as it related to the strategy.
8. Recycle the process when necessary.

EXERCISES

1. Select a strategic goal related to a logical strategic plan for your district, and develop a set of objectives supporting that goal.
2. Brainstorm alternatives to accomplish one or more of the objectives, and review them for greater-depth selection.
3. Elaborate upon the various activities that would need to be undertaken to accomplish one of the alternatives.
4. Develop a force field analysis for three of the alternatives, and do a cost/benefit analysis.
5. Select a likely alternative and develop an operational action plan for the alternative.
6. Assess the operational action plan through the summative evaluation process; relate the results to the district's strategic plan.

SELECTED REFERENCES

1. Pfeiffer, J. W., ed. 1986. *Strategic Planning.* San Diego, CA: University Associated, Inc., pp. 21–22.

2. Herman, J. 1989. "Strategic Planner: One of the Changing Leadership Roles of the Principal", *The Clearing House*, 63(2): 56–58.

3. Morrisey, G. L., P. J. Below, and B. L. Acomb. 1988. *The Executive Guide to Operational Planning*. San Francisco, CA: Jossey-Bass, Inc., pp. 65–66.

4. Kaufman, R. and J. Herman. 1991. *Strategic Planning in Education*. Lancaster, PA: Technomic Publishing Co., Inc.

5. Schmuck, R. A. and M. B. Miles, eds. 1971. *Organizational Development in Schools*. Palo Alto, CA: National Press Books, pp. 208–210.

6. Byars, L. L. 1987. *Strategic Management*. Second edition. New York, NY: Harper & Row, Publishers, p. 32.

7. Schmuck, R. A. and P. J. Runkel. 1988. *The Handbook of Organization Development in Schools*. Prospect Heights, IL: Waveland Press, Inc., p. 223.

8. Morrisey, G. L., P. J. Below, and B. L. Acomb. *The Executive Guide*, p. 69.

9. Kaufman, R. and J. Herman. *Strategic Planning*.

10. Herman, J. 1989. "School Business Officials' Roles in the Strategic Planning Process (Part II)", *School Business Affairs*, 55(3): 20–23.

11. Kaufman, R. and J. Herman. *Strategic Planning*.

12. Tushman, M. L., W. H. Newman, and E. Romanelli. 1986. "Convergence and Upheaval: Managing the Unsteady Pace of Organization Evolution", *California Management Review*, 29(1): 29–41.

13. Mace-Matluck, B. J. *Research-Based Strategies for Bringing about Successful School Improvement*. Austin, TX: Southwest Educational Development Laboratory (Office of Educational Research and Improvement, U.S. Department of Education). p. 6 (1986).

14. English, F. and B. Steffy. "Curriculum Mapping: An Aid to School Curriculum Management", *Spectrum*, 1(4): 17–26 (1983).

15. Stephens, G. and J. Herman. "Using the Instructional Audit for Policy and Program Improvement", *Educational Leadership*, 42(8): 70–75 (1985).

16. Lewis, A. *Restructuring America's Schools*. Arlington, VA: American Association of School Administrators, pp. 234–235. (1989).

17. Stephens, G. and J. Herman, "Using the Instructional Audit", pp. 70–75.

18. Tushman, M. L., W. H. Newman, and E. Romanelli, "Convergence and Upheaval", p. 41.

CHAPTER 5

Fitting the Employees to the Organization

THIS CHAPTER WILL develop a complete systems approach, which is depicted in Figure 5.1, to the tasks involved in a comprehensive approach to employee and organizational human resource *needs* (gap between "what is" and "what should be" or "what could be"). The topics discussed include: (1) determining the desired and required human resources, (2) designing and adopting favorable conditions related to hiring and maintaining high quality employees, (3) locating excellent employee candidates, (4) screening potential employees, (5) selecting employees, (6) assigning employees to a maximal position placement, (7) inducting employees, (8) supervising employees, (9) appraising employees to determine "fit" to organizational expectations, (10) providing training and staff development activities, (11) preparing the human resource inventory, (12) performing exit interviews upon separation from employment, and (13) projecting future human resource needs. After the projection of future human resource needs, the entire system is recycled [1].

The quality of the school district's or school building's instruction to students and the quality of the supportive services depends almost totally on the quality of those employees who are hired and retained and who are ultimately responsible for the quality of service delivered. Therefore, it behooves the school district's decision makers to expend whatever resources are required to locate, hire, place, assess, train, and retain high-quality school district employees. A systematic approach to the entire system of hiring and keeping quality people will pay big dividends when the outcomes of the school district's or school building's efforts are adjudicated. Let's now turn to a systems approach to this important human resource task.

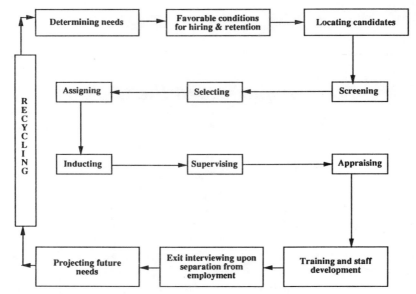

Figure 5.1 *A comprehensive systems model of employee and organizational human resource needs.*

DETERMINING NEEDS

A *need* is a gap or a discrepancy between "what is" and "what should be" or "what could be". A human resource need can be identified by carefully studying the programs offered by the school district, the current human resources available to cover them, and the changes in the numbers and types of student or community related services to be offered. Many examples of needs that have been identified by school districts include:

- the addition of programs for handicapped students
- the addition of programs for gifted and talented students
- an increase in service-related and information-related vocational courses and a decrease in vocational courses geared to manufacturing and agriculture
- a lengthening of the school day or school year
- an increase or a decrease in the student population
- a change in the racial mix or socio-economic mix of students attending a school district or school building

- an adjustment to societal or governmental demands for additional training in science, health, mathematics, or foreign language offerings
- a decision to expand the co-curricular activities offered by the school district or a decision to expand interscholastic sports for female students to the levels offered to the male students
- a decision to offer adult education and continuing education programs to the community at large
- the replacement of "key" employees who are about to leave employment because of retirement or transfer to another place of employment
- the inability to retain high quality employees for any length of time after their initial hire
- the inability to attract the quality level of new employees required
- the lack of a positive and effective systems approach to hiring and retaining the human resources desired and required to operate a high quality school district or school building

Most school districts that have problems hiring and retaining high quality human resources evidence problems similar to those listed. In most cases, those districts that experience problems in the human resource area possess a combination of the items listed [2]. Also, these districts probably do not have in place a high quality, effective systems approach to locating, hiring, and retaining the types of employees required. These school districts must start with a clear identification of the district's *needs* (gaps or discrepancies between "what is" and "what should be" or "what could be") related to human resources. Once the *needs* are clearly identified, the district's decision makers should dwell on those conditions that are required to hire and retain the type, quality, and quantity of employees they desire [3]. In exploring the conditions that are favorable to hiring and maintaining employees, the decision makers must realize they are in competition with other school districts and with other types of firms or organizations that offer employment opportunities to the existing or potential employees of the school district [4].

Once the needs are clearly defined, the next logical step is to discover what the district should have in place to attract and keep high quality employees. These conditions include: (1) salary, (2) fringe benefits, and (3) working conditions.

FAVORABLE CONDITIONS FOR HIRING AND RETAINING QUALITY EMPLOYEES

If your school district is located in a highly populated area where people wish to reside, if you pay very high salaries, if you have excellent fringe benefits, and if you have desirable working conditions, you should have little trouble locating, hiring, and retaining the quantity and quality of employees you desire. If, however, some or all of these conditions do not exist in your school district, you must create reasons for potential candidates to select your district; this is especially true in areas with shortages of skilled or certified employees, for example [5].

Certain situations provide advantages to the school district. For instance, if you are in an employment area where there are cyclical layoffs, you may be able to hire and retain maintenance specialists with the expectation of continuous employment even though your hourly wage would not match that of industry. Again, if your district is located in a college town, spouses may be available for a few years while their marriage partners are working on her/his degree(s). In addition to these highly specific favorable situations, all school districts can benefit by creating some favorable employment conditions, such as the following.

Flexible Working Hours

Working hours in many cases can be made to accommodate certain categories of employees. Many secretarial, food service, teacher aide, transportation, or custodial personnel will opt for a school year schedule rather than for a calendar year work schedule. Mothers or fathers who wish to be home with their children during the summers or who wish to start and end their work day at the same time as their children can create a major advantage to both the school district and to the parents. Of course, there are many additional reasons for selecting the school year and school day employment schedule, which may relate to the individual employee's desires [6].

Shared Positions

Shared positions can often be created, and they may attract employees in areas of shortages; or they may attract potential employees who may not, for personal reasons, desire to or be able to work full time. Making it easier for classroom teachers to share a job or for teacher aides to share a job are ways of increasing the supply of employees. Excellent teachers who previously hired on as full-time employees might like to work in just the mornings or the afternoons, or for two or three days per week [7]. Such combinations are more likely at the secondary level, specialty support areas (such as physical education or music) or in the case of half-day kindergarten arrangements; it is more difficult to split a traditional elementary classroom assignment due to the sustained teacher contact and instructional requirements. In these situations, the district can create a shared position for two high-quality employees. When this solution is utilized, the district must make certain that the two employees assigned to a shared job: (1) are compatible, (2) will unify their planning, and (3) will share the fringe benefit package in order to keep the district's fringe costs equivalent to those for a single full time employee.

Flex Schedules

Flex schedules are possible for certain categories of employees. For example, it is entirely possible to have certain custodial or maintenance employees work for four ten-hour days instead of five eight-hour days. Many variations on this theme can be developed for different employee categories by creative human resource decision makers [8].

Shifts

Shift differential assignments and pay are also possible means of attracting certain categories of school district employees. For example, it is reasonable to schedule most cleaning and maintenance shifts at times when the school buildings are not being utilized by students or the community. By going to a three-shift system and by allowing employees to select the shift they prefer (as much as possible), the quantity and quality of work done should improve. For instance, the district could offer a day shift that begins at 7:00 A.M. and ends at 3:00 P.M., an afternoon shift (with a pay differential of 50 cents or $1.50 per hour) which begins at 3:00 P.M. and ends at 11:00 P.M., and an evening shift (with a $2.00 or $5.00 per hour differential) that begins at 11:00 P.M. and ends at 7:00 A.M.

Salary Credit

Salary credit for new employees with previous experience is another way of attracting high quality, experienced employees who have recently moved into the area or who have recently decided to change jobs. Most school districts have salary schedules that pay higher salaries for years of experience; some of these districts (and perhaps many of them) will not hire new experienced employees and provide them any experience credit, or they will provide the new hire with limited experience credit as a means of saving budgetary expenditures related to employee costs [9]. This is a very short-sighted decision, especially for those school districts that are having difficulty in locating the quantity or quality of employees desired.

Fringe Benefit Options

Fringe benefit options are also important in attracting the type of employees desired. Fringe benefits can include such things as dental insurance, optical insurance, hospital and surgical insurance, drug riders, pension plans, investment options, life insurance, vacations, employee assistance programs for employees who are undergoing stressful situations in their lives, accidental death and disability insurance, liability insurance, income protection insurance, and optional employee paid or partially paid group benefits, such as universal life insurance. The types of fringe benefits that can be made available are increasing almost yearly. Three specific decisions can be made by a school district to increase the interest of potential employees: (1) if a spouse is covered by another employer, the school district can permit the school employee to opt for the average fringe benefit to be applied to areas not covered by the spouse's employer, or it can allow the school employee to enrich the fringe coverage by building better benefits on top of those already provided by the spouse's employer;

(2) it can allow family coverage in addition to coverage for the individual employee; and (3) it can allow the employee to participate in a cafeteria fringe benefit plan wherein the employee can choose the types and degree of fringes she/he wishes, while keeping the total amount allocated to the employee stable [10].

Fair Salary Paid

Salary paid is another very important factor in hiring and retaining quality employees. If a school district cannot pay salaries equivalent to the highest salaries paid in the area, it may be able to develop supplemental pay situations that will assist them in competing with the total income paid by competitors. A typical free-market inequity situation occurs in those rural/developing districts that surround the first outer-urban "ring" of affluent suburban districts; these school systems lack the tax base to be truly competitive. Yet because of their urban proximity, they cannot rely on any geographic monopoly effect to command and retain a ready supply of competent employees. Such districts must emphasize noncontractual or alternative salary enhancements. Examples are: (1) creating a great variety of supplemental contracts or salary enhancements for teachers who coach or sponsor a cocurricular activity for students; science, math, foreign language and environmental clubs, intramural sports sponsorship, or any variety of other opportunities that will enrich the students' experiences and supplement the teacher's pay. (2) Other areas might include employment for summer school teaching, staff development or training activities' employment, or employment related to curriculum development projects. (3) Weekend or after-school student enrichment or improvement activities add to the possibilities offered for increased pay. Such incentives must be matched with more climate-oriented and employee-supportive incentives, advantages larger and more affluent districts may lack [11].

Custodians, teacher aides, food service personnel, transportation personnel, and all other categories can receive supplemental pay for training or for staff development activities offered after normal work hours. The possibility of extra pay for project work of a related or alternate nature also could be provided. These paraprofessional and auxiliary positions are traditionally associated with lower pay or with part-time status. It is beneficial for the district to "package" full time assignments for these individuals in order to create combined positions that pay a living wage; this could therefore serve to retain able individuals. Fill-in hours during the school day and the summer normal down-time can be combined to offer a dual job description (supported with training) for an individual who can drive a school bus on the twice-daily routing, and work as a custodian or maintenance employee during the daily "between" hours and in the summer, for example. In the absence of any union shop restrictions, such hybrids could be effective for the district and for the employee.

Positive Working Environment

The working environment, if very positive and well-known, will oftentimes attract employees to a school district that may not be able to pay the highest salaries or offer the most extensive fringe benefits. This is an area that can be worked upon and developed by any school district in the nation. Regardless of the current working environment, this is one area that can always stand attention and improvement. The types of variables that make a school district or a school building desirable to potential or existing employees include the following: (1) they must have interesting work, (2) they must have opportunities for input into decisions that affect them, (3) they must have opportunities to improve and grow, (4) they must be recognized for their contributions, (5) they must be accepted by their peers, (6) they must buy into the vision and mission of the school district and of the school building or department to which they are assigned, (7) they must work in an environment that is safe and healthy, (8) they must feel that they are contributing to that vision and mission to a significant degree, (9) they must feel ownership, (10) they must feel that they are treated openly, honestly, and fairly, and (11) they must feel wanted, cared about, recognized and rewarded (not necessarily financially rewarded, although that is helpful as well) [12]. To summarize, current employees must feel that it is "a great place to work", and they will widely publicize, as a result, satisfaction with the job conditions in the school district and with their specific job assignments. Such positive communication will impact the community and potential future employees. Actions by the school district decision makers that attend to any of these variables will pay dividends. There are numerous action programs that can address each of these variables, and the success of the approach is only governed by the will and creativity of those who hold the responsibility for creating and maintaining a high-quality work environment [13].

Once the district's decision makers have: (1) identified their specific human resource needs and they have (2) created the best mix of salary, fringe benefits, and working environments they are able to create within the restrictions that exist in the local school district; they can move on to the next step in the systems approach to human resource planning. That next step involves the locating of candidates (potential employees) for the specific vacancies or openings that have been previously identified by the local school district's decision makers.

LOCATING CANDIDATES

Regardless of the local school district's needs or its available candidate pool, it is impossible to have too many candidates. The greater the supply, the better chance of hiring and retaining the top quality employees the district desires. If the candidate pool becomes very large, the only challenge to the persons responsible for human resources is that of developing a screening system that will discriminate among the candidates within a reasonable time and with a reasonable effort by those persons who are responsible for locating, hiring, and retaining employees.

Locating the employees who have been identified by the previously completed needs assessment depends on the specific type of employee the district is attempting to hire, the supply and demand situation that exists related to that specific type of employee, and the sources of the employee pool. In every case, both local and outreach sources should be thoroughly investigated [14]. In addition, specific sources of high-quality employees in specialized areas should be determined (for example, one may wish to hire a deaf or hard of hearing specialist who is well versed in signing from Gallaudet University, a mechanical engineer from General Motors Tech, or a school nurse from a highly specialized training center dedicated to the specific training of nurses who work in school district situations).

What are the sources of potential employees? There are many and we shall examine those available to school districts.

- *The school district's current employees* are an often overlooked source in locating high-quality potential employees. If they are pleased with the district and their work assignment and if they are notified of vacancies and asked to recommend candidates or make contacts with potential candidates, they can swell the pool of potential employees by telling friends or contacts in other school districts or other places of employment what a desirable place the district is to work in, and they can also suggest that they apply for positions that are open. They also may have contacts with universities that will be helpful in locating well qualified candidates. A personal contact is the best way to encourage people to apply.
- *Universities and other placement sources* can be helpful in locating potential employees. The school district's persons responsible for human resource activities would be wise to make visits to placement sources to talk to candidates, but they should also make themselves known to the placement directors and their staffs (don't overlook the placement office secretaries). Once they know you personally, you can send them vacancy notices, ask them to recommend specific candidates, get a list of graduates (if you are dealing with a university) and make direct phone requests to the placement office or to specific candidates they recommend.
- *State or national conventions* can be sources of contact, particularly those sponsored by professional organizations with memberships in the areas of your particular recruitment needs, such as minorities, women in administration, and critical certification fields (science, math, bilingual, English as a Second Language), etc. It is helpful to make contact with the staff of such organizations, and to maintain an open communications channel. These groups, such as the elementary and/or secondary principal associations, frequently have advance information about members or individuals desiring relocation. Additionally, such organizations frequently offer a job listing service in their professional publications that lists openings from various regions or states.

- *Neighboring school districts* are also sources of potential employees. By letting neighboring school districts know of your employee vacancies and asking them to post the vacancies, you may increase your pool of experienced people who will apply. This is especially true if a neighboring school district has to lay off (pink slip) employees due to financial difficulties or decreasing pupil populations. It also may offer the neighboring school district an opportunity to promote a rising star when there is no vacancy in their specific school district. Many intelligent employers will help employees who are to be laid off to find new employment opportunities, and many will assist others in advancing their careers elsewhere if the potential does not exist in their school district. A sense of reciprocity and professional courtesy with nearby colleagues is desirable for this reason, and for maintaining and networking local information pertaining to human resource management.
- *Advertisement of vacancies* in many market sources is another means of locating potential employees. Local and regional newspapers, TV announcements of job vacancies, placement bulletins from universities, announcements of vacancies to commercial placement firms, and placement of job notices at employment agencies are all possibilities. The state department of education or the area inter-mediate agency may be a source of highly-experienced, and, (more to the point) currently-certified individuals. In cases where the school system is experiencing a particular need in an area of highly specialized employment or in an area of severe job shortages, the district may wish to advertise in national sources such as the Sunday New York Times. Each of these sources will have to be decided upon based on the potential benefit as compared to the costs involved.

Once those who are responsible for human resource activities have investigated and decided upon the various methods to be used to locate potential employees and they have developed the formats required (affirmative action documentation, forms, records, etc.) to be submitted by interested candidates, they can turn to the task of screening the candidates who have applied [15]. Obviously, those who have applied have been previously sent a detailed job description, a position announcement, and a letter welcoming their application and explaining the procedures to be followed in selecting candidates who will be offered positions in the district.

SCREENING THE APPLICANTS FOR POSITION VACANCIES

If applicants are scarce, the district's decision makers can move immediately to the task of selecting one from the limited number of applicants; or they can refuse to hire anyone and subsequently re-advertise the vacancy. If, however, there are numerous applicants, the task of screening those to be given further consideration is the important next step to be addressed by the local school district's decision makers.

The vacancy announcement should have listed the specific criteria (skills, knowledges, attitudes, experiences, educational qualifications, and other criteria) desired of candidates who apply for the position vacancy [16]. These same criteria should be used by those persons responsible for screening the candidates down to a reasonable number to be further explored. The screening should be independently conducted by multiple persons using the criteria announced [17]; and, once their independent judgements on the top ten or five candidates, (or whatever number they previously agreed upon) have been made, these individuals should get together and reach consensus on those candidates to be pursued further. It is important to the unsuccessful candidates, and it is only professionally courteous, to inform them as soon as possible that they are no longer being considered; they should also be thanked for their interest in the school district.

At this point, those candidates selected for further interviews must undergo additional screening [18]. If we take, for example, an elementary principal candidate, that person should be contacted to see if she/he is still interested in the position; and the candidate should be told that contact will be made with the current employer. If that contact provides a favorable response to the criteria developed for the position, the candidate(s) will be invited for a full-scale personal interview. The interview team may consist of representative teachers, parents, central office administrators, and, in the case of a secondary principal, for example, students. While an individual interview should also be conducted with the potential employee's immediate supervisor, these group interviews can be a rich source of data, providing the advantages of bringing out information not previously reported, in being time-efficient, and in providing greater scope and depth than individual interviews [19]. This group, then, based upon questions geared to the specific criteria previously decided upon, will interview the three to five candidates, and they will make a specific set of recommendations to the final decision makers. At this point (let's assume that two candidates are truly outstanding), the final decision makers may visit the district where the candidate is currently a teacher or a principal to personally observe whether or not the criteria evaluated during the paper review and the interview sessions exist, indeed, in practice [20].

Once the candidate is decided upon, the human resource decision makers in the district must formally select and get the board of education to approve the selection and the contractual or employment conditions recommended. There are specific requirements to be met during this selection phase.

SELECTING AND CONTRACTING

Whether or not the new employee is to be hired under an individual written contract or simply with an agreed upon salary, work year and fringe benefits—these matters must be clear and agreed to by the potential new employee and they must be defended when a recommendation is made for formal approval to the school district's board of education [21]. There may be flexibility in terms of experience credit allowed or other variables, and the recommendation to the board of education would need to explain why one candidate is offered different entry employment conditions than another. Some reasonable deviations, as in the case of the principal, may be related to her/his years of experience, the current salary and fringe benefits at her/his place of employment, one-time moving expenses or resettlement costs if the principal is coming from a different geographical area [22], the educational level of the candidate, the regional or national reputation of the candidate, whether the candidate is from an area of particular need or critical shortage, or numerous other variables. In any case, the contracting conditions must be agreed upon by the candidate and the board of education, and the selection must be defended as the person being the "best fit" of all available candidates.

Once the selection has been made, the human resource decision makers must assign the new employee to a situation that will maximize the success of the new employee and that will also maximize the potential outcomes to the school district. Assignment of new employees should not be a routinized "first come, first served" situation, but rather a carefully thought-out process that considers both the best placement to benefit the district and the best placement for the new employee [23].

ASSIGNING THE NEW EMPLOYEE

If the school district has a building where the teaching staff is relatively young and can use the assistance of someone who is highly specialized in instructional supervision, and those skills are possessed by the newly hired elementary principal, then that is where the newly hired principal should be assigned. On the other hand, if the principal is not highly skilled in this area, but she/he is excellent at monitoring student performance and working with an experienced teaching staff in modifying the curriculum to meet identified student achievement needs, the best placement may be in a school with an experienced staff. If the principal possesses both skills and if there are numerous openings, the principal may choose which of the situations will be of most interest to her/him. Of course, the possibility of moving another principal (hopefully, with that person's agreement) to another school to create the "best fit" for the new person is also a possibility that should not be overlooked. Everything being equal, the best fit is that which matches the new employee's desires with the assignment and that which will be most productive for the school district and the school building to which she/he is assigned.

Once the new hiree has been selected and before that person is able to take over her/his responsibilities, the local human resource decision makers can greatly assist that new employee in her/his transition period. This action will not only assist the new employee, but it will also let the employee know that the district is interested in helping that person in any way possible [24].

INDUCTING THE NEW EMPLOYEE

New employees will feel that they have made a wise employment decision if they know that the local school district is not only interested in what they themselves can do for the school district, but that the school district human resource personnel are interested in assisting them in any reasonable manner with their personal needs. Some ways in which those persons responsible for the human resource activities of the local school district can assist new employees (the degree of assistance will vary with local employees versus out-of-district employees and with the category of new employee) are listed below. For this purpose, we will stay with the school principal example, and we will assume that the newly hired principal is from a different state or from a different location with the state, far removed from the local school district.

- *Provide personal in-district contacts* for the newly hired principal. Besides offering the newly hired principal the opportunity to call collect any employee of the human resource department of the school district, supply her/him with the names of persons who volunteer to assist in the transition. These names, addresses, and phone numbers should include the building secretary where the new principal will be assigned, a teacher from that building, and a well-respected, helpful and experienced elementary school principal in the school district.
- *Advance information should be mailed* to the new principal. Besides sending copies of the vitae of all employees in the building, the principal should be sent all curriculum guides, the budget, any plans that have been made by the preceding principal, any union contracts, a copy of board of education policies and building rules, a school calendar, the names and addresses of all other school district administrators, a listing of the names and addresses of PTA or other citizen leaders in his/her building's attendance area, or any other information that will be helpful in assisting the new person getting a head start on the job. Two other pieces of information may be especially helpful to the new principal: (1) copies of the previous year's minutes of staff meetings and any newletters or correspondence distributed to the staff, parents or community from the school building; and, (2) a district-paid temporary subscription to the local newspaper.
- *Offer to assist the newly hired person in locating housing.* This can best be done by: (1) asking the community to

assist the school district by listing available rentals in the district. The district should assign someone to check out the quality of these rentals prior to a visit by the new employee. Also, the district should offer to provide a school district-paid trip for the employee to transport the principal and family (if she/he has a family) to investigate possible housing; (2) the district can forward brochures of available housing for purchase and the names of reliable realty firms. The district can offer to make contact, if the new principal desires, with a realtor who will directly communicate with the principal and establish a schedule to look at housing.

- *Offer the new principal and her/his family a visit at district expense in order to become acquainted with the community.* During this visit, the principal and her/his family should be escorted around the community to locate sources of shopping, churches, entertainment or whatever else the family may wish to see. It would be wise to visit the school campuses the children would attend if any children are of school age, and it would be helpful to introduce the new principal and the family to persons with whom they might wish to become quickly acquainted.

- *Provide a welcoming ceremony* for the new principal (this should be done for all employees as a group, or individually when an individual welcome seems most appropriate). In the case of the principal, soft drinks, coffee, and cookies provided by the district or in cooperation with the teachers' union and PTA should be made available, the media should be asked to attend the event, and a short welcome should be given by the board president, the superintendent, someone representing the district's teachers union, a representative of the building's teaching staff, the PTA president, and (when possible) the mayor of the city. The principal should also be requested to give a brief response as this, in a very real sense, is a "coming out" ceremony.

Once this initial induction period has passed, the principal should be assured of continuing assistance by the central office's human resource department as she/he goes about the routine activities of the principalship. One of the best means of helping the new principal, or any employee, is by assessing her/his performance against the criteria that were used in developing the job description and the position vacancy announcement. These factors are those considered to be CSF's (Critical Success Factors). It is a truism that everyone can improve her/his performance, and it is with this in mind and a true desire to assist in that improvement attempt that employee supervision and performance appraisals should be conducted.

SUPERVISING AND APPRAISING EMPLOYEES

Although supervision and employee performance appraisal can be argued to be two separate functions, they are inextricably linked in a school district that sees them as functions designed (1) to assist employees, and (2) to improve performance. Both of these functions will be discussed under one topical heading. The key to a successful program of supervision, assessment, and employee performance improvement is to have a system that is developed by both those persons being supervised and those who are responsible for the supervisory activities [25]. Obviously, the assessment should rely mainly on those CSF's (Critical Success Factors) that were outlined in the job description and for which the person was selected as an employee. A specific schedule of events, a standard of performance and an action program should be decided upon. Also, each criterion that is considered critical should have indicators or descriptors listed upon which the supervisor can make an assessment of the quality of the employee's work [26].

By involving the employees in the development of the assessment instruments and in the structure and content to be utilized, the district has guaranteed that substantive due process has been accomplished; and by following the timelines and processes established, the district has guaranteed that procedural due process has been followed [27]. Although these guarantees are not crucial to the great majority of employees, they may become very important if a poor performing employee does not improve after being provided much assistance and after a reasonable time frame is provided within which the employee is to demonstrate improvement. Figure 5.2 represents a rational structural model for the supervision and assessment of employee performance.

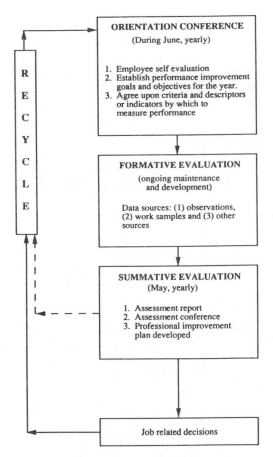

Figure 5.2 *A structural model for the supervision and assessment of employees.*

Let's briefly amplify upon the components outlined in Figure 5.2. Although each is important, none can stand alone and still provide a comprehensive high quality system of supervision and performance assessment.

The orientation conference at the beginning of the cycle is an important first step. At this conference, the supervisor and the individual supervised agree upon all the ground rules to be followed for the subsequent year. It is at this conference that the employee discusses her/his self evaluation with the supervisor; and, together, they establish the improvement goals and specific objectives for the year. They also develop the criteria and descriptors that are to be used by the employee and the employer in assessing the quality level of performance. Finally, they agree upon the timelines and procedures to be followed throughout the year [28].

The two major structures for assessing performance are: (1) achievement of specific, agreed-upon performance improvement objectives (an example for our principal example might be in the quality of conducting post observation conferences with teachers assigned her/his building as measured by (a)_____, (b)_____ and (c)_____); and, (2) the standard of performance achieved on specific criteria as determined by a series of descriptors or indicators for each of the criteria related to the CSF's (Critical Success Factors) for that specific position (elementary principal). One criterion and a few assessment descriptors or indicators, with a five point scale standard, is provided as an example.

An Example Criterion and Indicators for an Elementary Principal

standard: 1   2   3   4   5
                                                 (best)

Criteria: To monitor student achievement and to use the results to modify instruction.

Indicators

(*1*) Itemizes standardized student achievement scores to determine areas of successful achievement and areas in need of attention.

(*2*) Analyzes student criterion-referenced achievement testing to determine which desired outcomes (using mastery as 80 percent of the items related to each outcome objective) are being achieved and which are in need of additional attention.

(*3*) Disaggregates both norm-referenced and criterion-referenced student achievement test data by race, sex, socioeconomic level, and any other important variables to determine if there are significant discrepancies in achievement levels between: (1) students participating in particular programs (such as Chapter I); (2) gender groups; (3) student cohorts; (4) curricular or course areas; (5) grade levels; or (6) any individual students. This data analysis is done by the principal to make certain no students are "falling through the cracks" because their achievement is masked in group scores.

(4) Analyzes student achievement scores to locate "outliers" (those who fall above or below three standard deviations of the mean score). This is done to investigate why some are extremely successful and others are extremely unsuccessful. Further investigation of the positive outliers may provide information that will be useful in improving instructional delivery to the general student body. Further investigation of negative outliers is useful for the purpose of discovering what specifically is/are the problem(s), with the intention of improving delivery structures that will overcome the problem(s).

(5) Meets regularly with her/his teachers to study the monitored and arrayed student achievement data for the purpose of working with them to improve instruction wherever possible.

(6) Puts in place a follow-through procedure to determine if the instructional changes designed by and implemented by the teaching staff have had the desired positive impact on student achievement.

Formative evaluation is a year long continuous process that zeroes in on the quality of the employee's performance related to the specific objectives and the criteria agreed upon during the orientation conference. The supervisor performs a dual role during this formative process. The supervisor serves as a monitor of performance data that are provided the employee in a feedback conference for the purposes of analysis by the employee and the supervisor, and the supervisor is a helper and locator of human or material resources designed to assist the employee in her/his improvement efforts [29].

The formative evaluation process involves data collection through three sources: (1) *direct observations* by the supervisor (which may be geared to a specific request, such as clinical teacher/principal conferences, or which may be of a general nature, such as spending a few one-half days shadowing the principal). These may be announced or unannounced, but they are always followed by a feedback conference within twenty-four hours of the observation; (2) *work samples* which are minutes of meetings, samples of curriculum adjustments made, planning documents, studies, or whatever the principal feels should be shared with the supervisor as they relate to the performance improvement objectives or criteria agreed upon for the year; and, (3) *other sources of data*, which can include anything either the supervisor or the employee (principal) believes to be pertinent [30].

Summative evaluation is the end-of-year performance assessment based upon the initial objectives and criteria agreed upon at the beginning of the supervisory/assessment cycle, and the data for this summative assessment includes all the data collected throughout the year by the formative evaluation activities. As part of this summative evaluation process, or soon after the conclusion of the summative evaluation conference, a *professional improvement plan* (consisting of specific objectives and criteria) for the subsequent year is agreed upon by the employee and supervisor. Agreement upon that plan initiates a new supervisory and assessment cycle [31].

Sometimes a supervisor is also responsible for making salary, tenure, or placement decisions. If this is the case, these decisions will follow the summative conference, and the new cycle will be initiated after those decisions have been made by the supervisor.

As part of the supervisory assessment cycle, training and staff development requirements are designed and implemented to assist the employee in the performance improvement process. Let's now turn to a brief discussion of this topic. (For a more complete discussion, see Chapter 6.)

TRAINING AND STAFF DEVELOPMENT

Training and staff development activities are a joint responsibility of employees who are obligated to maintain and improve their skills and knowledge, and of the employer who is obligated to provide resources and opportunities that will allow the employees to upgrade their level of expertise. In addition, it is crucial that the employer provide training and staff development opportunities when new technology is introduced, or when the organization (school district) makes any major change in its structure or processes [32].

Training and staff development activities, to be maximally effective, should zero in on the *needs* (gaps or discrepancies between "what is", and "what should be" or "what could be") at three levels: (1) the individual employee level, (2) the group level, and (3) the total organizational (school district) level [33]. The district level may involve such activities as assisting all employees in adjusting to new laws, a new school board policy, or the introduction of a new technology into the total school district operation. The group level may involve such matters as the entire group of employees in the business office being trained on an improved accounting system. The individual employee's training or staff development program should include those specific helps related to the objectives and criteria developed for that employee's annual improvement plan.

If we stay with our example of the elementary principal who has a need to improve her/his skill in post-observation conferences with teachers, we may develop a combination of training or staff development activities geared to assisting the principal to improve her/his performance in this area. Someone from the office may cover the principal's building for a few days while the principal observes another elementary principal who is an expert on post-observation conferencing, the district may purchase books or videotapes to assist the principal, the district may pay for the principal to attend a week-long workshop on teacher observation and conferencing led by nationally known experts, an expert elementary principal in the district may be asked to observe the principal and provide feedback and suggestions throughout the school year, or there could be other ways of assisting the elementary principal in improving her/his skills in post-observation conferencing with teachers.

Up to this point we have talked about: (1) determining our human resource needs; (2) providing favorable conditions for hiring and retaining employees; (3) locating candidates; (4) screening potential employees; (5) selecting those to be hired from the candidate pool; (6) assigning the newly hired employee; (7) inducting the employee; (8) supervising the employee; (9) appraising the employee; and (10) providing training and staff development activities. There comes a time, however, when an employee will leave the district because of retirement, a change of geographic location, a promotional opportunity or any other number of valid additional reasons. We should not let those who leave exit without taking advantage of the knowledge and attitudes they possess about the district. It is highly recommended that as part of the formal separation procedure (final check, transfer of records, etc.) an exit interview be conducted.

EXIT INTERVIEWING

If the employee who is leaving employment with the district truly believes that the human resource staff is interviewing her/him for the sole purpose of trying to improve the work environment for all new and existing employees, a great deal of very valuable information can be gained by interviewing each person who is terminating employment with the school district. The exit interview should be structured around the following type of questions, after a sincere thank-you is given the employee for her/his contribution to the district during her/his employment (an appropriate memento would also be appreciated). Questions appropriate for such an interview could include:

- Did you enjoy your employment in the district?
- What things did you enjoy most?
- Do you feel that we treated you well and fairly during your employment with us? (If the answer is "no" or "yes", ask for specific examples.)
- Do you feel that we used your knowledge, skills, and leadership to the district's and to your best advantage? (If the answer is "no" or "yes", ask for specific examples.)
- Did you feel that the process we used to select you from the candidate pool was fair and professionally done? (If the answer is "no" or "yes", ask for specific examples.)
- Do you feel that we did enough to help you as you started your job (induction)? (If the answer is "no" or "yes", ask for specific examples.)
- Do you feel that we provided you with sufficient resources and training or staff development opportunities to assist you in performing your job well? (If the answer is "no" or "yes", ask for specific examples.)
- Do you feel our salary schedule and fringe benefits are fair and adequate? (If the answer is "yes" or "no", ask for specifics.)
- Did you get the supervisory and other help that you felt you needed? (If the answer is "yes" or "no", ask for specifics.)

- What can we do to make working here better for your replacement and for all of the school district's employees? (Ask for specifics.)

When a sufficient number of exit interviews are conducted, patterns and trends can be discerned. Whenever these data define a *need* (gap or discrepancy between "what is" and "what should be"), those responsible for the human resource activities within the district should develop action plans to meet the need(s) identified. Many times this will involve OD (Organizational Development) activities that lead to restructuring the district's organization or its processes.

Now that we have taken an employee throughout the entire system, we must recycle by determining the existing needs and projecting future human resource needs. This new starting place is best accomplished by: (1) developing a matrix of the skills, knowledges and attitudes required; (2) analyzing the skills, knowledges and attitudes possessed by the current group of employees; and (3) taking heed of the information gathered from the exit interviews. For, only to the extent that those responsible for OD (Organizational Development) and HRD (Human Resource Development) see this as an interrelated systems process that is cyclical and ongoing, can a school district truly reach its vision of "what should be"—the degree of excellence desired.

SUMMARY

This chapter has presented the development of a systems approach and an overview of the tasks involved in a comprehensive process of dealing with employee and HRD needs. *Needs* (gaps or discrepancies between "what is" and "what should be" or "what could be") are identified by reviewing the district's program, resources, and variables that impact employees. The next logical step is to determine favorable conditions for hiring and retaining quality employees. Specific conditions to be considered include working hours, shared positions, flexible schools and assignments, salary ranges related to experience, fringe benefits, and the quality of the working environment.

Potential sources of employee recruitment include current-employee personal contacts, university placement offices, professional organizations and conventions, and adjacent districts. Once applicants are located, the screening process should winnow the initial candidate group down to those selected for interview through a multiple-criteria and multiple-judge search committee process. Group interviews should be conducted, paired with an individual immediate-supervisor interview.

Clarity of terms is critical to the (legal) selection and contracting process, and subsequent care should be taken to assign the new employee to maximize both district benefit and employee success. Assistance for the new employee should be supported with peer contacts and supervisor-provided transitional activities that will facilitate the induction experience. The provision of vital co-worker and other contacts, personal relocation assistance, and a formal welcome are also appropriate.

The formal supervisory and appraisal process, as did previous functions, should directly relate the the CSF's (Critical Success Factors) of the job criteria; and all the protocols of appraisal scheduling, performance standards, and a training program should be determined. Employee involvement in the development of supervisory and appraisal procedures is vital for morale and for due process purposes. Both the formative and summative evaluation processes should be documented, and they should be aimed at professional growth. Training and staff development are logical operational components of such an appraisal system, focused on needs at three impact levels: individual, group, and district. As a final system component, exit interviews are suggested as sources of information to assist in the discernment of patterns and trends, which will provide data that can be used by the district's decision makers to improve the entire program.

GUIDELINES

1. Employee and HRD needs should be viewed within the framework of identified needs, which are determined by studying the gaps or discrepancies between "what is" and "what should be" or "what could be".

2. The conditions affecting the desirability of the district as a place of employment should be considered and analyzed.

3. Traditional and nontraditional sources of information for recruitment should be identified and employed.

4. The recruitment and screening process should be designed for legal and maximum participatory purposes.

5. Contracting with the new employee should result in clarity of terms and agreements, and the assignment of these individuals should maximize both their professional experience and the district's benefit.

6. A professional and personal induction system should be provided.

7. The cyclical supervisory and appraisal process should begin with orientation, and it shall include formative and summative evaluation.

8. Training and staff development are a joint responsibility of employer and employee, and they should be needs-focused.

9. An exit interview should precede separation from the district in order to obtain vital feedback from an employee perspective, which will assist the decision makers in improving the program.

EXERCISES

1. Develop a system to determine the human resource needs for all categories of employees in the school district.

2. Develop an analysis of sources to locate and contact potential candidates for teachers, administrators, and all categories of classified (auxiliary) employees.

3. Write a job description for an: (a) administrator position and (b) teaching position.

4. Write a position announcement for an: (a) administrator position, and (b) teaching position.

5. Design an interview schedule for an: (a) administrator position, and (b) teaching position. (Remember to ask questions related to those Critical Success Factors pertaining to the specific job. Also, remember to ask follow-up questions related to what they have experienced in the past related to the Critical Success Factors.)

6. Determine how you would go about deciding which candidates to offer contracts, and how you would notify unsuccessful candidates.

7. Develop a year-long induction program for new employees and list critical checkpoints throughout the year.

8. Develop systems for evaluating a custodian, secretary, teacher, and a principal.

9. Determine how you as a supervisor would balance the helping relationship and the evaluative relationship in your appraisal system.

10. Develop an exit interview procedure, using questions that will provide you with feedback information which will assist in improving all aspects of your HRD operation.

SELECTED REFERENCES

1. Castetter, W. B. 1986. *The Personnel Function in Educational Administration*. New York, NY: Macmillan Publishing Company, p. 48.
2. Rebore, R. W. 1987. *Personnel Administration in Education*. Second edition. Englewood Cliffs, NJ: Prentice-Hall, pp. 104–106.
3. Castetter, W. B. *The Personnel Function*, p. 184.
4. Deutsch, A. 1979. *The Human Resources Revolution: Communicate or Litigate*. New York, NY: McGraw-Hill Book Company, p. 102.
5. *Business Week*. May 2, 1988. "Perspective of the Problem," pp. 126–127.
6. Schuster, F. E. 1985. *Human Resource Management*. Reston, VA: Reston Publishing Company, Inc., p. 9.
7. Webb, L. D. et al. 1987. *Personnel Administration in Education*. Columbus, OH: Merrill Publishing Company, p. 53.
8. Sloane, A. A. 1983. *Personnel-Managing Human Resources*. Englewood Cliffs, NJ: Prentice-Hall, Inc., p. 563.
9. Castetter, W. B. *The Personnel Function*, p. 452.
10. Sloane, A. A. *Personnel*, pp. 312–323.
11. Sloane, A. A. *Personnel*, p. 257.
12. Dyer, W. G. 1983. *Contemporary Issues in Management and Organizational Development*. Reading, MA: Addison Wesley Publishing Company, pp. 67, 126.
13. Sikula, A. F. and J. F. McKenna. 1984. *The Management of Human Resources*. New York, NY: John Wiley & Sons, pp. 113–115.
14. Deutsch, A. 1979. *The Human Resources Revolution*, p. 118.
15. Harris, B. M. et al. 1979. *Personnel Administration in Education*. Boston, MA: Allyn and Bacon, Inc., pp. 108–110.
16. Sikula, A. F. and J. F. McKenna. *Management*, p. 167.
17. Sikula, A. F. and J. F. McKenna. *Management*, p. 171.
18. Harris, B. M. et al. *Personnel Administration*, pp. 110–111.
19. Horwitz, J. and H. Kimpel. 1988. "Taking Control: Techniques for the Group Interview", *Training and Development Journal*, 42(10): 52–54.
20. Sikula, A. F. and J. F. McKenna. *Management*, pp. 80–81.

21. Rebore, R. W. *Personnel Administration*, pp. 320–322.

22. Sloane, A. A. *Personnel*, p. 118.

23. Rebore, R. W. *Personnel Administration*, p. 137.

24. Sloane, A. A. *Personnel*, pp. 167–175.

25. Schneier, C. E., R. W. Beatty, and L. S. Baird. 1986. "How to Construct a Successful Performance Appraisal System", *Training and Development Journal*, 40(4): 38–42.

26. Schneier, C. E., R. W. Beatty, and L. S. Baird. 1986. "Creating a Performance Management System", *Training and Development Journal*, 40(5): 74–79.

27. Castetter, W. B. *The Personnel Function*, pp. 356–381.

28. Human Resources Forum Supplement. Sept. 1989. "Entry-Level, Support Staff Need Training, Survey Shows", *Management Review*, pp. 1–4.

29. Harris, B. M. 1986. *Developmental Teacher Evaluation*. Boston, MA: Allyn and Bacon, pp. 20–21.

30. Harris, B. M. *Teacher Evaluation*, pp. 108–110.

31. Harris, B. M. et al. *Personnel Administration*, pp. 240–242.

32. Harris, B. M. et al. *Personnel Administration*, pp. 182–183.

33. Rebore, R. W. *Personnel Administration*, pp. 170–171.

CHAPTER 6

Evaluating, Developing and Training Employees

THE PRIMARY REASON for staff development and training programs is to improve the performance of employees based upon clearly identified needs. This has particular impact for the field of education, given the implied importance and need for continued growth in competence of public school personnel [1]. Human Resource Development (HRD) is the goal, and staff development and training programs are the means of accomplishing that goal.

When developing programs for adults, it is important to realize that planning for andragogy (the teaching of adults) is significantly different than planning for pedagogy (the teaching of children). Adult education as a field has grown over the last fifty years. It is characterized by such need factors as self-directed learning, a collaborative mode, opportunities for critical and reflective thinking, self-direction, and empowerment [2]. When planning staff development activities for adults it is important to consider the following:

- Adults come to the learning environment with a great deal of background experiences and much prior knowledge, which should be utilized.
- Adults should be *actively involved* in the learning process.
- Adult learners can help each other learn.
- Adults desire training activities that relate directly to their job responsibilities; particularly those that employ problem posing and solving [3].

It may be necessary, given the more traditional pedagogical process expectations of trainees with substantial experience in staff development and training, to reorient these individuals towards andragogical instructional methods; to assess and address their developmental stage of learning style receptivity [4].

Once we have established the goal of HRD and staff development and training as the means of achieving the goals and once we are aware of some of the most important factors to consider when planning staff development activities for adults, we can move to; (1) conducting a staff development needs assessment, (2) planning the overall staff development program, and (3) planning the details of a specific example staff development program.

CONDUCTING A STAFF DEVELOPMENT NEEDS ASSESSMENT

A *need* is the gap between "what is" and "what should be" or "what could be". In other words, a *need* is the discrepancy between current results and the required results. The *means* of closing the identified gaps are the staff development programs that are created.

There are three important dimensions of needs assessment within a school district that require staff development programs. They relate to the total school district, sub-groups within the school district, and individual employees of the school district. This relationship is demonstrated in Figure 6.1.

The needs (gaps between "what is" and "what should be") that affect everyone in the *total school district*, and for which staff development activities are appropriate interventions, might well come from technological or demographic changes [5]. The change of a school district's student composition from one of practically all white students to one comprised mostly of a mix of black, Asian, and Hispanic students should trigger the need for staff development activities among all employees. These could be related to the culture and should promote the communication skills required to successfully deal with a different student body mix.

Once the school district is committed to making all of its students computer literate, it requires staff development activities related to computer use and operation by every teacher, teacher aide, and administrator in the total school district. Computer instruction and management packages can greatly improve the effectiveness and efficiency of the district's operations, if the personnel responsible for delivery are well trained.

Sub-group needs can come from a wide variety of sources, and each identified need can be met by a staff development activity geared to that specific identified need. Examples include: (1) the

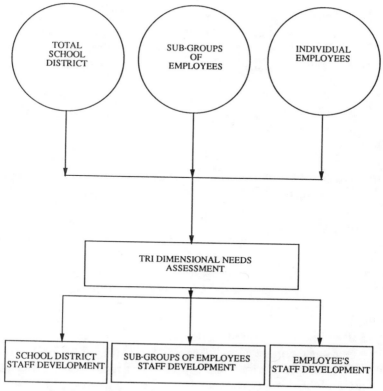

Figure 6.1 Tri-dimensional needs assessment model.

training of all industrial teachers in the use of robotics, once the school district has included robotics in its machine-related industrial courses; (2) the training of all elementary teachers in the whole language approach to language arts; (3) the training of school bus drivers to control vehicle slides during severe winter weather; (4) the training of all teachers in the technique of cooperative student learning (where students of different abilities are formed into a team); and (5) the training of all food service workers in dietetics.

Individual needs can best be identified on a continuous basis by utilizing staff evaluation as the method of needs assessment. Evaluation, in this case, is formative in nature, and it is a cooperative activity between the individual employee and the supervisor. In the case of a teacher, it is a cooperative identification of needs for improvement between the individual teacher and her/ his principal. In the case of an administrator, it is a cooperative identification of needs between the administrator and her/his immediate supervisor. Once the needs are identified, an individualized staff development program can be devised. Both individual and subgroup needs can be considered micro needs, in the sense of being intended for a smaller group, rather than for systemwide needs [6].

When evaluation and staff development are intricately interwoven into a complete system of needs assessment and performance improvement activities for each employee, a complete cyclical systems approach to performance improvement exists [7]. A series of graphics displays a holistic model of staff evaluation and staff development (see Figures 6.2 through 6.9). The elements of a holistic system include: (1) overlap between staff evaluation and staff development, (2) prerequisite conditions, (3) questions requiring answers, (4) types of needs, (5) positive assumptions for program development, (6) human needs, (7) sequential order of change, and (8) the completed holistic model. Each of the elements are crucial, and each of them apply to both the staff evaluation and staff development activities.

The feedback and overlap between the staff evaluation loop and the staff development loop are depicted in Figure 6.2 [8]. The staff evaluation loop depicts the continuous nature of formative evaluation for the purpose of needs assessment for the individual employee, the staff development loop depicts the continuous staff development activities that are undertaken by the individual to meet the needs that were identified, and the feedback and overlap area between the evaluation and development loops indicate

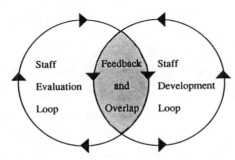

Figure 6.2 *Holistic model of staff evaluation and staff development.*

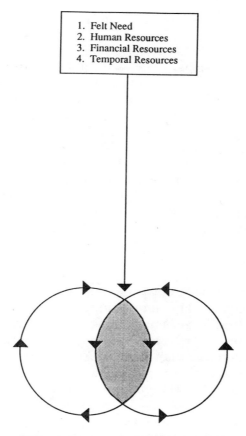

Figure 6.3 *Prerequisite conditions.*

the two-way cyclical interaction between the two loops. The overlap and feedback area indicates that the needs identified during evaluation are addressed during the development activities. Once the staff development activities have assisted the individual in meeting the identified needs, the individual can move on to other needs that have been identified, and staff development activities can be provided that will assist the individual in becoming even more productive.

Before any program of staff development or, for that matter, of staff evaluation can take place, there are four prerequisite conditions that must be present if the program is to be successful. Figure 6.3 illustrates the four prerequisite conditions of: (1) felt need, (2) human resources, (3) financial resources, and (4) temporal resources.

A *felt need* must exist before any program can be begun successfully. If the individual teacher does not feel a need to use a computer with her/his students, that teacher will probably not be interested in spending time and effort in staff development activities related to computer knowledge and usage. On the other hand, an employee in the business office who uses the computer to do the day-to-day work will readily participate in training sessions to learn the new upgraded software applications because that knowledge is an absolute necessity to allow her/him to perform the job well. A curriculum director may see no need to participate in a staff development program directed at improving the skill of administrators in the conduct of formative evaluation conferences with teachers. On the other hand, the principal who agreed with his supervisor during a formative evaluation session that one area of operation where much improvement could and must be made was that of conducting formative teacher evaluation conferences, would readily volunteer to participate in a self improvement staff development program geared to this clearly identified need.

The bottom line message is clear. If people perceive a need to improve, they will gladly participate in staff development activities that will improve their performance in the areas of needs (gaps between "what is" and "what should be") that have been clearly identified by themselves and by their supervisors during formative evaluation activities [9]. On the other hand, if the individual employee does not feel it necessary to participate in a staff development program focused on an area of no interest to the employee, the staff development specialist will either have to come up with some motivational device, such as a learning contract, to get that person to participate, or to omit involving that individual in that specific staff development program [10].

Once the felt need has been established, the other prerequisite conditions of human resources, financial resources, and temporal resources have to be met if the staff development program is to be successful. The *human resources* required might include a critical mass of employees to make the staff development cost effective, it may include the freeing of some of the district's employees who have specific skills to act as trainers, or it may include the hiring of out-of-district consultants to perform the specific training required. There is a wealth of human resources available in the parents, students, and community citizens, as well [11]. *Financial resources* will probably include money to hire substitutes for the employee during the staff development training periods, money for consultants, and money for the necessary equipment, supplies and housing for the participants. (One cost that is often overlooked by novices planning their first staff development activity is that related to meals and drinks for breaks during the training sessions.) *Temporal resources* not only include the released time for the district's employees who are taking the training or who are serving as trainers, but it should also include time for administrators to be present to provide visible and active support for the employees who are involved in the staff development activities. In fact, some of the most successful staff development activities will be those where administrators and teachers attend staff development activities as teams.

Once the prerequisite conditions have been met, six questions should be addressed before proceeding with the staff development plans. The questions of why?, who?, how?, what?, when?, and where? must be answered whether one is planning a staff evaluation system or a staff development system. Figure 6.4 demonstrates how these questions fit into a holistic system.

Why should a school district operate comprehensive staff evaluation and/or staff development programs? The why of staff evaluation should be to identify areas where improved performance can be made, and the why of staff development should be to provide training that will help the individual employee improve the areas identified as needs through the formative evaluation process [12].

Who should be involved in evaluation can include peers, supervisors, students, and outside evaluators, in terms of teachers. In terms of administrators, those involved can include teachers and other employees, supervisors, peers, and outside evaluators. For classified personnel, evaluation can include peers, supervisors, and outside evaluators. Who should be involved in staff development activities should include in-district trainers, supervisors, out-of-district consultants, and those who are participating in the training activities.

The *what* question depends on the specific activities to be evaluated, the specific needs (gaps between "what is" and "what should be") that are identified during the formative and summative eval-

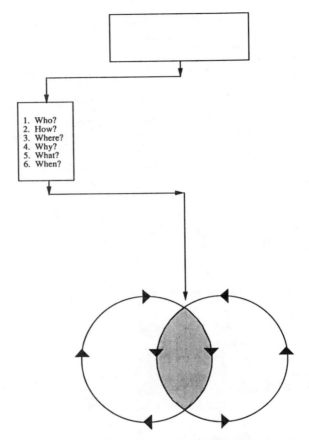

Figure 6.4 *Questions requiring answers.*

uation processes, and the specific staff development activities that are designed to address the specific needs identified.

The *where* will emphasize the workplace during the formative evaluation phase, but the staff development activities will vary from the workplace to off-site locations, depending on the specific needs being addressed and the specific environment desired. The location for the training should reflect training requirements rather than preferences [13]. Use of school facilities—an individual campus site itself—has been recommended in order to facilitate trainee awareness of application and participation [14].

When evaluation shall take place will generally be during the working day activities of the employee. The when for staff development may take place during the work day by hiring substitutes to release employees during training period, but many times this is not desirable because students should not be deprived of their regular teacher too frequently or for long time periods. Many other employees also cannot be separated from their normal duties frequently or for long periods of time. In these cases, it is many times more reasonable to offer staff development activities during after school hours, during weekends, or during normal vacation periods. There is evidence, however, to support a choice of time that will maximize the participants' motivation. The delivery of staff development at a noncontractual time and under the assumption of participants' willingness to volunteer the hours, has almost a guarantee of failure. Some compensation for the volunteered time, whether monetary, in the form of staff development credit hours, or through other compensatory measures, should be provided [15].

The *how* of formative evaluation can include peer observation, feedback from students or other employees, observation by supervisors, analyses of lessons or work plans, reviews of portfolios, or reviews of videotaped activities. The how of staff development will vary with the specific needs being addressed. For example, if the development activity is to train teachers to develop or use video disks in their teaching, the activity would be specifically geared to developing and utilizing video equipment during the training. If, however, the training is designed to improve the administrators' ability to carry out formative evaluation conferences, the how might well combine analysis of videos depicting examples of administrators conducting formative conferences with specific practice activities conducted during the training sessions. Effective staff development programs, in general, include such characteristics as: participant involvement and positive attitude; planning for training transfer support and mechanisms; an activities orientation; a tangible-results focus; and the provision for specificity and concreteness of instruction [16].

Once the questions requiring planned answers have been dealt with, it is time to move on to the categories of needs that can be addressed through staff development activities. Figure 6.5 illustrates the three categories of needs identified as: (1) maintenance

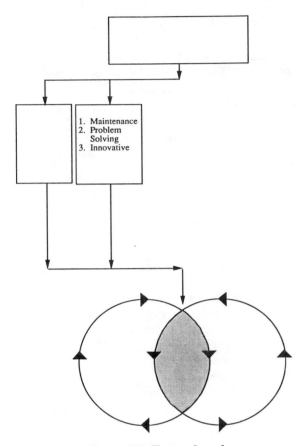

Figure 6.5 *Types of needs.*

related, (2) problem solving related and (3) innovation related activities. Obviously, the needs identified during formative or summative evaluation activities in each of these categories are those
addressed with specifically focused staff development activities.

Maintenance related staff development activities can be numerous. A few examples will indicate the variety of maintenance activities that can be addressed through staff development programs [17].

Example #1: Many teachers are not proficient at performing a
task analysis prior to planning the details of the lessons they are
providing students.

Example #2: Custodians must be trained in the operation and maintenance of the newly installed computerized heating and cooling systems in all of the district's school buildings.

Example #3: Teacher aides are newly assigned to the task of collecting and arraying student achievement data, which can be used by classroom teachers to adjust the instruction offered students whenever the data indicates a requirement for modification in content or method of instructional delivery.

Problem-solving staff development activities can be district wide, sub-group related or related to an individual employee. One example from each level will serve to illustrate problem-solving needs that can be addressed through staff development activities [18].

Example #1: An individual teacher has difficulty in checking for understanding of the knowledge absorbed by the students in the teacher's class. This need can be met by hiring a substitute teacher, and thus allowing the teacher to spend a week with another teacher who has demonstrated superior ability to use the techniques of checking students' understanding. This one-to-one counseling is a very effective method to use in solving certain identified needs.

Example #2: A group of food service personnel is having difficulty using the new computerized ovens. Because of this difficulty much food is wasted, and the food service, which operates on a self supporting basis, is in danger of seeing its budget going into a deficit condition. The solution exercised is to have the manufacturer send a trainer in for two weekend training sessions, during which the food service personnel prepare and evaluate small portions of food using the new computerized ovens. The food service workers are paid for their weekend training, and the decrease in wasted food will more than make up for the cost of the two weekend training sessions.

Example #3: There is difficulty in the district's ability to do effective problem solving, which affects the classroom, building, and central office levels. The solution is to train selected personnel from each of these levels to operate as vertical problem-solving project teams.

Innovative needs are sometimes identified when external or internal changes require adjustments and the employees are not sufficiently prepared to implement the innovations. A good example might well be the decision to implement a district-wide TESA (Teacher Expectations and Student Achievement) program [19]. The need was identified when student achievements were on a downward trend, and it was determined that the trend was caused by an attitudinal rather than a knowledge deficit. A two week workshop on TESA was offered to all teachers who volunteered to attend a summer workshop for which they received pay. Also, four one day renewal sessions were scheduled during the subsequent school year. All principals and central office administrators also attended these staff development sessions [20].

The assumptions that affect the attitudes of those planning and operating the staff evaluation and/or staff development programs of the school district are very important in determining the approaches used in the training and in the receptivity of the participants of the staff development activities. Figure 6.6 illustrates the positive attitudes that any staff developer must possess if she/he is to successfully work with employees. The assumptions about participants that are crucial to success include the following: (1) all employees desire to perform well, (2) employees desire feedback, (3) employees wish to improve, (4) they can do anything well if they wish to do it, (5) people want meaningful work and meaningful staff development activities, (6) they want to help others succeed and they want the district to continually improve, (7) employees are a most valuable human resource, and (8) all employees have a present state that is accepted by trainers, and everyone has future desires that staff developers can help them to achieve.

There are also a number of human needs that must be addressed by those responsible for staff evaluation and staff development. Figure 6.7 illustrates how these fit into the holistic model of staff evaluation and staff development. The human needs include those related to: (1) information, (2) technology, (3) strategies and techniques, (4) social acceptance, (5) professional acceptance, (6) physical health, (7) psychological health, (8) security and (9) self esteem [21]. Let's elaborate a bit on each of these needs.

Information is needed in terms of basic knowledge and in terms of methodology. Feedback is a very important means of providing information on performance. This structure provides the basis for need identification. Once the need has been identified, staff de-

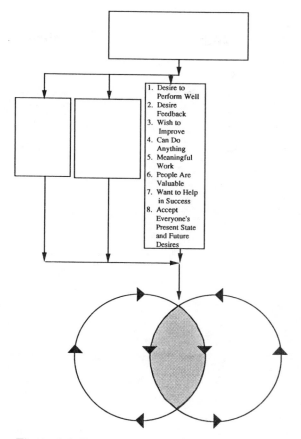

1. Desire to Perform Well
2. Desire Feedback
3. Wish to Improve
4. Can Do Anything
5. Meaningful Work
6. People Are Valuable
7. Want to Help in Success
8. Accept Everyone's Present State and Future Desires

Figure 6.6 *Positive assumptions about employees.*

velopment activities can provide the information required to meet the identified need.

Technological advances become important needs when they affect the ability to perform in a high qualitative manner.

Strategies and techniques are important employee needs when they relate to the ability to deliver services or instruction, or when they are important to successfully deal with job related problem solving.

Social acceptance is an important human need, *and*, when coupled with *professional acceptance*, it provides the feeling of caring and worth that is crucial for any person to operate successfully and comfortably within the work environment.

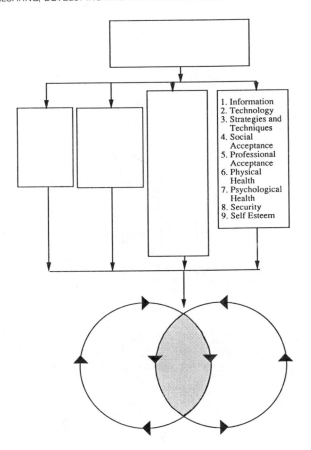

1. Information
2. Technology
3. Strategies and
   Techniques
4. Social
   Acceptance
5. Professional
   Acceptance
6. Physical
   Health
7. Psychological
   Health
8. Security
9. Self Esteem

Figure 6.7 *Human needs.*

Physical health is another important human need. A *Wellness* staff development program that concentrates on the identified physical health needs of the district's employees can be an important and an appreciated addition to a comprehensive staff development program. Examples include smoking cessation clinics, weight loss clinics, and a wide variety of exercise programs.

Psychological health is also important, as an employee who is suffering from psychological stress cannot perform well on the job. Staff development programs that offer stress reduction clinics or that include an *Employee Assistance Program* (which refers, in a confidential manner, employees who are experiencing psychological problems to psychologists, psychiatrists, or other mental health specialists) can be career-saving and human capital-saving additions to a staff development program. Stressful psychological times arise during situations where an employee experiences the death of a close relative, when a close relative is found to have an incurable disease, when a divorce is impending, or when other psychological stress situations arise.

Security is another basic human need. If an employee is uncertain about having a position for the subsequent year due to budget cutbacks, that employee will not benefit from participation in a staff development activity during that time period. The basic need for security will probably consume all of the mental and psychological energy available to that employee during this time period.

Self-esteem is also one of the most basic needs of any employee. If someone does not feel good about herself/himself, a staff developer cannot expect that person to gain maximum benefit from involvement in a staff development activity. In this case, the staff developer must devise means of building a positive ego within that participant by complimenting the participant on the quality of her/his efforts, by using the participant to demonstrate a skill for the other participants, or by any other means of building self-esteem while also providing the staff development activity.

Once all the matters previously discussed have been considered by the staff developer, there is one more crucial element that must be considered *before* starting staff evaluation or staff development activities. Staff developers must be cognizant of the *order by which change takes place*. Figure 6.8 illustrates the sequential order of change. Before an employee or an organization can initiate a change, there must be a reason for and a method of unfreezing the status quo. Once the status quo is unfrozen, the initial step is that the employees who are to make the change must become aware of the need to change. Next, those employees must have sufficient interest to cause them to volunteer to involve themselves in the change process [22].

Once they are convinced enough to involve themselves in the change process, they must take action to cause the desired change to take place. The action steps involved are: (1) diagnosing the situation, (2) arriving at tentative solutions, (3) making application of the preferred solution, (4) revising the initial application to improve it, and (5) re-applying the revised change solution. Once the enacted change is satisfactory the change pro-

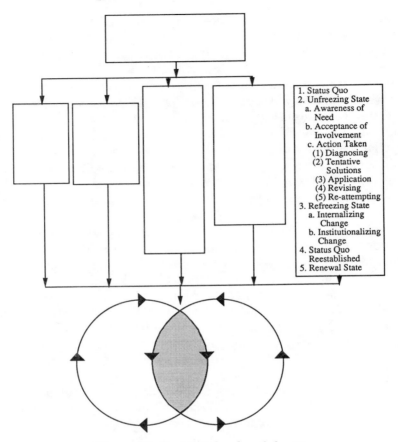

1. Status Quo
2. Unfreezing State
   a. Awareness of
      Need
   b. Acceptance of
      Involvement
   c. Action Taken
      (1) Diagnosing
      (2) Tentative
          Solutions
      (3) Application
      (4) Revising
      (5) Re-attempting
3. Refreezing State
   a. Internalizing
      Change
   b. Institutionalizing
      Change
4. Status Quo
   Reestablished
5. Renewal State

Figure 6.8 Sequential order of change.

cess must be refrozen in order to stop the change process at the solution level enacted [23].

Once the change process is re-frozen, the change must be internalized by the employees; and once the critical mass of employees accept the change, the change will become institutionalized. Once the change becomes institutionalized, the status quo is reestablished; and the status quo remains until another renewal state is required [24].

If we add: (1) the cyclical nature of staff evaluation and staff development to the fact that there is a considerable overlap and feedback between the two, (2) the prerequisite conditions to be met, (3) the questions to be answered, (4) the type of program needs that must be considered, (5) the positive assumptions about people, (6) the human needs that must be considered, and (7) the sequential order of change; we have all the elements that should be considered before planning and operating a staff development program for the school district. Putting all of this together, we arrive at a Holistic Model of Staff Evaluation and Staff Development, as illustrated by Figure 6.9.

Once all of the items in Figure 6.9 have been considered, the district's staff developers can begin planning a comprehensive long term district-wide staff development program, and they can also begin planning for specific staff development activities.

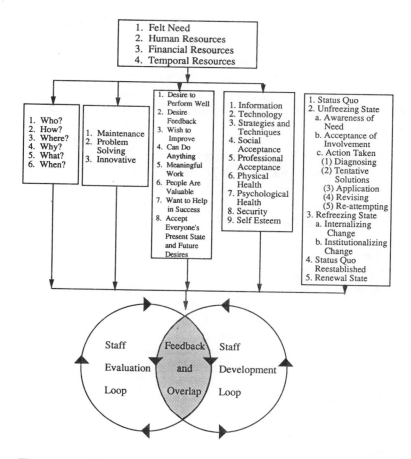

Figure 6.9 *Holistic model of staff evaluation and staff development.*

PLANNING THE OVERALL STAFF DEVELOPMENT PROGRAM

In addressing all levels of an educational organization, a comprehensive staff development program is a constant component of the HRD structure. Based on sound strategic planning and originating in the goals and objectives of the individual school district, the comprehensive program receives its impetus from board of education and planning team direction. Board funding, allocation of other resources, and appropriate policies for staff development implementation should follow. The central office administration, through those individuals responsible for human resource development, provide a master plan (including any macro needs) and the district-wide supervisory function. The site managers—principals and supervisors—are responsible for identifying and specifying those micro needs that will support the overall goals and objectives. Other administrators and supervisors, from support and noninstructional areas, should likewise identify those needs particular to their areas. Teachers, paraprofessionals, and classified employees are responsible for participation in staff development which is aligned with both their micro needs and the larger macro needs of the district [25]. A primary distinction that should be made is that between training—which "is the process of learning a sequence of programmed behaviors", and education, which involves the understanding and interpretation of knowledge [26]. In school districts, it is more likely that the professionally-certified employees' needs will require staff development that is designed to provide an educational experience, while the classified employees' needs will require staff development that is designed to provide a training experience. For example, the involvement of campus principals in staff development aimed at instructional leadership skills will require educational experiences, while the provision of staff development for those custodians who will be maintaining a new district-wide type of gymnasium flooring will require training experiences.

DETAILED PLANNING FOR A SPECIFIC STAFF DEVELOPMENT ACTIVITY

An example is provided of planning for staff development that is macro in need and aimed at professionally-certified employees.

A school district board of education and strategic planning team may decide to support the general goals of the felt needs of instructional improvement and academic achievement through the provision of a comprehensive staff development experience in a coordinated, multiple-research model of effective teaching practices. This type of staff development is innovative as a categorical need. The initial step is publicizing and "selling" the project to the district employees and to the community, outlining the projected benefits, obtaining up-front commitment and marshalling the required human, financial, and temporal resources, and beginning the process of incorporating acceptance of such a major effort (unfreezing and freezing the change process) into the district culture. After consideration of the six-question prerequisite conditions, national and state consultants are engaged to lead an extensive turnkey training session involving a selected group of district professionals. Key personnel to include in such a kickoff session are selected board members, central office personnel involved with instruction, all principals, and master teachers and lead paraprofessionals from each school building. Community leaders should be invited to attend, for publicity and awareness purposes. The training session is intended, over the period of days required to reach proficiency level in the content, to produce a cadre of peer coaches who follow the initial content training session with an application session intended to allow them to practice being peer coaches and observers of teaching practices. Within this cadre is also developed a corps of volunteer master trainers who will serve as the designated effective teaching practices training team for the district.

The district then initiates the process of providing the multiple training sessions needed (because of staff development training group size limitations) to bring all professionals and paraprofessionals through the training, which is conducted by the corps of master trainers. The content is paced so that the trainees have the opportunity to practice individual segments of the new learning in their classrooms, while being observed and coached by those knowledgeable campus-based professionals—principals and teachers—who have already been through the training. Depending on the size of the district, cohort after cohort of professionals and paraprofessionals experience the training, until all individuals have completed it. As the training proceeds, the pool of trained individuals per campus becomes larger, and the resultant demands for peer coaching and observation more distributed. Important considerations for such an undertaking are: (1) the inclusion and "mixing-in" of central office personnel (not just the central office instructional personnel) with the successive cohorts of trainees, in order to provide leadership modeling and for the symbolic effect on the district culture; (2) the timing of the training to take place during the normal contracted staff development days, to insure compliance and total participation; and, (3) the development of a modified and support-oriented effective teaching practices awareness program for the classified employees, to enlist their participation, and to further infuse the goals of the training into the district culture. The human needs of the participants are provided for in the feedback-oriented strategies and techniques, in the collegiality and camaraderie nature of the training; and in the positive, professional self-esteem focus of the program.

SUMMARY

Performance improvement upon clearly identified needs is the primary reason for staff development – a goal achieved through Human Resource Development. As a conceptual framework for that goal, the requirements of andragogy demand a more collaborative and experience-based staff development design. Three dimensions of needs assessment for staff development should be considered: total school district needs, sub-group needs, and individuals needs. When these needs comprise the substance of a system that is interwoven between evaluation and staff development, a complete cyclical systems approach to performance is achieved. A model was provided that displayed the feedback and overlap interaction of formative and summative evaluation and staff development. Prerequisite conditions for a successful program are the existence of a felt need as an impetus for performance improvement and the provision of human, financial, and temporal resources to support the training response to that felt need.

The considerations of reasons for staff development (evaluation-identified needs shaping programs); the participants and specific activities; and the design specifications of staff development location, time, and procedures should precede planning for training. Three categories of identified staff development needs that can be addressed by training are maintenance-related activities, problem-solving activities, and innovative activities. Assumptions about participants' positive attitudes regarding performance, feedback, and training are crucial to success, as is consideration of a number of human needs. The holistic staff development model was augmented to include the needs for information, technological advances, strategies and techniques coupled with professional acceptance, physical health, psychological health, security, and self-esteem. A final consideration prior to the initiation of staff development activities is the providers' comprehension of the order by which change takes place; a recognition of the unfreezing and refreezing steps that precede and follow change solutions in organizations. Internalization and institutionalization of staff development-caused change are part of the cyclical nature of staff evaluation and staff development, and this is displayed in the holistic model.

GUIDELINES

1. There should be a constant awareness that the purpose of staff development is performance improvement, and that HRD activities achieve that purpose through an andragogically-designed staff development and training system.
2. There should be a constant awareness that the three important dimensions of needs assessment that require staff development programs are total school district needs, sub-group needs, and individual needs.
3. Evaluation and staff development should be interwoven into a cyclical systems approach.
4. A felt need is a prerequisite condition to staff evaluation and staff development, and the provision of human, financial, and temporal resources must address that need.
5. The six questions of why?, who?, what?, where?, when?, and how? should be addressed prior to proceeding with staff development plans.
6. Three categories of identified need should be addressed through staff development activities—maintenance-related, problem solving-related, and innovation related.
7. Staff developers must have positive attitudes and assumptions about participants' motivation for performance improvement.
8. Staff developers should address human needs—information,

technological advances, strategies and techniques, social and professional acceptance, physical health, psychological health, security, and self-esteem.

9. Staff developers must be cognizant of the order by which organizational change takes place.

EXERCISES

1. Analyze a recent staff development experience of yours in terms of andragogical recommendations, and make recommendations on how it could be improved.

2. Identify five needs for your school district for each of the three dimensions of needs assessment (total school district, subgroup, and individual).

3. Project several felt needs for your school district, and briefly describe appropriate staff development activities to address those needs.

4. Using one of the projected felt needs and staff development activities from the previous exercise, list the human resources within the school district and external to the school district that could be tapped to support the staff development experience.

5. Using the same need and activities, list the financial resources within the school district and external to the school district that could be tapped to support the staff development experience.

6. Using the same need and activities, list the temporal resources within the school district that could be tapped to support the staff development experience.

7. Select another felt need from Exercise 3, and use it to address the six questions of why?, who? what?, where?, when?, and how? regarding planning for staff development.

8. Provide three examples of maintenance-related staff development activities, three examples of problem-solving staff development activities, and three examples of innovative staff development activities for your district.

9. Consider the human needs that are prerequisite to successful staff development, and assess the status of each as it exists within a particular group of employees or within a particular school building in your district.

10. Describe a scenario of the change process in your district, tracing a staff development change through the action steps of (1) diagnosing the situation, (2) arriving at tentative solutions, (3) making application of the preferred solution, (4) revising the initial application to improve it, and (5) re-applying the revised change solution.

SELECTED REFERENCES

1. Harris, B. M. 1989. *In-Service Education for Staff Development*. Boston, MA: Allyn and Bacon, Inc., p. 12.

2. Moore, J. R. 1988. "Guidelines Concerning Adult Learning", *Journal of Staff Development*, 9(3): 2–5.

3. Moore, J. R. "Guidelines", pp. 4–5.

4. Feuer, D. and B. Geber. 1988. "Uh-Oh . . . Second Thoughts about Adult Learning Theory", *Training*, 25(12): 31–38.

5. Harris, B. M. *In-Service Education*, p. 12.

6. Laird, D. 1978. *Approaches to Training and Development*. Reading, MA: Addison Wesley Publishing Company, p. 47.

7. Harris, B. M. 1986. *Developmental Teacher Evaluation*. Boston, MA: Allyn and Bacon, Inc., p. 201.

8. Shroyer, M. G. 1990. "Effective Staff Development for Effective Organization Development", *Journal of Staff Development*, 11(1): 2–6.

9. Oliva, P. F. 1976. *Supervision for Today's Schools*. New York, NY: Longman, Inc. p. 400.

10. Moore, J. R. "Guidelines", pp. 3–4.

11. Harris, B. M. *In-Service Education*, p. 15.

12. Moore, J. R. "Guidelines", pp. 4–5.

13. Harris, B. M. *In-Service Education*, p. 31.

14. Hinson, S., M. S. Caldwell, and M. Landrum. 1989. "Characteristics of Effective Staff Development Programs", *Journal of Staff Development*, 10(2): 48–51.

15. Duttweiler, P. C. 1989. "Components of an Effective Professional Development Program", *Journal of Staff Development*, 10(2): 2–6.

16. Hinson, S., M. S. Caldwell, and M. Landrum. "Characteristics", pp. 50–51.

17. Laird, D. *Approaches*, pp. 50–51.

18. Laird, D. *Approaches*, p. 47.

19. Kerman, S. and M. Martin. 1980. *Teacher Expectations and Student Achievement Teacher Handbook*. Bloomington, IN: Phi Delta Kappa.

20. Laird, D. *Approaches*, pp. 47–48.

21. Harris, B. M. *In-Service Education*, pp. 107–108.

22. Hoy, W. K. and C. G. Miskel. 1987. *Educational Administration*, Third Edition. New York, NY: Random House, p. 412.

23. Shroyer, M. G. "Effective Staff Development", pp. 3–4.

24. Hampton, D. R., C. E. Summer, and R. A. Webber. 1987. *Organizational Behavior and the Practice of Management*. Glenview, IL: Scott, Foresman and Company, p. 688.

25. Rebore, R. W. 1982. *Personnel Administration in Education*. Englewood Cliffs, NJ: Prentice-Hall, p. 171.

26. Rebore, R. W. *Personnel Administration*, p. 161.

CHAPTER 7

Employee Involvement and Empowerment

EMPOWERING EMPLOYEES TO make decisions related to their assigned work tasks and to the development of district-wide answers to organizational problems or challenges initially involves an OD (Organizational Development) intervention strategy that ultimately changes the existing culture of an organization. A traditionally structured school district, which sees itself as a top-down, closed, authoritarian organization, must be culturally modified to let the light of involvement shine upon it. The inherent rigidity of any existing organizational culture requires specific targeted interventions for the initiation of empowerment [1]. Obviously, this means that the district's decision makers must have a changed philosophy towards employees, and they must plan interventions that cause their newly acquired employee empowerment philosophy to become operational.

This chapter will provide insight into intervention structures that will empower employees at the site level, and Chapter 9 will present strategies that will provide examples of intervention structures and strategies applicable to a district level approach to employee involvement and empowerment. Chapter 7 will discuss: (1) beliefs about people and employees, (2) collaboration as a means of developing employee ownership and employee leadership, (3) the advantages of employee involvement, empowerment and collaboration, (4) quality circles, (5) site level vertical experiential teams, and (6) project teams and other collaborative structures.

BELIEFS ABOUT PEOPLE AND EMPLOYEES

In order to have a successful culture that involves employees in productive decision making and development, and that causes employees truly to buy into the organization, *owners*—the people who possess positional power [2] (the superintendent of schools and board of education members at the school district level, and the building principal or director at the site level)—must subscribe to positive beliefs about people and about the roles and motives of employees [3]. Barring these positive beliefs, the traditional top-down authoritarian model will prevail to the detriment of employees, administration, and, ultimately, the students for whom the school or school district exists.

An administrator who possesses positional power must truly believe that people are good, kind, trustworthy, and valuable [4]. She/he must believe that employees possess these characteristics; but also that they want to improve themselves, they want to assist other employees to improve, they want their school building and their district to be the best they can be, they want to assist in decision making that is intended to improve themselves and the school building's and school district's quality, and they want to do whatever they can to improve the education of their students [5].

If the building principal truly believes positively about people and employees, she/he can use involvement and collaborative intervention strategies that will empower the employees. By promoting a collaborative empowerment culture, the principal will also experience a broadened leadership base within the building [6].

COLLABORATION AS A MEANS OF DEVELOPING EMPLOYEE OWNERSHIP AND EMPLOYEE LEADERSHIP

If the building principal promotes a culture of involvement and empowerment and the employees are not accustomed to the freedom and the opportunity to involve themselves in decisions that affect them and the school building's operation, the principal must *sell* this new culture until the employees buy in and develop an *ownership* mind set. By utilizing collaborative intervention strategies, not only are better decisions and fully-owned decisions made; but, over time, a dispersed ownership will develop. In other words, each employee, within a culture that promotes collaborative involvement, will eventually be provided with and will assume a leadership role within the school building [7].

Examples of this dispersed leadership are: (1) a teacher chairs a curriculum development committee, (2) a school cook serves as a consultant or a presenter on healthy dietary habits to the elementary teachers, (3) a teacher serves as a trainer of the other district teachers and the principal on specific areas with which they are not knowledgeable, such as TESA (Teacher Expectations and Student Achievement) [8], (4) a custodian assists a teacher and students in the construction of a set for a play they are presenting, and (5) a couple of teachers, a couple of custodians, a couple of food service personnel, a couple of secondary department heads, and an assistant principal work as a committee to develop a recommendation on procedures and a structure to officially and systematically recognize outstanding contributions by the school building's employees. Collaborative involvement of all employees in meaningful decision making and meaningful activities will not only encourage ownership of the school building's programs and operations, but it also provides ample opportunities for each employee to assume leadership [9]. In summary, then, what are the advantages of employee involvement, empowerment, and collaboration? The following description outlines those advantages, and suggests some characteristics of productive employee collaborative teams.

ADVANTAGES OF EMPLOYEE INVOLVEMENT, EMPOWERMENT AND COLLABORATION

Employee involvement can exist without empowering the employees to make final decisions, and involvement and empowerment can exist without utilizing a collaborative structure of employee decision making. However, it is clear that all of these elements must co-exist if the maximum advantages are to be reaped by the employees and the school building's operation. The major advantages are listed below:

- Employees accept accountability when they are given authority [10].
- Employees enjoy working in an environment that provides them with opportunities for input, improvement and leadership [11].
- Employees enjoy the opportunity to improve themselves, to

help improve their colleagues and to improve the school building's operation [12].

- Employees take pride in high-quality outputs and outcomes that come about because of their efforts [13].
- Employees enjoy being recognized for their contributions by their colleagues and their principal [14].
- Employees are highly motivated when they feel they are a valued part of a collaborative employee team [15].
- Leadership builds more leadership, and diversified leadership is more productive than positional leadership by a single person—the principal [16].
- Positive experiences in leadership promote additional leadership desires and opportunities [17].
- Employees prefer to be partial owners of an institution that believes in utilizing all its human resources as part of a productive work family that achieves high quality results [18].

Now that the advantages are clear, what are some of the characteristics of productive employee collaborative teams? If one wishes to measure whether or not a productive collaborative employee team exists, she/he should be able to observe the following characteristics as one visits the school building and talks to the employees.

- Employees listen to and are open to the ideas of others.
- Employees take pride in the employee team's achievement.
- They are free with their praise of one another.
- There is a feeling of ownership, work family, and empowerment.
- They are alert to ways in which they can assist and support each other.
- Employees act as a unified group by using a diagnostic and positive approach to problem solving and program development.
- Employees look for opportunities to share with one another.
- Each employee operates as a full and valued member of the employee team.
- Each employee feels successful and feels that she/he is an integral part of a successful work family.

- The team exhibits distributed skillful and positive leadership.
- The team has clearly defined goals and objectives.
- The team members have many creative and innovative ideas that prove to be successful.
- They have a well-developed structure for realistic planning and conflict resolution.
- They exhibit positive, effective, and persuasive communication techniques.
- They exhibit success, which leads to the desire for greater success [19].

To this point we discussed: (1) the beliefs about people and employees that are required to have a winning employee team, (2) how collaborative structures develop ownership and leadership among employees, (3) the advantages of employee involvement, empowerment and collaboration, and (4) the advantages to the school building's operation when employees are involved and empowered in collaborative efforts. We now turn to specific intervention structures that cause winning employee collaborative teams to become operational. We begin with a discussion of the common structures of quality circles.

QUALITY CIRCLES

Quality Circles are site-based organizational structures that are designed to involve employees in arriving at solutions of problems that exist in the workplace [20]. They can also be utilized as groups that develop new approaches to old problems or new programs to replace existing ones that are outdated or that do not meet the current *needs* (gaps between "what is" and "what should be" or "what could be") of the students, employees or the school building's operation.

A *quality circle* is generally made up of six to eight job-alike members, a leader and a recorder. Its primary purposes are to improve the work environment in which the employees work and to improve the products or outcomes of their efforts [21]. Membership is voluntary, and the circle generally meets on school time for one or two hours per week (if teachers are involved, the circle time may have to be scheduled after normal student attendance hours) [22]. A building can have multiple quality circles, and there may be various job-alike quality circle groups functioning at the same time in any school building. Occasionally, there may even be a quality circle comprised of members of two or more job-alike groups.

In order to be as effective as possible, part of the time during which the circle meets is spent in training activities [23]. Extended training activities are usually conducted for multiple days, and away from the school districts' sites. The initial skills training areas should be heavily focused upon:

- communication techniques
- problem identification methods
- problem analysis techniques
- information gathering methods
- evaluation techniques
- recommendations and reports writing
- presentation techniques [24]

A few examples of skill training are: (1) brainstorming, (2) force field analysis, (3) graphing, (4) "I" messages, (5) active listening, (6) survey techniques, and (7) nonverbal behavior analysis. To these areas can be added any other training activities desired by the members of the quality circle [25].

When the circles are initially organized, they should be given a written charge which clearly outlines that the problems they address or the program recommendations that they may recommend, which must be limited to the workplace and to those areas within the circles' authority and control. Quality circles' intervention into an organization has typically addressed problem solving at three levels: (1) Type I problems, over which members have control; (2) Type II problems, over which members have limited control and require some outside influence, and (3) Type III problems, which are beyond circle solution or influence [26]. For example, the circle should be prohibited from dealing with personality-related or union/management-sensitive problems. Some guides for problem selection are:

- Are the problems MEANINGFUL?
- Are the solutions potentially AFFORDABLE?

- Are they DOABLE?
- Are they MEASURABLE (that is, can we collect information to determine whether or not the solutions worked)?
- Are sufficient RESOURCES available (human, temporal, financial and material)?
- At the initial attempts by the circle stage, do the solutions have a predictable 75 percent chance of success [27]? (Later, more difficult problem-solving probabilities may be attempted.)

Operationally, the circle can call for assistance from experts (other employees) within the school building or the school district. They also can request that the principal obtain out-of-district expert help if such assistance is not available in the district [28].

In the operation of a circle, decisions are always made by *consensus*. Consensus, in this sense, means that all members of the circle have to agree on the solution or the activity; or, at least, all members agree to let the circle proceed. [29] The building principal is always welcome to sit in on any circle meeting. The principal can be invited by the circle's leader to attend, or the principal can decide, on her/his own, to attend the circle meeting as a nonmember.

At the circle meetings it is clear that every circle member has a responsibility to contribute leadership to the circle. At these meetings the circle will consider the ideas of its members, but it will also consider ideas suggested by other quality circles, by the principal or central office administrators, or by outside sources. Once the circle has developed a proposed solution to a problem they have isolated, the circle members will make a presentation to the building principal. If the solution is accepted, the building principal will then do whatever is necessary from her/his power position to implement that solution or suggested program [30].

As related to other quality circles in their building or anywhere in the school district, the quality circle: (1) can suggest training activities that are applicable to all quality circle members in the school district and (2) will cooperate with the district-wide quality circle steering committee.

Now that we have discussed the basic structure, training, and activities related to quality circles, let's turn to the specific ways in which a quality circle identifies problems, generates solutions, and does effectiveness follow-up on those solutions. Following this process discussion, we will indicate some measures that can be used to evaluate the effectiveness of the quality circle structure within the individual school building.

Quality Circle Problem Identification and Problem-solving Sequence

(1) The circle members list all the problems that they collectively believe exist in their workplace.

(2) They list all the problems in the order of priority to be attacked.

(3) They select the first problem to be approached, and they stay with this problem until it is resolved. They then go on to the second priority problem that they have agreed upon. They select each problem utilizing the decision rules:
   • Is it meaningful?
   • Is it affordable?
   • Are sufficient human, temporal, financial and material resources available?
   • Is it doable?
   • Is it measurable?

(4) They analyze the problem and identify the cause(s).

(5) They then collect information and data related to each of causes.

(6) They array and analyze the data for accuracy, for completeness, and for clues that will assist the circle in exploring solutions to the problem.

(7) They then use the *brainstorming technique* to generate a wide variety of potential solutions in a relatively short time period [31].

(8) They narrow down the potential solutions to those most likely to assist in eliminating the problem. These are usually three to five in number.

(9) They then collect more data, if this is deemed necessary, on these solutions.

(10) The circle members next do a *force field analysis*, which is a technique for the listing of supporting factors and restraining factors related to each solution [32].

(*11*) They review this analysis and select the one, in their judgement, best solution to the problem.

(*12*) If the solution is within the quality circle's arena of independent authority, the circle will implement the preferred solution.

(*13*) If the solution is not within the quality circle's arena of independent authority, the circle members will develop a presentation to be given at a meeting with the school building's principal.

(*14*) The circle members make the presentation of the problem and the preferred solution they are recommending to the principal. This presentation should clearly state the problem, the steps taken, the data collected to study and analyze the problem and preferred solution, and it should include the structure and costs, if any, related to implementing the preferred solution.

(*15*) If the principal agrees to the preferred solution, the circle members and the principal implement the solution.

(*16*) After the preferred solution has been in place for a specified period of time, data are collected to evaluate the degree of effectiveness of the solution.

(*17*) If the follow-up data indicate that the problem is successfully resolved, the quality circle moves to its next highest priority problem. If it is not successful, or if is just moderately successful, the quality circle goes back to the drawing board with the original problem [33].

Once the quality circle organization has been implemented for a reasonable amount of time in the individual school buildings across the school district, how can the effectiveness of the quality circle empowerment structure be evaluated? Some of the major ways in which the effectiveness of the quality circle operation can be evaluated as to its effectiveness are:

- Are the problems attacked by the quality circles effectively solved?
- Is the workplace improved for employees and for students?
- Do employees indicate that they are happier and more satisfied than they were before the quality circles were initiated?
- Are the attitudes of employees and administrators improved?

- Is the quality of the work performed improved?
- Is there improved communications in the workplace?
- Do more employees have the opportunity for leadership, and have they exercised that opportunity?
- Are there progressively fewer problems or less severe problems to deal with in the workplace?
- Is there a reduction in employee absenteeism and tardiness?
- Is there a reduction in employee turnover?
- Is there an increase in positive employee suggestions?
- Is there measurably increased employee morale?
- Are there reductions in errors and less-than-desirable work products?
- Is there a reduction in employee-employee and in employee-management conflicts?
- Is there a reduction in employee complaints and grievances [34]?

If we wished to check out employee and management attitudes towards the work environment before and after the quality circles' operation, we might develop a simple and brief opinionnaire to determine the attitudinal changes. An example is provided that captures some general measures of attitudes towards both satisfaction and productivity.

Job Satisfaction Questionnaire

Instructions: Please rate your personal feelings toward your work and the place where you work by drawing a circle around the number on the scale point below that best describes your current feeling. "4" is the "best" feeling and "0" is the "worst" feeling.

Communication	4	3	2	1	0
Decision Making	4	3	2	1	0
Training	4	3	2	1	0
Morale	4	3	2	1	0
Assistance	4	3	2	1	0
Caring	4	3	2	1	0
Trust	4	3	2	1	0
Respect	4	3	2	1	0
Chance for Improvement	4	3	2	1	0
Administration	4	3	2	1	0
Resources	4	3	2	1	0
Quality of Work Completed	4	3	2	1	0
Other (Please List)	4	3	2	1	0

Site-Based Vertical Experiential Terms

The horizontality of the quality circle organizational structure has its particular strength as an intervention vehicle; one aimed at affording a problem-solving process for a homogeneous work group. However, the types of problems school quality circles can typically solve are those that are within the immediate control of the group members and those problems that can be addressed by that control group, plus the influence of an administrator or other professional outside of the circle. The normal maturing process of the school quality circle involves a progression of problem-solving skills, ranging from addressing the simple to the more complex problems. Problems and issues will occur sooner or later that will demand the attention of more than one district or organizational department's quality circle(s), and they may require assistance or intervention from a different organizational level. Many school-based concerns or issues are beyond the scope of control of individual campuses or departments (the Type III problems noted earlier); they must be addressed by policy change, by interdepartmental collaboration or cooperation, or by major structural changes. A logical and recent development is a type of quality circle and a group structure more empowered to solve complex problems—the vertical team [35].

This type of team is vertically representational of top-to-bottom levels of the school district, with single or multiple members drawn from the ranks of the school board, patrons, superintendent(s), central office personnel, supervisors or coordinators, principals, teachers, students, and classified personnel. The range of the team provides organizational level representation and affords a district vertical view of the impact of issues and concerns that the team addresses. As an innovation, it should be approved and chartered by the school board to take appropriate action (within policy discretion), and it should be publicized as accessible and enabling intervention structures. The strong empowerment effect and the symbolic leadership effect on the district climate and culture are additional benefits.

Peer selection can be used to determine members, or the superintendent may design teams by requesting volunteers from the vertically descending levels. The superintendent can also solicit individual board member participation. Multiple vertical teams are possible; variations to an initial "charter" team can address problems of a more specific nature. For example, very successful vertical teams in a large district can be comprised of each individual high school principal (accompanied by staff, parent, and student body representation), and the principals and representative staff, parents, and students of the feeder middle/junior high schools and elementary schools. Such a team can create a community feeling, plan in a collaborative manner, process problems that are common to the district, and customize solutions that involve the combined neighborhoods and attendance areas.

The vertical team can be created on an "as-needed basis", to serve as a support structure to an existing base of quality circles, or it can be created as a permanent planning-oriented and/or troubleshooting school district team. The distinctive characteristic of these teams is their degree of operational freedom due to the multiple-level access to administrative intervention. While their problem-solving strategies may be the same as those of the quality circle, they have board-bestowed autonomy and access to vertically-substantial information, both of which can facilitate a rapid and comprehensive response to district needs.

PROJECT TEAMS AND OTHER COLLABORATIVE STRUCTURES

From the education reform movement of the early 1980s came the recommendation of restructuring, which was initially comprised of a number of disparate proposed school changes. Mostly, these were aimed at redesigning the fundamental structure of education as a social system—long term, comprehensive changes that require a rethinking of the learning environment and, almost invariably, a move to deregulation and to a shifting of control from top-down to bottom-up [36]. In order to bring about such restructuring, the early participants in the movement have created new, site-based governance structures—planning teams that are empowered by the existing district leadership and that are aimed at campus instructional improvement projects, curriculum revitalization on a campus basis, or other site-tailored efforts.

One example is a project of the NEA-sponsored National Foundation for Improvement of Education, which supports restructuring via teams that begin as small units within schools and that spread to other (or feeder) schools, creating a network of school-based shared decision-making structures. This borrowed concept of decentralization through team collaborative management came from industry, and it is currently in vogue in school reform. Effective school restructuring efforts during the late 1980s have focused on meaningful, shared decision making by developing and empowering collaborative and collegial teams. The campus-based empowerment that can be accomplished through team-building will require the management of human resources [37]. The project and collaborative team structures will require support through temporal and financial resources that allow for significant periods of time away from instructional and routine duties to develop collaborative team skills, to engage in professional discourse, and to address problem solving [38].

Chapter 9 will discuss a QWL (Quality of Work Life) structure that operates on a school district wide basis. The quality circles, vertical teams, and project and other collaborative structures that have been discussed in this chapter should be synchronized with the district level QWL structure if one exists, and they should work in tandem to improve the work environment for employees and students alike.

SUMMARY

This chapter has provided insight into the intervention structures that empower employees at the site level. Individuals in the school district with positional power must subscribe to positive beliefs about employee motivation, and they must believe in involvement and collaborative intervention strategies. Employees must develop an ownership mindset about assuming a leadership role within a collaborative involvement culture. The advantages of this involvement and empowerment are the enhancement of the working environment, the development of employee pride and motivation, and the encouragement of leadership opportunities. Productive employee collaborative teams are characterized by open lines of communication, pride in team achievement, development of a feeling of ownership, mutual support, and successful group problem-solving and planning skills.

Quality circles (site-based organizational structures) were described in detail as job-alike problem-solving teams designed to involve employees in addressing workplace problems. These are teams that require initial training skills, that are charged with clearly-outlined powers, and that are provided with district resources and contacts for assistance. Consensus decisions and member-wide leadership are expected, and there must be a specific problem identification and solution sequence. The outcomes of the implementation of effective quality circles in a school district should be a diminishing of workplace problems and an enhancement of morale.

Vertical teams were proposed as a logical outgrowth of quality circles, and they address problems beyond the effective range of job-alike horizontal teams. They are composed of multilevel, top-to-bottom representation of the administrative and employee layers of a school district, and they are empowered by the board to solve more comprehensive and broad-impact problems. Project teams and other collaborative structures were described as representative of the recent school reform movement toward restructuring and site-based teaming aimed at improving the quality of instruction through empowerment for meaningful, shared decision making.

GUIDELINES

1. In order to have true organizational involvement in productive decision making and empowerment, district people who possess positional power must subscribe to positive beliefs about people and about the roles and motives of employees.

2. In order to achieve better and fully-owned decisions, a broadened leadership base within a building or organization must be promoted within a collaborative empowerment culture.

3. Building visitation and observation should be done to obtain an accurate measure of the presence of productive employee collaborative teams.

4. Quality circle membership should be voluntary and should include extended training activities on communication techniques and problem processing strategies.

5. Quality circle problems should be appropriate for the limits of the group's authority and control.

6. The effectiveness of the quality circle empowerment structure should be evaluated.

7. Vertical teams should be representational of multiple district or-

ganizational levels and should be empowered by the school board to act on specific issues and concerns.

8. Project and collaborative team structures should be supported with district resources and empowered by the district leadership.

EXERCISES

1. Assess the level of positive leadership beliefs in people that exists in your school district, and informally measure the productivity of any collaborative team structures that are presently in place in your district.

2. Select the most appropriate school building or department in your district to initiate a quality circle approach; assess the staff, and select members to serve effectively on the circle.

3. Assign appropriate tasks to the imaginary (or actual) quality circle in your district, tailoring your choices to those that the circles could effectively address.

4. Form a quality circle at your own campus, and practice some problem-solving strategies aimed at real campus issues. Invite the principal or some other administrator to participate, focusing on a problem that would require his/her intervention.

5. Experiment with an initial vertical team arrangement in your district, and use it as a prototype to present a multiple team proposal to the school board.

6. Organize a project team for your campus's instructional improvement, and collaborate with district leadership to implement the team's recommendations.

SELECTED REFERENCES

1. Hampton, D. R., C. E. Summer, and R. A. Webber. 1987. *Organizational Behavior and the Practice of Management.* Glenview, IL: Scott, Foresman and Company, p. 809.

2. Hampton, D. R., C. E. Summer, and R. A. Webber. *Organizational Behavior*, p. 197.

3. Lewis, A. 1989. *Restructuring America's Schools.* Arlington, VA: American Association of School Administrators, pp. 233–235.

4. Lewis, A. *Restructuring*, pp. 233, 236–237.

5. American Association of School Administrators. 1988. *Challenges for School Leaders.* Arlington, VA: American Association of School Administrators, pp. 11–12.

6. Killion, J. P., J. P. Huddleston, and M. A. Claspell. 1989. "People Developer: A New Role for Principals", *Journal of Staff Development*, 10(1): 2–7.

7. Buchholz, S. and T. Roth. 1987. *Creating the High Performance Team.* New York, NY: John Wiley & Sons, Inc., pp. 30–31.

8. Kerman, S. and M. Martin. 1980. *Teacher Expectations and Student Achievement Teacher Handbook.* Bloomington, IN: Phi Delta Kappa.

9. McGreal, T. 1989. "Necessary Ingredients for Successful Instructional Improvement Initiatives", *Journal of Staff Development*, 10(1): 35–41.

10. Hampton, D. R., C. E. Summer, and R. A. Webber. *Organizational Behavior*, pp. 334–335.

11. Hampton, D.R., C.E. Summer, and R.A. Webber, *Organizational Behavior*, pp. 335.

12. Maeroff, G. I. 1988. "A Blueprint for Empowering Teachers," *Phi Delta Kappan*, 69(7): 473–477.

13. Webb, L.D. et al. 1987. *Personnel Administration in Education.* Columbus, OH: Merrill Publishing Company, p. 179.

14. Killion, J. P., J. P. Huddleston, and M.A. Claspell. "People Developer", pp. 4–5.

15. Buchholz, S. and T. Roth. *Creating the High Performance Team*, p. 40.

16. American Association of School Administrators. *Challenges*, p. 15.

17. Kimberly, J. R. and R. E. Quinn. 1984. *New Futures: The Challenge of Managing Corporate Transitions.* Homewood, IL: Dow Jones-Irwin, p. 15.

18. Lawler, E. E. III, and Mohman, S. A. 1989. "High-Involvement Management", *Personnel*, 66 (4): 26–31.

19. Buchholz, S. and T. Roth. 1987. *Creating the High Performance Team.* New York, NY: John Wiley & Sons, Inc., pp. 67, 88, 150.

20. Webb, L. D. et al. 1987. *Personnel Administration*, p. 178.

21. Hampton, D. R., C. E. Summer, and R. A. Webber. *Organizational Behavior*, p. 331.

22. Hampton, D. R., C. E. Summer, and R. A. Webber. *Organizational Behavior*, p. 332.

23. Warrick, D. D., ed. *Contemporary Organization Development.* Glenview, IL: Scott, Foresman and Company, pp. 331–333.

24. Berger, R. W. and D. L. Shores, eds. 1986. *Quality Circles.* New York, NY: Marcel Dekker, Inc., p. 94.

25. Berger, R. W. and D. L. Shores, eds. *Quality Circles*, p. 124.

26. Metz, E. J. 1981. "The Verteam Circle", *Training and Development Journal*, 35(12): 79–85.

27. Berger, R. W. and D. L. Shores, eds. *Quality Circles*, pp. 264–265.

28. Webb, L. D. et al. *Personnel Administration*, pp. 178–179.

29. Schmuck, R. A. and M. D. Miles, eds. 1971. *Organization Development in Schools*. Palo Alto, CA: National Press Books, pp. 323–325.

30. Warrick, D. D. *Contemporary Organization Development*, pp. 334–339.

31. Buchholz, S. and T. Roth. *Creating the High Performance Team*, p. 142.

32. Schmuck, R. A. and M. B. Miles. *Organization Development*, p. 382.

33. Schmuck, R. A. and M. B. Miles. *Organization Development*, pp. 301–304.

34. Berger, R. W. and D. L. Shores. *Quality Circles*, pp. 186–187.

35. Metz, E. J. "The Verteam Circle", pp. 79–85.

36. Lewis, A. *Restructuring*, pp. 2–5.

37. Lewis, A. *Restructuring*, p. 184.

38. Lewis, A. *Restructuring*, p. 226.

CHAPTER 8

Developing a Win-Win Attitude between Unions and Management

THE DEVELOPMENT AND maintenance of a healthy organization, whether it be a school district or any other, depends on that organization's ability to successfully adjust to changes in its external and internal environments. As previously addressed in Chapters 1, 2 and 6, as the organization makes changes because of technology or some other variable, it is crucial that the employees be trained to utilize this new technology. On the other hand, as the type of employee changes or as the employees' attitudes change, the organization must modify its structure to fully capitalize on the changes that have taken place within the employees.

There is another important employee element to be considered in most school districts. That element is the existence of employee unions within the school district. Many school districts have multiple union organizations, which may include separate unions for administrators, teachers, custodians, food service employees, transportation employees, maintenance personnel, teacher aides or other sub-groups of employees [1]. In addition, many of the local unions, especially teacher unions, are directly tied to state level or national level union groups [2]. In some cases, the master contracts are negotiated by a state official, and the local employee is represented by a state level union employee during grievance hearings. If one is to develop and maintain a healthy, productive, efficient, and effective school district and school buildings, it is crucial that the union leadership be effectively involved in those areas of the school district's operation that legitimately involve decisions related to the union's welfare, as well as those related to the school district's welfare [3].

Union/management relations within any school district can

usually be described as collaborative (win-win) or confrontational (adversarial); and it behooves the school district's decision makers to do everything within reason to develop a *win-win* approach to union/management relations. For only as the union leaders, administrators, and board of education members develop positive relations and comfortable day-to-day decision-making procedures, will the school district, its component parts, and its employees display the positive attitudes and environments that make winners of everyone [4].

Let's turn our attention at this juncture to: (1) defining *win-win* union/management, (2) outlining the differences between win-win and adversarial relations and the application of both of these approaches to union/management relations, (3) discussing a variety of structures that promote *win-win* labor management relations, and (4) elaborating upon the reasons why collaborative attitudes and relationships by union officials and management personnel are crucial to developing and maintaining a healthy organization and happy and productive employees. First, let's develop operational definitions of *win-win* union/management relations and adversarial union/management relations.

WIN-WIN OR ADVERSARIAL UNION/MANAGEMENT RELATIONS

Win-Win union/management relations are those that are collaborative in nature, that approach matters as problems to be solved by a give-and-take attitude, and that make both parties winners [5]. On the other hand, *adversarial* union/management relations can best be described as those that are confrontational in nature, that are approached in a manner such that each party must win as much as possible regardless of the consequences to the other party, and that are decided by strategies and emotions rather than by logic and mutual problem solving [6]. The basic approach to union/management relations is not only emphasized during the negotiations of a new labor contract, but it colors the day-to-day operations of the entire school district, its component parts and the employees' attitudes [7].

Even though there was a movement during the early 1960s to differentiate professional (teacher) negotiations from collective bargaining, that basic approach of classic labor/management collective bargaining has prevailed in educational systems during the past few decades [8]. Taking extreme scenarios, a list of descriptors can dramatically display the differences between the *win-win* and *adversarial* atmospheres and procedures that exist between unions and management when extreme conditions prevail—the same conditions that are historically derived from the confrontational legacy of private sector labor relations.

Descriptors of Win-Win and Adversarial Union/Management Relations

Win-Win	Adversarial
Trust	Mistrust
Fact	Propaganda
Respect	Disrespect
Information	Emotion
Mutual problem solving	"Beat them" strategies
Professional colleague	Enemy
Arrive at consensus	Push for 100 percent of your solution
Flexibility	Rigidity
Share information	Hide information
Disclose your position	Hide your bottom line position
Avoid contests of will	Apply maximum pressure
Make offers of solutions	Make threats
Change your position easily	Dig in to your position
Make concessions	Demand concessions
Be soft on people, hard on problem solving	Be hard on people and on problem solving
Invent multiple options	Insist on one solution
Identify shared interests	Insist on your interest
Give credit to the other party	Take all credit for yourself
Make winners of both parties [9]	Be the winner, and make them the loser [10]

It should be clear when viewing this list that the *win-win* approach to union/management relations is the preferred alternative. On the other hand, if an *adversarial* approach is selected by either party or both parties, the collective bargaining (negotiations) will be long, unpleasant, and destructive [11]. More importantly, however, a negative atmosphere will pervade the day-to-day operations, and the school district, its component parts (school buildings and departments) and the employees will remain in an unhealthy, unproductive, inefficient, and unpleasant state. Let's explore two examples from the view of negotiations and two examples from the view of day-to-day operational decision making.

Example #1: Adversarial Negotiations

Union At-the-Table Positions

(1) We demand a 15 percent salary increase.
(2) We demand fully paid hospital, surgical, medical, optical, dental, and auditory benefits.
(3) We demand that class size be reduced to fifteen students maximum per teacher, and that all special education students (regardless of category) be counted as equivalent to four students.
(4) We demand final veto power over any policy adopted by the board, any curriculum change, or any staff development activity.

Board of Education (Management) At-the-Table Positions

(1) We offer a 2 percent increase in salary.
(2) We propose that each employee pick up the cost of any increases in insurance premiums, and that we go to a $250 deductible clause in all our insurance coverages.
(3) No other changes shall be made in our existing union/management master contract.

Union Strategies

(1) Get a ground rule agreed to that keeps negotiation discussions closed (no media publicity or position releases).
(2) Paint the board members, superintendent of schools and the

board of education's negotiation team members as bad people and as enemies.

(3) Paint the board's proposals as being unreasonable, uncaring of the employees, and unconcerned for the children of the school district.

(4) Use the school districts with the highest pay and the best benefits as comparisons with which the school district should compete.

(5) Pay no attention to the taxpayers' ability to pay or to the amount of taxes already being levied to support the schools.

Board of Education (Management) Strategies

(1) Don't agree to closed negotiations, and insist upon publicizing the unreasonable requests of the union.

(2) Use the lowest paying districts as the comparable group as to where the school district should be competitive.

(3) Paint the union leaders and the negotiating team members as self-serving and power-hungry individuals.

(4) Paint the union positions as unreasonable and uncaring about the effect of those proposals on the taxpayers in the community.

(5) Insist that the board of education's negotiation team is trying to protect the long term interests of the students and the employees.

The Union's Negotiation Team's Membership

The union's negotiation team is comprised of the following members, and their roles are briefly described.

(1) *Spokesperson:* this is the most important of all members, in that she/he does all the at-the-table talking and controls the roles played by other members. This person also has the final say on strategies utilized at-the-table.

(2) *Language Specialist:* this person makes certain that all languages included in the union's proposals and those included in the proposals of the management team are analyzed for all specific meanings. That is, such words as "shall" and

"will" are mandates, whereas such words as "may" and "might" convey a permissive state.

(3) *Financial Expert:* this person's role is to figure the immediate and long term financial costs of all proposals made by the union and by management. For example, the union may wish to present the lowering of the average class size from twenty-five students per teacher to fifteen students per teacher as a non-economic issue; but, in reality, this can be a very costly proposal to implement.

(4) *Observer:* this person's role is to observe the behavior of the management team's members to determine if there are members who *telegraph* (display their feelings) by verbal or non-verbal behaviors. If such a person serves on the management team, this can be helpful in determining the effect of the union's proposals. If someone on the union's team is telegraphing, that person should probably be removed from the team. On the other hand, having someone fake emotion is sometimes an effective tactic.

(5) *Recorder:* this team member's job is to keep detailed records of everything that is written by either party, and to keep detailed notes on the verbal transactions during at-the-table discussions.

(6) *Rationalizer:* this person's role is to develop the union's rationale for each proposal made by the union, and to develop the rationale for each reaction to the proposals made by the board of education's negotiation team.

(7) *Publicist:* this member is responsible for the specific wording of any communication given to the total group of employees, or to any media source, or to the community in general.

(8) *Historian:* this member analyzes the existing contract, all previous contracts and the proposals made during prior contract negotiations by both the union and management.

(9) *Other specialists:* others may be desirable for the immediate negotiations' circumstances.

The Board of Education's Negotiation Team's Membership

The board of education's team might well have the identical team members as the union, but it may wish to vary its membership to the extent that it may desire to have a lawyer serve as a spokesperson (of course, also the union may wish to utilize a labor attorney or a state level Uniserve director as its spokesperson), or the board may wish one of its members to sit in on the negotiation sessions as a communications link to the total board of education's membership.

The At-the-Table Conduct of Either or Both Parties

In all probability, the at-the-table manner will be one of controlled discussions—a lot of proposals being made that are *trade offs* (not really expected as end results) or unreal initial requests (the union wants a 25 percent raise, and the board of education offers a 1 percent raise); and an emotional approach to the enemy (rather than a problem-solving approach with the professionals representing the board of education).

The Predictable End Results of Adversarial Collective Bargaining

The following results are most common after the collective bargaining has resulted in a contract.

(1) There are winners and losers.
(2) The loser takes the attitude that "we'll get you next time".
(3) The other party is still seen as the enemy.
(4) The current negotiations are seen as one battle in a continuing power war.
(5) Sadly, many times the community loses faith in both parties, and the students attend in an atmosphere that is unhealthy. In reality, all parties are losers: union, employees, board of education, administrators, community residents, taxpayers, and, especially, students [12].

Example #2: Win-Win Negotiations

Union At-the-Table Positions

The union's positions and proposals are based upon:
(1) The high priority items determined by the total employee membership

(2) Comparability with like unions groups in the geographic area

(3) Knowledge of the prior positions of the board of education and management on issues

(4) Knowledge of the community's attitudes towards the board of education, management, the union and the employees

(5) Knowledge of the board of education's high priority items

(6) Knowledge of the financial ability of the school district and the priorities built into the total budget of the school district

Board of Education (Management) At-the-Table Positions

The board of education's negotiating team's positions are based upon:

(1) Knowledge of the union's high priority items

(2) The board of education's high priority items

(3) Comparability of union contracts in like districts in the geographic area

(4) Knowledge of the union's prior positions on issues

(5) Knowledge of the affordability of any contract settlement

(6) Knowledge of the community's attitudes towards the union, the board of education, management, and the employees

Union and Board of Education (Management) Strategies

The ground rules agreed to include the fact that all information will be correct and shared, that any member of either team can speak at any time, that they can contribute to a solution to the problem being studied, and that neither party will attempt to propagandize the process.

Both parties will present proposals that are based upon factual information and logic. There will be no one-upmanship strategies attempted. Rather, both parties will involve themselves in collaborative problem solving.

Membership of the Union's and Board of Education's Teams

Both groups shall be selected on the basis of their having credibility with the other team's members, on their desire to solve problems in a collaborative fashion, and on their ability to bring factual information and rationality to the problem solving process.

At-the-Table Conduct of Both Parties

The conduct of both groups is geared to a friendly cooperative approach to problem solving based upon shared information and logic. In fact, many sub-groups are organized to develop resolution proposals to the total membership of both teams. In addition, *side-bar agreements* (agreements away from the table) are often reached by the spokespersons, and ratified by both negotiations groups. There is no need for caucuses of either body, as all information is shared openly for the benefit of both parties.

The Predictable End Results of Win-Win Collective Bargaining

The following results are most common after the collective bargaining has resulted in a master contract:

(*1*) Both parties are winners, and everyone realizes that neither party was trying to beat the other.

(2) All parties are seen as co-professionals who reached the best agreement possible under the situations that existed.

(*3*) The community is not upset, and knowledgeable members of the community appreciate the approach taken by both parties.

(*4*) The day-to-day interface among teachers and administrators and among union and management officials is positive.

(5) The master contract is reasonable and affordable.

(6) The work environment for students and employees is upbeat and positive [13].

A win-win approach to contract negotiations, then, achieves the following:

- It produces a wise agreement that assists both parties.
- A ratified contract is reached within a reasonable time period and with a reasonable use of the human resources by both parties.
- It improves, or at least does not damage, the relationship between the parties.

- It meets the legitimate interests of both parties.
- It resolves conflicting interests in a fair manner.
- It is durable and avoids grievances during the life of the contract.
- It takes the community interests into consideration.
- It treats the welfare of the students as a serious quality control element.

Now that we have explored the differences between win-win and adversarial bargaining during the period of contract negotiations, let's explore two examples of how a *win-win* union/management and an *adversarial* union/management attitude can affect the daily operation of a school district. Although many examples could be utilized, we will confine our two examples to that of dealing with an employee (in this case, a teacher) who is not performing adequately.

Example #3: A Poorly Performing Teacher During a Period of Adversarial Union/Management Attitudes

Situation

Instrumental Teacher, Jim O'Jones, is performing poorly; and the principal's summative evaluation, on the instrument developed with teacher representatives, indicates that Mr. O'Jones' performance is not up to the minimally accepted standard. Mr. O'Jones is told by administration that even though he holds a tenured position, specifications will be written for dismissal if improvement is not made soon.

Union Position

The union suggests that the teacher file a grievance, and the union steward attends the grievance hearings at all levels of the grievance procedure to represent the teacher. (At this juncture, it is important to mention that the union and its officials can be sued by a member if that member's interests are not represented by the union and its officials.) At the various stages of the grievance hearings, the union representative makes the following points:

(1) Management has to prove that no other teacher performing at or below the level of Mr. O'Jones is being evaluated at a higher performance level than that of Mr. O'Jones.

(2) The principal is not a music specialist and therefore is not qualified to judge the quality of Mr. O'Jones performance. In addition, the principal has not been a classroom teacher for fifteen years, and the principal, therefore, is not updated on current teaching methods.

(3) Sufficient time and assistance is not being provided Mr. O'Jones [14].

Management's Position

Management states that the official warning of termination, if rapid improvement does not take place, will remain in the employee's official personnel file. It also presents the following evidences:

(1) A series of memos indicating all specific pertinent information provided to Mr. O'Jones.

(2) A detailed chronology of events that proves that the teacher is not performing up to the minimum standard. The information chronicled includes complaints from parents and students, the lowering of adjudication ratings in competition with other school district's similar performing units, and a trendline that displays a drastic drop in the number of students registering for the elective program in instrumental music [15]. Of course, Mr. O'Jones was given copies of all the information as it was placed in his official personnel file.

Union Followthrough Procedures

The union solicits teachers within the building to testify that Mr. O'Jones is an excellent teacher, in case management attempts to fire Mr. O'Jones; and the union asks the state level union's attorneys to investigate and assist in preparing a case against the principal, superintendent, and the board of education. The union collects data to verify that Mr. O'Jones was not provided with sufficient assistance or time to improve, and the union collects information that indicates that Mr. O'Jones meets the minimum requirements for performance.

Management Followthrough Procedures

The principal is directed to keep copies of every phoned or written complaint filed against Mr. O'Jones, to verify the decline in the numbers of students signing up for his elective courses, to tape record his practice sessions, and to keep a record of all adjudications of all of Mr. O'Jones' performing groups. The principal is also to share each of these with Mr. O'Jones as he builds a case for dismissal, with the assistance of central administration and the school district's attorney [16].

Predictable Results of This Adversarial Approach

The predictable results of this approach are:

(*1*) A public trial will probably take place in the media, and the teacher, teacher union, and management will be damaged by the publicity.

(*2*) Warfare between the union and management will accelerate.

(*3*) Neighboring union groups and, perhaps, state and national groups will put their political pressure into the local environment.

(*4*) A great deal of money and human effort will be spent trying to win this case.

Example #4: A Poorly Performing Teacher During a Period of Win-Win Union/Management Attitudes

The Union's Position

The union's position in this case involves:

(*1*) Talking to the teacher to get Mr. O'Jones' story

(*2*) Meeting with management to review all the information possessed by management

(*3*) Offering to assist in solving the situation by cooperating with management in any improvement strategies, while notifying management of procedures that will be necessary to represent a union member if satisfactory improvement is not made. On the other hand, if the performance of Mr. O'Jones is clearly unsatisfactory, the union leadership may attempt to counsel Mr. O'Jones to improve or to resign [17].

Management's Position

Management's position in this case involves:

(1) Specifying exactly what is expected of Mr. O'Jones

(2) Specifying the timeline allowed for improvement of performance to be displayed

(3) Specifying the specific assistance to be provided Mr. O'Jones over this time period

(4) Specifying the types of records of performance to be kept and the procedures for collecting and sharing those records with Mr. O'Jones [18]

Union Followthrough Procedures

The union induces other music teachers to unofficially provide assistance to Mr. O'Jones, and the union leaders monitor the situation and counsel Mr. O'Jones at each step in the process. The union leaders also share helpful improvement related information with management [19].

Management Followthrough Procedures

Management followthrough with the specific program elements are shared in writing with Mr. O'Jones; management also keeps the union's officials continually informed of Mr. O'Jones' progress or lack of progress; and management unofficially welcomes any assistance given Mr. O'Jones.

Predictable Results of This Win-Win Approach

There are three very important end results of this win-win approach:

(1) The quality of teaching standards is considered important, and both parties attempt to help the teacher attain that quality level which is at least at a minimum level of acceptability.

(2) Both parties join forces to solve an important problem.

(3) The community at large is spared the negative and emotional hearing trials.

(4) Financial and human resources are not wasted, and they are used to improve the teacher and the classroom environment for students.

Again, the advantages of a *win-win*, rather than an adversarial approach to union/management operational problem solving is evident. Not only are both parties attempting to resolve problems at a highly professional level using fact and logic, but the students and community are spared from the unpleasant by-products of union/management power wars.

Now that we have explored the dramatic differences between a *win-win* approach to union/management and an *adversarial* approach, we can turn to a discussion of various union/management structures that can be put into place to make and keep a healthy school district organization in existence. Some of the most productive structures that can be originated to develop and keep positive union/management relations are:

(1) Union/management bi-weekly leadership meetings

(2) Problem-solving union/management teams

(3) Joint union/management data gathering teams to be organized prior to contract negotiations

(4) Joint grievance investigatory union/management teams

(5) Regularly shared, accurate information that is of interest to the union or to management

(6) Methodologies to isolate and work together on areas of school district improvement that are of interest to both parties [20]

STRUCTURES THAT PROMOTE A WIN-WIN UNION/MANAGEMENT RELATIONSHIP

Union/management bi-weekly leadership meetings are extremely helpful in avoiding any surprises to either party. They can be used to share important information, to alert the other party to potential problems that may arise, or they can be used to help establish trust, respect, and rapport between the leadership members of the union and management. In any case, continuous scheduled meetings, with the provision that either party is free to contact the other party at any time, is the key to communication and to the maintenance of *win-win* attitudes.

Problem-solving union/management teams can greatly assist in keeping the relationship between management and union a positive and helpful one. Either party can signal the other party that a problem exists or that a problem is evolving. In this case, both parties clearly define the problem and its dimensions. Once the problem is clarified, both parties can discuss alternate solutions to the problems, and the impact of each of these solutions on the students (if applicable), on the community (if applicable), on individual employees (if applicable) and on the union and management organizations. Once the alternatives and their impacts are determined, the *best* solution under existing conditions can be mutually decided upon, and both the union and management can act in a manner that maximizes the positive effects of the chosen solution.

Joint union/management data gathering teams can be organized well before the time contract negotiations are scheduled to commence. Some of the data that can be collected are:

(*1*) Any applicable new laws that might affect the upcoming contract

(*2*) The anticipated cost increases in such matters as health and other fringe benefits

(*3*) The predicted increases (or decreases) in income from local taxes, state sources, and federal sources

(*4*) Comparable data from other school districts in the area

(*5*) A summary of those items that were identified as problems and/or grievances during the life of the current master union/management contract, and any mutually agreeable resolutions that were achieved on these issues during the life of the existing contract

Joint grievance investigatory union/management teams can assist in keeping the temperature of the parties down during serious employee grievance situations. These joint grievance investigatory union/management teams do not attempt to determine the stance to be taken on the grievance on the other party, but they do collect data that is accurate and that will be used by both parties as the grievance proceeds. In other words, the facts will not be in contention, but the positions that both parties take on the basis of mutually agreed-upon facts may differ.

Regular sharing of accurate information that is of interest to the union and/or to the management avoids suspicion, avoids confusion, avoids positioning and avoids misunderstandings. Information on such matters as increases in health insurance premiums and other fringe costs, increases or decreases in energy costs, upcoming impacting legislation, and many other crucial pieces of information should be automatically shared. These informations not only impact future contract negotiations, but they also may impact operational problems to be mutually investigated and solved by the union's and management's leadership.

Developing methodologies to isolate and work together on areas of school district improvement that are of interest to both parties also makes a great deal of sense. Such matters as desirable staff development programs, community information services, or student "phone-in" homework assistance are win-win opportunities that not only assist union and management, but that also present both union and management in a favorable light with both students and the community's residents [21].

The structures that can be developed by well-intentioned and innovative union and management personnel who desire to have a win-win environment that will assist both parties, the students, and the community are limited only by the creative talents of the individuals representing both union and management. The *key* is the desire to develop and maintain a *win-win* union/management environment; the means are any structures that can be devised to achieve that goal.

Now that we have explored the dimensions of a *win-win* and an *adversarial* approach to contract negotiations and to a potential grievance, and we have outlined some structures that can assist in causing a *win-win* state to be created and maintained, we can end this chapter by discussing why a win-win attitude between union and management is necessary in order to develop and maintain a healthy school district, healthy school building environments, healthy, happy and productive employees, a supportive student body, and a supportive community. The alternative is to have continuous problems, low levels of satisfaction by all parties, and a non-productive school district.

WHY A WIN-WIN UNION/MANAGEMENT IS CRUCIAL TO A HEALTHY SCHOOL DISTRICT ORGANIZATION

A union/management *win-win* attitude and operation is crucial for many reasons. Some of the most important of these reasons are:

- Trust, caring and professionalism are important to the operation of any healthy organization.
- Program solving on the basis of data and logic is much preferred within any organization to problem solving by power plays, emotionalism, and win-lose approaches. A win-lose approach only favors one party over a very short time period, and this approach causes long term negative results.
- A *win-win* approach most likely will bring support from students, all employees, and the community at large.
- A *win-win* approach uses human, financial and material resources in an efficient and positive manner.
- It causes those items that are identified by research to exist in effective organizations. That is, a win-win approach assists in meeting the requirements for: the creation and maintenance of a safe and healthful environment; a mutual problem-solving operation that allows input opportunities for employees, an environment that promotes innovation; an environment that is built upon a helping relationship; and an environment in which all individuals and groups are seen as desirable and valuable resources to be utilized in continuously improving the organizational health of the school district, its constituent parts, and the individuals who study and work within the school district [22].

The almost half-century-long history of collective bargaining in education began as a protective measure, and, as union growth increased, it has "augmented the rights and protections of teachers, limited the prerogative of principals, and promoted the centralization and standardization of district personnel practices" [23]. As the profession enters the 1990's, some major universities and educational organizations have begun to respond to the reform and restructuring demands that emerged during the

1980's by creating professional agendas addressing current negotiation issues, and by initiating an endorsement of the win-win attitude. This more integrated approach to collective bargaining can be described as having the capacity to produce more enduring settlements. A move from the borrowed, historical, industrial model of negotiations to the integrated bargaining process, focused on problem solving, has implications for key employee organizational representation on the team structures and empowerment models proposed in Chapter 7. If a new generation of labor relations is arriving, educational policy will be its focus as unions work collaboratively with administration/management. This reform of the atmosphere and substance of negotiations will require mutual adaptation, which is clearly the very essence of win-win.

SUMMARY

Many school districts have multiple unions or other employee organizations, functioning unofficially or officially, (through legislative requirement), as the compensation or bargaining agents, or as procedural and grievance resources for employees. Union/ management relations within any district can be described as collaborative (win-win) or confrontational (adversarial). The more desirable win-win relationship was defined (and descriptors were provided) as being more collaborative in nature, while the adversarial relationship was described as confrontational. Union and management at-the-table positions and conduct, strategies, and membership descriptions for each style of relations were contrasted. A scenario of unacceptable employee performance was traced through the grievance procedure with both the adversarial and win-win approaches being utilized. Structures that promote the win-win relationship include bi-weekly leadership meetings; union/management teams for problem solving, data gathering, grievance investigation, and information sharing; and the development of methodologies to collaboratively focus on school district improvement. A win-win union/management attitude and operation that supports the development of a healthy organization is more logical, and is supported by the students, employees, and community. Also, it promotes the most efficient use of human, financial, and material resources. There is evidence mounting that a more rational, collective gaining attitude has been forming in the educational labor relations within the last decade.

GUIDELINES

1. An organization must effectively include and involve union leadership in areas of the school district's operation that legitimately involve decisions related to the union's welfare.
2. Positive attitudes and environments require union/management positive relations and comfort in day-to-day decision-making procedures.
3. It should be kept in mind that the basic approach of union/management relations will color the day-to-day operations of the entire school district.
4. It should also be kept in mind that the end results of adversarial collective bargaining will many times cause a sense of disaffection in the students and in the community.
5. Aim for win-win collective bargaining; this will create a more positive and supportive school and community climate.
6. Proactive and standard union/management structures, such as focused, collaborative teams, are appropriate preventive measures that can support a win-win attitude.

EXERCISES

1. Assess the labor/management relationship in your district, and determine which elements are adversarial and which are win-win.
2. Investigate board minutes or records to trace the district history of any salary or benefit negotiations, whether with a legally recognized bargaining unit or with a "meet-and-confer" employee organization.
3. Trace the grievance procedure(s) of your district, and assess their adversarial or win-win application.
4. Contact the local or state offices of any district employee organization to obtain an overall picture of the union/management relationship in your district, and across the state's district.

5. Redesign an existing district union/management collective bargaining procedure to cause it to be more win-win in nature.

6. Suggest several possible district structures that will promote a win-win relationship.

SELECTED REFERENCES

1. Johnson, S. M. 1984. *Teacher Unions in Schools*. Philadelphia, PA: Temple University Press, p. 25.

2. Webb, L. D. et al. 1987. *Personnel Administration in Education*. Columbus, OH: Merrill Publishing Company, pp. 95–98.

3. Kohler, L. T. 1980. "Basic Points for Negotiators", *AS & U*, 52(9): 40–41.

4. Pennington, R. 1989. "Collaborative Labor Relations: The First Line Is the Bottom Line", *Personnel*, 66(4): 78–83.

5. Yoder, D. and P. D. Staudohar. 1982. *Personnel Management and Industrial Relations*. Seventh edition. Englewood Cliffs, NJ: Prentice-Hall, Inc., p. 469.

6. Johnson, S. M. 1984. *Teacher Unions in Schools*. Philadelphia, PA: Temple University Press, pp. 28–29.

7. Johnson, S. M. *Teacher Unions*, pp. 166–167.

8. Webb, L. D. et al. *Personnel Administration*, p. 93.

9. Smith, P. and R. Baker. 1986. "An Alternative Form of Collective Bargaining", *Phi Delta Kappan*, 67(8): 605–607.

10. Smith, P. and R. Baker. "An Alternative Form", pp. 605–606.

11. Nyland, L. 1987. "Win/Win Bargaining Pays Off", *Educational Digest*, 53(1): 28–29.

12. Webster, W. G. 1985. *Effective Collective Bargaining in Public Education*. Ames, IA: Iowa State University Press, pp. 105, 145.

13. Kohler, L. T. "Basic Points", pp. 40–41.

14. Neal, R. G. 1988. "Justice Favors the Well Prepared," *The Executive Educator*, 10(11): 17–18.

15. Johnson, S. M. *Teacher Unions*, pp. 108–110.

16. Johnson, S. M. *Teacher Unions*, p. 13.

17. Neal, R. G. "Justice", pp. 17–18.

18. Johnson, S. M. *Teacher Unions*, pp. 120–123.

19. Webb, L. D. et al. *Personnel Administration*, pp. 155–156.

20. Johnson, S. M. *Teacher Unions*, p. 125.

21. Kohler, L. T. "Basic Points", pp. 40–41.

22. Smith, P. and R. Baker. "An Alternative Form", pp. 605–607.

23. Nyland, L. "Win/Win Bargaining", pp. 28–29.

CHAPTER 9

Developing and Maintaining a Healthy Organization

IT IS IMPORTANT to develop and maintain a healthy central district organization as well as healthy individual buildings and departments. If attention is not paid to the whole and the sum of its parts, one could have a district wherein some individual buildings have extremely healthy cultures and other buildings have very unhealthy cultures. If this situation exists, then the total school district will not display the degree of organizational health that is required to maintain a highly productive and effective school district operation [1].

Chapter 7 dealt with means of involving employees in empowerment activities focused on collaborative planning, employee training, two-way communications, and developing an OD (Organization Development) and HRD (Human Resource Development) unified strategy that promoted the organizational culture that makes for a first class culture focused primarily on the school building and departmental levels. Chapter 8 discussed ways of involving employee unions in collaborative efforts that promote a healthy organizational culture.

This chapter discusses means of OD (Organizational Development) interventions and HRD (Human Resource Development) activities focused on the central level of a school district's operation. Chapter 9 specifically discusses the following:

(1) The definition of a healthy organization
(2) Assessing the existing culture and climate within your school district and within each school site within the district
(3) OD strategies that help create and maintain a healthy organization
(4) District-wide vertical teams

(5) District-wide horizontal matrix means

(6) QWL (Quality of Work Life)—a comprehensive approach to developing and maintaining a healthy school district

DEFINITION OF A HEALTHY ORGANIZATION

A healthy organization can be defined as one that includes the following characteristics:

(1) It is an open organization wherein both employees and clients have opportunities for significant input.

(2) It is one in which human contributions are valued and recognized.

(3) It is one that provides meaningful work for students and employees.

(4) It is one that has a clear vision and mission that all stakeholders know and buy into as owners.

(5) It is one in which data are collected to monitor progress towards its vision, mission, and strategic goals; and these data are used to modify objectives, strategies and processes.

(6) It is one that produces high quality student and staff outputs and quality, long-term outcomes.

(7) It is one that has high levels of satisfaction and active support from all stakeholder groups. A less complex definition is one stating that a healthy organization is one that is both highly productive and possesses positive human relationships and a positive "feeling tone" [2].

Using the two measures of *productivity*, and *positive relationship and "feeling tones"*, let's explore some of the specific ways to assess these measures. Obviously, the productivity measures can be assessed by analyzing data from trends in student test scores, and by collecting data related to employee productivity (contributions to students, to the community, and to the professions). The relationship and "feeling tone" can be collected by surveys and observations [3]. This leads to assessing the "what is" state of the climate and culture in the school district and in the individual school buildings that comprise the school district. Periodic and uniform assessments can provide trends which then can be used to plot the requirement for OD interventions if improvements appear to be required [4].

ASSESSING THE CULTURE AND CLIMATE

While serving as superintendent of schools in Greece, New York (a district of approximately 12,000 students) one of the authors developed a series of opinionnaires that assessed the "feeling tone"–climate and culture factors related to the school district and to the individual buildings within the district. These opinionnaires were developed with input from the stakeholders, and they were developed for students, parents and employees. They were analyzed for use in determining the "what is" health quotient of the total district and of each building within the district [5]. Periodic administration of the opinionnaires revealed trends, after the initial administration provided the base data related to the initial "what is" state. All instruments were pre-tested, and they were administered to a stratified random sampling of fifth grade elementary students and a random sampling of all secondary students and parents. For political reasons and to avoid any suspicions, all employees were asked to respond to the employee opinionnaire anonymously.

The responses were coded on computerized answer sheets, and the entire operation was conducted under the direction of the director of research. Obviously, anonymity of respondents was guaranteed. It should be noted that the student and parent responses related to the specific building(s) while the employees responded to both the building and district levels. Below are the instruments utilized to measure climate and culture.

The Elementary Student Climate/Culture Survey Instrument

Directions to principal: The sampling procedure used this year is likely to require no more than twenty-five students in each school to be given the survey. The survey should be administered by a teacher or teacher aide (pretests indicate that the total time required should not exceed 30 minutes).

The survey is intended to be self-administered. However, grade five students should be offered the opportunity to have a word or phrase read to them individually if necessary. This available assistance should be announced prior to administration of the survey. Also, stress the importance of making sure the responses are recorded on the correct line of the answer sheet. As students complete the survey, briefly scan the answer sheet for completeness and the absence of extraneous marks.

When answer sheets seem to be in good condition for machine scoring, please put them in the confidential envelope provided and return them to the Research Office.

Elementary Form

School _____ Return to Research Office by_____

Directions to students: The purpose of this survey is to find out how you feel about your school. In this survey there are 56 statements. Please read carefully each statement. Then, for each statement, select the responses which best represents how you feel about that statement, and put an "X" in the space under the column which indicates your response to that statement. Respond by using one of the following:

☐ **SA** (strongly agree)
☐ **A** (agree)
☐ **D** (disagree)
☐ **SD** (strongly disagree)

There are no right or wrong answers, so respond to each statement as honestly as you can.

	SA	A	D	SD
1. Students in this school help one another and share.	☐	☐	☐	☐
2. Our principal really cares about the students.	☐	☐	☐	☐
3. Most people in this school are kind.	☐	☐	☐	☐
4. Teachers often spend their informal time with students.	☐	☐	☐	☐
5. The principal spends some of her/his time working with students.	☐	☐	☐	☐
6. People in this school seem to care about me as a person.	☐	☐	☐	☐
7. Teachers in this school often show their appreciation for the work of other employees.	☐	☐	☐	☐
8. Teachers often embarrass students in front of the class.	☐	☐	☐	☐
9. Custodians here are seen by students as helpful, friendly, and caring.	☐	☐	☐	☐
10. School secretaries greet visitors, students, and employees in a warm, friendly manner.	☐	☐	☐	☐
11. People in charge here enforce the rules consistently but are considerate when they do.	☐	☐	☐	☐
12. Teachers in this school try hard to have learning "come alive" for students.	☐	☐	☐	☐

	SA	A	D	SD
13. Many classes here are dull and boring.	☐	☐	☐	☐
14. Teachers in this school encourage students to speak up on issues and problems they study.	☐	☐	☐	☐
15. Students have frequent opportunities to express personal opinions in class.	☐	☐	☐	☐
16. Teachers often ask students to share personal experiences related to their learning.	☐	☐	☐	☐
17. In this school students are encouraged to think critically about the information they acquire.	☐	☐	☐	☐
18. Students feel they can express opinions freely, even if they are not in agreement with teachers or other students.	☐	☐	☐	☐
19. The principal and staff seem to work as a team.	☐	☐	☐	☐
20. The principal of this school is concerned about how I learn.	☐	☐	☐	☐
21. The principal in this school supports and helps the teachers whenever she/he can.	☐	☐	☐	☐
22. The principal sets an example by working hard.	☐	☐	☐	☐
23. The principal spends extra time in the building.	☐	☐	☐	☐
24. The principal in this school is often difficult to understand.	☐	☐	☐	☐
25. I feel I can be myself when I talk to the principal.	☐	☐	☐	☐
26. The principal's influence in the building is recognized by most people.	☐	☐	☐	☐
27. Most students here can learn a lot when they try.	☐	☐	☐	☐
28. Teachers here usually encourage students to do their best.	☐	☐	☐	☐
29. Teachers in this school expect a lot from students.	☐	☐	☐	☐
30. Teachers here routinely tell students how they are doing.	☐	☐	☐	☐
31. Teachers usually make sure students really learn something before going to something new.	☐	☐	☐	☐

	SA	A	D	SD
32. It's clear what has to be done to get a good grade.	☐	☐	☐	☐
33. Only a handful of students in this school really care about learning.	☐	☐	☐	☐
34. All in all, students here learn much less than they could.	☐	☐	☐	☐
35. People in this school believe that you can learn a lot, no matter who you are.	☐	☐	☐	☐
36. Awards, citations and other honors are available to ALL students.	☐	☐	☐	☐
37. Teachers here can be heard frequently to say such things as "keep up the good work".	☐	☐	☐	☐
38. Students here fail to appreciate the work of custodians, nurses, aides, and cooks.	☐	☐	☐	☐
39. Teachers in this school don't really know students as individuals.	☐	☐	☐	☐
40. Students and teachers in this school can be found talking with one another in small groups.	☐	☐	☐	☐
41. Teachers here try very hard to understand young people.	☐	☐	☐	☐
42. Students have the opportunity to make some suggestions as to how this school is run.	☐	☐	☐	☐
43. Teachers here are fair with students, even when they do poorly in some school work.	☐	☐	☐	☐
44. Teachers and students in this school respect one another.	☐	☐	☐	☐
45. Teachers here clearly explain how assignments are to be done.	☐	☐	☐	☐
46. In this school students usually master most of the content covered in reading, language arts, and math.	☐	☐	☐	☐
47. Teachers here know a lot about the prior achievement of their students and use it to help students learn.	☐	☐	☐	☐
48. Just about every student in this school gets involved in the day to day work in class.	☐	☐	☐	☐

	SA	A	D	SD
49. In this school test results are reported in ways people can understand.	☐	☐	☐	☐
50. Teachers here don't help students practice new skills they have just learned.	☐	☐	☐	☐
51. Teachers have a system to keep track of student achievement and progress on important instructional objectives.	☐	☐	☐	☐
52. Teachers in this school make a point of letting students know when they have done well.	☐	☐	☐	☐
53. Teachers in this school try hard to show students how new ideas and skills are connected to what they already know.	☐	☐	☐	☐
54. Students in this school do homework and other practice activities without understanding what they are doing.	☐	☐	☐	☐
55. In this school results of achievement tests are used to improve the way certain things are taught.	☐	☐	☐	☐
56. In this school system the school board sets goals that are directly related to student achievement.	☐	☐	☐	☐

Cover Letter to Parents

Dear Parent:

We in Greece are justifiably proud of the levels of performance attained by our students. Recent research on effective schools clearly indicates that although *what* students can do continues to be extremely important, two additional factors are also very important—namely, how we relate to students as we serve them, and the "feeling" or "atmosphere" in a school building. Collectively, these factors have come to be known as "school climate".

As one who has a vital interest in our school, you are asked to complete the enclosed *School Climate Survey*, along with teachers, other employees, and students who are randomly selected.

Specifically, we ask you to respond *anonymously* to a number of statements concerned with such things as respect, vitality in instruction, academic expectations, school leadership, and other matters related to school climate and to effective schools.

With the help of our data processing department, the research office will analyze the information and will provide district data by the respondent groups cited above. This information should be available by early March. Later, at the request of individual school building staffs, *confidential* analyses by school will be provided.

We urge you to take the necessary 20–30 minutes to read the directions for recording your responses and to complete the survey. With your help we can take further steps to make our schools even better.

We thank you in advance for your cooperation.

Sincerely,

_____ (Building Principal)

_____ (Director of Research)

School Climate/Culture Survey
(Secondary Student, Employee and Parent Form)

Please return to the Research Office by _____.

Directions: The purpose of this survey is to collect some information about how you see your school and its atmosphere. Please check here which type of respondent you are:

__ Parent   __ Teacher   __ Non-teacher employee   __ Student

Since you are not asked to supply your name, your responses are completely confidential. However, we do ask you to respond as honestly as you can to each statement so the survey will provide accurate information.

You are provided with this survey booklet, a separate answer sheet called the "general purpose" answer sheet, and a confidential envelope.

Your reaction to each statement is expressed by selecting one of four indications of agreement: **SA** (strongly agree), **A** (agree), **D** (disagree) or **SD** (strongly disagree). Here is an example:

	SA	A	D	SD
Pride in this school is often demonstrated	☒	☐	☐	☐

Final reminders:

(1) Be careful to record your response to each statement on the correct line of the answer sheet.

(2) All statements are not expressed the same way. Read each carefully and answer as honestly as you can.

(3) Use a number 2 pencil to fill in the answer spaces properly; and if you erase, please do so completely.

(4) When finished, place the answer sheet inside the booklet and return both in the confidential return envelope provided, being careful not to fold the answer sheet.

Your cooperation is sincerely appreciated.

	SA	A	D	SD
1. Students in this school help one another and share.	☐	☐	☐	☐
2. Our principal really cares about students.	☐	☐	☐	☐
3. Most people in this school are kind.	☐	☐	☐	☐
4. Teachers often spend their informal time with students.	☐	☐	☐	☐
5. The principal spends some of his/her time working with students.	☐	☐	☐	☐
6. People in this school seem to care about me as a person.	☐	☐	☐	☐
7. Teachers in this school often show their appreciation for the work of other members of the school staff.	☐	☐	☐	☐
8. Teachers here often embarrass students in front of the class.	☐	☐	☐	☐
9. Custodians here are seen by students as helpful, friendly, and caring.	☐	☐	☐	☐
10. School secretaries greet visitors, students and faculty in a warm, friendly manner.	☐	☐	☐	☐
11. Vice principals here seem as concerned with understanding student problems as they are with enforcing rules.	☐	☐	☐	☐
12. People in charge here enforce the rules consistently but are considerate when they do.	☐	☐	☐	☐
13. Teachers in this school try hard to have learning "come alive" for students.	☐	☐	☐	☐
14. Many classes here are dull and boring.	☐	☐	☐	☐
15. Teachers in this school encourage students to speak up on issues and problems they study.	☐	☐	☐	☐
16. Students have frequent opportunities to express personal opinions in class.	☐	☐	☐	☐
17. Teachers often ask students to share personal experiences related to their learning.	☐	☐	☐	☐
18. In this school students are encouraged to think critically about the information they acquire.	☐	☐	☐	☐
19. In several courses here we do things a lot as they are done in the work world.	☐	☐	☐	☐

	SA	A	D	SD
20. Students feel they can express opinions freely, even if they are not in agreement with the teacher or other students.	☐	☐	☐	☐
21. The principal and other employees seem to work as a team.	☐	☐	☐	☐
22. The principal of this school is concerned about how I learn.	☐	☐	☐	☐
23. The principal in this school supports and helps the teachers whenever she/he can.	☐	☐	☐	☐
24. The principal sets an example by working hard.	☐	☐	☐	☐
25. The principal spends extra time in the building.	☐	☐	☐	☐
26. The principal in this school is often difficult to understand.	☐	☐	☐	☐
27. I feel I can be myself when I talk to the principal.	☐	☐	☐	☐
28. The principal's influence in the building is recognized by most people.	☐	☐	☐	☐
29. Most students here can learn a lot when they try.	☐	☐	☐	☐
30. Teachers here usually encourage students to do their best.	☐	☐	☐	☐
31. Teachers in this school expect a lot from students.	☐	☐	☐	☐
32. Teachers here routinely tell students how they are doing.	☐	☐	☐	☐
33. Teachers usually make sure students really learn something before going on to something new.	☐	☐	☐	☐
34. It is clear what has to be done to get a good grade.	☐	☐	☐	☐
35. Only a handful of students in this school really care about learning.	☐	☐	☐	☐
36. All in all, students here learn much less than they could.	☐	☐	☐	☐
37. People in this school believe that you can learn a lot, no matter who you are.	☐	☐	☐	☐
38. Awards, citations, and other honors are available to ALL students.	☐	☐	☐	☐

	SA	A	D	SD
39. Teachers here can be heard frequently to say such things as "keep up the good work".	□	□	□	□
40. Students here fail to appreciate the work of custodians, nurses, aides, and cooks.	□	□	□	□
41. Teachers in this school don't really know students as individuals.	□	□	□	□
42. Students and teachers in this school can be found talking informally with one another in small groups.	□	□	□	□
43. Teachers here try very hard to understand young people.	□	□	□	□
44. Students have the opportunity to make some suggestions as to how this school is run.	□	□	□	□
45. Teachers are fair with students even when they do poorly in some of their school work.	□	□	□	□
46. Teachers and students in this school respect one another.	□	□	□	□
47. Teachers clearly explain how assignments are to be done.	□	□	□	□
48. In this school students usually master most of the content covered in reading, language arts, and math.	□	□	□	□
49. Teachers here know a lot about the prior achievement of their students and use it to help students learn.	□	□	□	□
50. Just about every student in this school gets involved in the day to day work in class.	□	□	□	□
51. In this school test results are reported in ways people can understand.	□	□	□	□
52. Teachers here don't help students practice new skills they have just learned.	□	□	□	□
53. Teachers in this school have a system to keep track of student achievement and progress on important instructional objectives.	□	□	□	□
54. Teachers in this school make a point of letting students know when they have done good work.	□	□	□	□

	SA	A	D	SD
55. Teachers in this school try hard to show students how new ideas and skills are connected to what they already know.	☐	☐	☐	☐
56. Students in this school do homework and other practice activities without understanding what they are doing.	☐	☐	☐	☐
57. In this school results of achievement tests are used to improve the way certain things are taught.	☐	☐	☐	☐
58. In this school system the school board sets goals that are directly related to student achievement.	☐	☐	☐	☐

You will note that the questions are identical or similar for each respondent group, whether they are elementary students, secondary students, parents, teachers, or non-teaching employees. This is done to compare responses between and among response groups. Also, certain items are replicated in order to determine whether or not the respondent(s) answers the same questions in an identical manner.

In addition to the surveys duplicated above, an additional survey instrument was administered to every employee of the district. The survey instrument duplicated below was designed to get a picture of employees' attitudes at both the building and district levels on the identical questions.

Employee Climate/Culture Survey

Directions: Please complete each item in this survey for BOTH your building level and for the district level by placing an "X" in the space provided that most closely represents your attitude towards each item. Anonymity is assured. When you complete the survey, please return it in the *confidential* envelope provided to the Director of Research.

	Bldg. Level				District			
Cluster 1: Morale	SA	A	D	SD	SA	A	D	SD
1. Nearly everyone who works in this location is happy to be here.	☐	☐	☐	☐	☐	☐	☐	☐
2. Teacher morale here is high.	☐	☐	☐	☐	☐	☐	☐	☐

	Bldg. Level				District			
	SA	A	D	SD	SA	A	D	SD
3. ALL employees here share a certain sense of pride.	☐	☐	☐	☐	☐	☐	☐	☐
4. Where I work we don't seem to have the "we" spirit.	☐	☐	☐	☐	☐	☐	☐	☐
5. Students, teachers and parents here often display symbols of school pride.	☐	☐ ·	☐	☐	☐	☐	☐	☐
6. Most of us around here, including me, care a great deal about Greece Central.	☐	☐	☐	☐	☐	☐	☐	☐
7. I use a wide range of skills in the work I do.	☐	☐	☐	☐	☐	☐	☐	☐
8. Lately I often think of quitting my job.	☐	☐	☐	☐	☐	☐	☐	☐
9. My job is challenging and makes good use of my abilities.	☐	☐	☐	☐	☐	☐	☐	☐
10. Keeping my job and making money are not the only reasons I try to do my job well.	☐	☐	☐	☐	☐	☐	☐	☐
11. My work used to be more enjoyable than it is now.	☐	☐	☐	☐	☐	☐	☐	☐
12. All in all, I am very satisfied with my job.	☐	☐	☐	☐	☐	☐	☐	☐

Cluster 2: Involvement and Influence

1. All in all, this district encourages people to exchange opinions and ideas.	☐	☐	☐	☐	☐	☐	☐	☐
2. Most of the time people here are asked for their ideas before decisions are made.	☐	☐	☐	☐	☐	☐	☐	☐
3. Work objectives and plans in my area are announced and explained, but rarely discussed beforehand.	☐	☐	☐	☐	☐	☐	☐	☐
4. I influence decisions related to my job.	☐	☐	☐	☐	☐	☐	☐	☐

	Bldg. Level				District			
	SA	A	D	SD	SA	A	D	SD
5. As long as I do my job well, I have a great deal of freedom as to how it gets done.	☐	☐	☐	☐	☐	☐	☐	☐
6. Generally, I find those above me are receptive to ideas and suggestions I make.	☐	☐	☐	☐	☐	☐	☐	☐
7. High level administrators are the only people who have the "say" around here.	☐	☐	☐	☐	☐	☐	☐	☐
8. Work standards and expectations are usually clear to everyone.	☐	☐	☐	☐	☐	☐	☐	☐

Cluster 3: Trust

	SA	A	D	SD	SA	A	D	SD
1. People here don't always agree, but we share concerns with each other.	☐	☐	☐	☐	☐	☐	☐	☐
2. People who work here trust students to use good judgment.	☐	☐	☐	☐	☐	☐	☐	☐
3. Students can count on adults who work in the district to listen to their side of the story and be fair.	☐	☐	☐	☐	☐	☐	☐	☐
4. Immediate supervisors and other administrators take time to tell people when they have done outstanding work.	☐	☐	☐	☐	☐	☐	☐	☐
5. Generally, I feel that those who get ahead here deserve it.	☐	☐	☐	☐	☐	☐	☐	☐
6. In general, district management seems genuinely interested in me and my work.	☐	☐	☐	☐	☐	☐	☐	☐
7. I have difficulty in seeing my supervisor as someone who actively tries to help me do my job better.	☐	☐	☐	☐	☐	☐	☐	☐

	Bldg. Level				District			
	SA	A	D	SD	SA	A	D	SD
8. My current job is helping me progress toward my career goals.	☐	☐	☐	☐	☐	☐	☐	☐
9. My co-workers seem very willing to provide the information and assistance I need to plan and carry out my work.	☐	☐	☐	☐	☐	☐	☐	☐
10. Generally speaking, day-to-day operation around here goes on in a climate of cooperation and mutual trust.	☐	☐	☐	☐	☐	☐	☐	☐

Cluster 4: Individual Respect

	Bldg. Level				District			
1. Other people here seem to care about me as a person and not just as a worker.	☐	☐	☐	☐	☐	☐	☐	☐
2. On most occasions the equipment, supplies, or other resources I need are in good condition and available.	☐	☐	☐	☐	☐	☐	☐	☐
3. Work is organized around here in a way that considers my human needs.	☐	☐	☐	☐	☐	☐	☐	☐
4. My work area is a suitably laid out, reasonably comfortable, and generally free from annoying distractions.	☐	☐	☐	☐	☐	☐	☐	☐
5. I am treated with dignity and respect.	☐	☐	☐	☐	☐	☐	☐	☐
6. Sometimes I feel my good work is minimized because of difficulties related to activities at work which I can't control.	☐	☐	☐	☐	☐	☐	☐	☐
7. The amount of work I have to do sometimes interferes with how well I do it.	☐	☐	☐	☐	☐	☐	☐	☐
8. Around here I never get the feeling I am being "hassled".	☐	☐	☐	☐	☐	☐	☐	☐

	Bldg. Level				District			
Cluster 5: Relations with My Immediate Supervisor	SA	A	D	SD	SA	A	D	SD
1. My immediate supervisor is friendly and easy to talk to.	☐	☐	☐	☐	☐	☐	☐	☐
2. My immediate supervisor shows me she/he has confidence in me.	☐	☐	☐	☐	☐	☐	☐	☐
3. My immediate supervisor listens to what I have to say and is genuinely interested.	☐	☐	☐	☐	☐	☐	☐	☐
4. My immediate supervisor really knows her/his job and does it well.	☐	☐	☐	☐	☐	☐	☐	☐
5. I am encouraged to find new ways to improve what I do.	☐	☐	☐	☐	☐	☐	☐	☐
6. Some of the suggestions I have made have been included as changes in work routine.	☐	☐	☐	☐	☐	☐	☐	☐

Cluster 6: Work Relations with Others

1. People in my work group are friendly and helpful.	☐	☐	☐	☐	☐	☐	☐	☐
2. I know I am trusted to get the job done.	☐	☐	☐	☐	☐	☐	☐	☐
3. Everyone is treated fairly around here.	☐	☐	☐	☐	☐	☐	☐	☐
4 People in my immediate work group share ideas.	☐	☐	☐	☐	☐	☐	☐	☐
5. My co-workers seem very willing to provide the information I need to plan and carry out my work.	☐	☐	☐	☐	☐	☐	☐	☐
6. Almost everyone would do more work on their jobs if they were paid to do it.	☐	☐	☐	☐	☐	☐	☐	☐
7. Most of my fellow workers are very conscientious about their work.	☐	☐	☐	☐	☐	☐	☐	☐

	Bldg. Level				District			
Cluster 7: Confidence in Management's Understanding	SA	A	D	SD	SA	A	D	SD
1. In general, district administrators seem genuinely interested in me and my work.	☐	☐	☐	☐	☐	☐	☐	☐
2. Central office administrators too often seem concerned only with their own projects and activities.	☐	☐	☐	☐	☐	☐	☐	☐
3. The concerns of administrators in this district often seem far removed from my own.	☐	☐	☐	☐	☐	☐	☐	☐
4. Generally I am satisfied with the amount of recognition I receive for doing my job.	☐	☐	☐	☐	☐	☐	☐	☐
5. Most of the time I am satisfied with information I get regarding what is going on in the district.	☐	☐	☐	☐	☐	☐	☐	☐
6. Generally, I would characterize this district as well managed.	☐	☐	☐	☐	☐	☐	☐	☐
7. Most people who work here understand that the overall organization has "needs" just as they do.	☐	☐	☐	☐	☐	☐	☐	☐
8. In day to day operation, administrators here do a good job of considering *both* organizational and personal needs.	☐	☐	☐	☐	☐	☐	☐	☐

Survey instruments can provide much assistance in deciding whether or not the school district would benefit from an OD (Organizational Development) intervention, a HRD (Human Resource Development) activity, or a combination of both OD and HRD activities. Periodic and systematic surveys provide the following valuable information that assists those in charge of the school district's OD and HRD functions [6].

- Trends are developed which can be analyzed.
- Outliers (those areas where there is unanimous positive or negative agreement) can be identified. The negatives can be studied to determine interventions or training activities that will improve them. The positives can be studied to determine the reasons for success, and these can be used as models for other areas [7].
- Comparisons can be made among a single group's responses, between groups, or among all groups. Discrepancies can be identified and analyzed. These identified "needs" (discrepancies or gaps between "what is" and "what should be") can signal the need for OD or HRD, or for both types of intervention activities [8].
- Periodic "snapshots" of the district's and individual school buildings' or individual department's health assist in making required corrections, and a series of such "snapshots" assist in determining whether or not the school district and its constituent parts are becoming more healthy or less healthy. This organizational health assessment provides information related to general health, as well as information related to all important sub-areas of organizational health (trust, caring, productivity, openness, and many other indicators of health) [9].

Once the needs (gaps between "what is" and "what should be") of the organization and the employees within the organization have been identified, the district's decision makers next must decide the intervention actions that can be taken to enable the employees and the entire organization and its sub-parts to approach and ultimately reach the desired "what should be" state. The intervention options are only limited by the creativity of the decision makers [10].

STRATEGIES THAT HELP CREATE AND MAINTAIN A HEALTHY ORGANIZATION

Although literally hundreds of intervention activities could be discussed, including such techniques as focus problem-solving groups or employee/management planning groups, this section will limit the discussion to three major wide-range intervention strategies. One of these, a QWL (Quality of Work Life) intervention strategy will outline a strategy that is a permanent way of thinking about and of utilizing people to improve their work life and to improve the operation of the total school district and its sub-parts (campuses and departments). The other two interventions–those of vertical teams and horizontal matrix teams–generally are utilized for specific time periods, and they are terminated when it is determined that other vertical or horizontal teams should be organized for specific purposes.

Development of Vertical Teams

Vertical Teams (described in Chapter 7) can be organized for the purpose of dealing with discrepancies between "what is" and "what should be" as the total district's functions relate to the individual sub-system's (school building or department level) functions. The composition of these teams usually involves a representative cross section of all employee groups who are, or should be, involved in investigating the problem, program, or plan, and those who should be involved in arriving at suggested solutions to improve the operation of the school district and its sub-systems.

Team members will generally include teachers, non-teaching employees, principals, and central office administrators, although the composition will vary with the specific problem, program, or plan being addressed. In addition, there are sometimes outside experts assigned to assist the team as OD intervention strategists. Before the team is officially appointed, the district's decision makers have carefully analyzed the "need" (gap between "what is" and "what should be"), and they have outlined the specific charge for the vertical team [11]. They have also stated the product that is to be produced by the team, the resources allocated for the team's work, and the time period allotted to develop the desired product.

If the *need* is one that can be addressed rapidly, the team members can be provided with some released time or be paid an additional stipend. If, however, the *need* is one that is complex, arrangements should be made to relieve the team members from their routine assignments and duties until the desired product is produced.

Now that we have outlined the structure and purpose of vertical teams, let's turn to another type of intervention strategy. This strategy deals with matters that cut across horizontal functions performed with a school district.

Development of Horizontal Teams

Horizontal Matrix Teams are those that deal with needs (gaps or discrepancies that exist between "what is" and "what should be") related to overall district functions such as personnel, business, and instruction. These teams are usually organized in a manner such that representatives of each functional area or division are involved in developing a product to solve the problem, improve the planning, or create a required program. The same considerations for released time, the team's charge, the required resources, and the time period allotted to complete the product, as were given to the vertical teams, apply to the horizontal teams [12].

If we operated a manufacturing company that made the decision to produce and market an innovative gidget; we would have, at a minimum, involvement of the departments of (1) engineering, (2) manufacturing, (3) packaging, and (4) marketing. Let's assume that the engineering department did an excellent job, and the manufacturing and packaging areas provided management with a firm completion date. The marketing people, based on this date, began a sales campaign and took orders for thousands of the new gidgets that were to be delivered by the firm date. However, a problem developed—the engineers made a little modification to assist the manufacturing department but the packaging department was never given this information. They developed the package for the original design. The result was disastrous: (1) the manufactured gidget and the package didn't fit together, and there was a loss of $1,000,000 in useless packages; and (2) the reputation of the firm was severely damaged when the gidgets, which were so highly touted by the marketing department, were not delivered even close to the date they were promised.

In school districts we often think of the organizational pattern as that of line and staff, wherein every decision is made in a vertical line from top to bottom—or, on occasion, from bottom to top. In reality, school districts are matrix organizations, and there usually are many different fingers in the organization's decision pie [13]. That is, for example, a decision made by the instructional department to add a new curriculum area really involves, at a minimum, the (1) personnel department to assist with staffing, (2) business department to allocate funds to implement the new program, and (3) the building and grounds department if modifications have to be made in the physical plant. In addition, the superintendent of schools and the school district's board of education are probably going to be involved in formally approving the new curriculum program that is suggested.

In a medium to large school district, very few major decisions that are made within a school district involve only a single functional area. Even at the building level, a principal receives: (1) a budget, supplies, custodial and maintenance service from the business department; (2) teachers, teacher aides, substitute employees, secretaries and other personnel with the assistance of the personnel department; (3) curriculum help from the instructional department; (4) staff development assistance from the training department. She/he may also have to interact with the superintendent's office, the board of education, the transportation department, the purchasing department, the food service department, or other central departments that have been established within the school district.

With this complexity outlined, it should be clear that within a matrix organization, which is exemplified by the school district organization, matrix horizontal teams are crucial to solving problems, doing planning, or developing programs that involve operation activities from two or more departments within the school district. This coordination is crucial if the school district and its department are to function as an efficient and effective whole.

Now that we have outlined the desirability of creating vertical and horizontal teams to solve problems or develop programs by being organized into temporary work groups, let's investigate a long term involvement OD (Organizational Development) intervention scheme that also includes the opportunity for HRD (Human Resource Development) activities. This scheme, generically named QWL (Quality of Work Life) is primarily designed to involve employees in improving their work environment. As a by-product, the school district total organization is generally improved as well.

DETERMINATION OF QUALITY OF WORK LIFE

QWL (Quality of Work Life) is a method that serves school districts that desire to involve all their employees and employee organizations in the decision-making processes of the district and in arriving at methods and means of improving their work life and the organizational health of the school district [14]. A specific example that one author lived through for a ten year period will help to amplify upon the advantages of this broad based, long-term improvement-focused involvement strategy.

Employees' Communications and Development Council[1] (A Quality of Work Life Approach to Employee and Organizational Improvement)

While serving as the superintendent of schools for the West Bloomfield School District of Michigan, one of the authors developed a QWL program that involved the voluntary participation of six union groups and all non-unionized employee groups. This very affluent suburban Detroit school district of approximately 6,000 pupils (at the time the author served as superintendent) will demonstrate the effectiveness of combining both OD interventions and HRD activities within an organization such as a school district. The specific steps and structures taken to create and maintain the ECDC (Employees' Communication and Development Council) will be related.

The purposes of attempting to organize this intervention strategy were three in number: (1) It provided an opportunity to implement a PHILOSOPHY which proposes that people are talented, and that they wish to assist in improving themselves, their work environment and the school district; (2) It attempted to achieve a "what should be" GOAL of improving the work environment for all employees, and thus improving the effectiveness and efficiency

---

[1]Based in part upon Herman, Jerry J. 1982. "Improving Employee Relations", *Michigan School Board Journal*, 29(7):10–13. Used with permission.

of the school district and its constituent parts; and (3) It was an attempt to initiate and sustain a PROCESS that used the talents and interests of employees to improve their own work environment and the effectiveness and efficiency of the school district [15].

The beginning was initiated when the superintendent hired a very skilled speaker, who was a public relations specialist, to spend an entire day with every employee of the school district discussing (1) what was good about education, (2) what was good about the West Bloomfield School District, (3) how they as employees could work together to improve their own work environment and the school district's operations, and (4) how they held a significant responsibility for positive communications with the public and with other employees [16]. At the end of this inspirational day, the superintendent asked if the employees would like to continue such discussions.

Following an enthusiastic "yes" response to the question, each of the six unionized employee groups and each of the non-unionized employee groups were asked to select two of their members to meet regularly with the superintendent to explore ways to improve their work environment. Very soon, following this initial day, leaders of QWL programs from industrial unions and management were brought in to talk to the board of education, union leaders, and other interested parties to explain what QWL was all about, to tell of the advantages of a QWL program, and to stress the pitfalls to avoid when initiating such an employee involvement program.

The second step was initiated once each employee group selected its two representatives to meet with the superintendent. This group was taken to an off-site location for a two-day intensive planning work session. The purpose of this session was to develop the basic structures necessary prior to involvement of all employees of the district and prior to launching the full-fledged effort. All employee representatives and management agreed that it was important not to rush into this effort without sufficient pre-planning of the structural and process decisions [17].

At this two day work session, numerous thoughts and ideas were exchanged, and some exercises helped elaborate on a definition of what the group was seeking. Some of the major thoughts, ideas, and exercises were as follows.

Basic Guiding Beliefs

- In order to succeed in this endeavor we must believe that: (1) people are good, (2) people want to succeed, (3) people want to work hard at success, and (4) people want to help improve each other and the school district.
- In order to motivate employees, we must: (1) develop possibilities that will allow them to grow, (2) provide meaningful and rewarding work, (3) delegate decision-making responsibilities, (4) recognize employee contributions, and (5) allow each employee to experience a personal sense of achievement.

Once these basic ideas were explored, the group turned to consideration of the prerequisites to be considered prior to initiating the full-blown employee involvement program. Some of the major points of this discussion are listed below.

The representatives also agreed to a name for the group. They called themselves the Employees' Communication and Development Council.

Prerequisite Considerations

- A well planned and motivational starting activity is important.
- Employee leadership as well as management should be involved in the planning and evaluation activities [18].
- Starting with one employee group or with all employee groups is a decision to be determined by estimating which approach will best enhance the probability of a successful beginning.
- It is important to have a central district-wide employee council involving representatives of all employee groups, and each school building site should have representation [19].
- It is also important to have school site employee units (generically these have been entitled "Quality Circles").
- Decisions related to this program must be made by consensus; this is defined as all parties agreeing to allow the decision to go forward (even if they disagree with the

decision). Also, all participants must have equal status and power when making decisions [20].

- As part of the activities undertaken by the employee group, ongoing employee training should be provided in such areas as leadership skill development, problem-solving techniques, and effective communication methods [21].
- An outside OD consultant (one from a major corporation was enlisted) should be hired to assist in the planning, initiation, and evaluation stages of this program [22].
- A trained central level liaison (the superintendent's project manager was trained and assigned) should be made available to assist and help the elected leadership with training needs and to help coordinate the building and site levels employee groups [23].
- Meetings and planning sessions should be conducted on school district time, at least the majority of the time [24].
- A budget should be provided to facilitate the operation of this employee involvement program [25].
- A board of education policy should be written and adopted to guide this venture into employee involvement [26].
- Bylaws should be drafted and approved by the participating groups *before* the program is implemented [27].
- There was agreement that certain areas should not be addressed by employees involved in this program since other avenues (such as union master contracts and grievance procedures) already existed. These excluded areas that were agreed upon included: (1) wages, salaries and fringe benefits, (2) employment practices, (3) disciplinary policies, (4) personality-related problems, (5) termination policies, (6) grievances, and (7) collective bargaining items

Once these prerequisites were thoroughly addressed, an exercise was provided to help define more completely what this group of representatives considered to be a "what should be" goal of improving the employees' work environment. For this purpose, the planning group was given the task of deciding the descriptors of the *best* job they ever had and the *worst* job they ever had. Each participant was asked to individually list words or short phrases that defined the best and worst job situation she/he had had. These were then discussed in groups of eight people, and each group was asked to reach agreement on the descriptors they would use. Ultimately, the total group of participants was asked to agree on the appropriate descriptors.

Since the *worst* descriptors were almost always the opposite of the *best* descriptors, only examples of the *best* descriptors are related below.

Best Job Descriptors

- Good leadership exists.
- Trusting relationships are evident.
- Input opportunities are readily available.
- Meaningful work is provided.
- Employee recognition is consistent.
- Respect for each other is evident.
- Communication is open and positive.
- A helping relationship exists.
- Group cohesiveness is the norm.
- Opportunities exist to improve oneself and the school district.
- Commonality of vision, goals, and concerns is evident.
- Shared power is the norm.
- Ownership by all exists.
- Goals and objectives are clear, agreed upon, and understood by all.
- People are comfortable.
- There is a search for improvement.
- Success of the individual, the group, and the district is desired.
- Caring for one another and for the quality of products is evident.
- There is a willingness to invest.
- Successes and failures are shared by all parties.
- New ideas are welcomed, and all ideas are considered.
- Good planning and organization exists.
- Everyone knows what is expected and what is going on.
- There is a feeling tone of "togetherness".
- Innovation and flexibility are encouraged.
- Agendas are open.

At the end of the two day work session, it was agreed that volunteers would work with the superintendent's appointed liaison to draft bylaws for the group and to draft a policy to be proposed to the board of education. Once the drafts were completed, they were brought back to the total planning group for consensus approval; ultimately, the board of education adopted the proposed policy. The final versions are displayed below.

Employees' Communication and Development Council Bylaws

The employees' Communication and Development Council shall be an on-going committee, advisory to the superintendent, representing all employees, and responsible for assisting in:

(1) Planning staff development

(2) Solving problems

(3) Improving communications for the purpose of making the West Bloomfield School District a better place to work, live, learn, and GROW.

(4) Participation in the Employees Communication and Development Council is limited to employees of the West Bloomfield School District.

(5) Participation in the Employees Communication and Development Council shall be voluntary.

(6) The Employees Communication and Development Council shall act in an advisory capacity, promoting rather than directing.

(7) The Employees Communication and Development Council welcomes ideas from all employees.

(8) The Employees Communication and Development Council does not take the place of the legitimate roles of other groups in the school district such as employee bargaining groups, Curriculum Council, Communications/Governance Councils, Administrative Council, and others.

Representation

- Two (2) representatives from each employee group including at least one (1) representative from each work site.

- Two (2) representatives at large may be added if the committee deems it necessary.
- One (1) superintendent's administrative designee, ex officio member.
- One (1) board of education member, ex officio member.

Employee Groups

- West Bloomfield School Association of Educational Secretaries
- AFSCME School Aide Bargaining Unit, Local 1284, Council 25
- West Bloomfield Cafeteria Employees Association
- West Bloomfield Education Association, Affiliate of the Michigan and National Education Associations
- West Bloomfield Schools Team Management (Administrators) Association
- AFSCME Custodial-Maintenance Bargaining Unit, Local 1384, Council 25
- AFSCME Transportation Bargaining Unit, Local 1384, Council 25
- Non-unionized Secretarial-Clerical
- Non-unionized Administrators-Supervisors

Work Sites

- West Bloomfield High School
- Orchard Lake Middle School
- Abbott Middle School
- Ealy Elementary School
- Doherty Elementary School
- Green Elementary School
- Scotch Elementary School
- Roosevelt Elementary School
- Transportation Facility

Representative Rotation

- Terms are September–August.
- Each employee group will be requested to select two (2)

representatives by May 1 of each year. One will serve a three (3) year term, and one will serve a two (2) year term.
- After the second year all terms will last two (2) years.
- Work site and at-large representatives will be appointed by the chairperson for a one (1) year term.

Roles and Responsibilities

(1) The superintendent's administrative designee shall:
- Keep and distribute minutes
- Monitor budget, keep within the allocation, and process expenditures
- Arrange for meetings
- Communicate information
- Maintain records
- Accept agenda items

(2) Chairperson:
- Develop agenda
- Chair meetings
- Appoint sub-committees
- Call meetings
- Act as spokesperson
- Appoint work site and at-large representatives

(3) Assistant chairperson
- Replace chairperson in her/his absence

(4) Secretary
- Take minutes
- Maintain correspondence

The Employees' Communication and Development Council will elect its officers in May of each year from the selected employee representatives who have served at least a one (1) year term on the Council. Terms of office to be one (1) year from September through August.

Meetings

- Regular meetings will be held from 3:00–5:00 P.M. on the first working Thursday of each month.
- Special meetings may be called by the chairperson.

- The chairperson will notify members at least five (5) working days in advance of special meetings.
- Business will be conducted using a simplified *Roberts Rules of Order.*
- All meetings will be open.

Amendments

- Amendments to the bylaws may be proposed by any member of the Council and they will be accepted by a simple majority of those present.

Now that the bylaws of the Employees' Communication and Development Council have been reviewed, let's turn to the board of education policy that provided the official go-ahead to begin implementing this employee involvement program [28].

West Bloomfield School Policy Personnel:
Employees' Communication and Development Council

Policy #4135

The West Bloomfield Board of Education recognizes that the competency and satisfaction of all its employees affects the quality of the West Bloomfield Schools. In seeking to obtain the greatest degree of competence and satisfaction, assessment of the needs of employees shall be identified in terms of:

(*1*) District-wide operations

(*2*) Sub-groups within the district

(*3*) Individual employees

The board desires to establish a systematic process for the assessment of employee needs, and the development of programs to meet the needs and measurement of results.

Furthermore, the board desires to support a climate in which the district's employees participate in such a process, especially as it relates to:

(*1*) Planning for employee development

(*2*) Solving problems

(*3*) Improving communication

Therefore, the board supports a program for employee development and recognizes its obligation to provide funds to carry out such a program as an integral part of the total school district operation.

The Board of Education directs the West Bloomfield Superintendent of Schools to implement an employee involvement program for all employees of the West Bloomfield School District.

Rules and Regulations (Which Were Developed by the Superintendent to Implement the Policy)

(1) The superintendent shall establish an advisory committee consisting of representatives of employee sub-groups within the district. Participation in the advisory committee shall be voluntary.

(2) The program shall encompass employee training needs as well as conditions related to the quality of employee work environment.

(3) The program shall not infringe on the rights established under collective bargaining agreements.

(4) Programs shall attempt to serve the needs of the total district organization, employee sub-groups, and all employees of the West Bloomfield School District.

The implementation step first involved each member of the planning committee taking time at employee meetings to explain the purposes, structure, and how the ECDC (Employees Communication Development Council) was developed and organized. Once the ECDC became operational, many excellent programs and activities took place.

Examples of the programs and activities that were developed by ECDC include the following examples from the three areas of: (1) planning employee development, (2) solving problems, and (3) improving communications.

The responsibility for improving *communications* included activities such as the establishment of an internal welcome-wagon type structure to assist and greet new employees, ECDC suggestion boxes placed at each work site, meetings held at each work site, open access provided to work site ECDC members in order to have problems or suggestions forwarded to the District ECDC, and the establishment of duplicate ECDC units at the work site level. Also, ECDC sponsored such events as a district-wide employees' meeting where the superintendent explained the details of the succeeding year's budget, where employees were asked to discuss means of making more efficient the district's operations, and where employees were asked to provide ideas for improving communications between and among employee groups.

The responsibility for *problem solving* took on a wide variety of activities. Four examples will provide a sense of the efforts of this important ECDC function.

(1) *Relating to the Whole Child.* Bus drivers for special education students met with teachers of special education students. Some drivers had transported the same child for 5–10 or more years, and they knew the home environment quite well. Some new teachers only knew what the the written information in the student folder provided. Such meetings proved very beneficial to both groups, but they proved to be especially beneficial to the students and their parents.

(2) *Set 'em Up Again, Charlie.* With over 10,000 people using the schools after normal day student hours, it was important that all rooms and equipment were properly set up for use by residents. The custodial staff used to get the sixth copy of the buildings-use form; this last copy was practically unreadable, causing many setups to be missed or botched. The solution to this problem was one of simply giving the custodian the first (clear) copy, and letting the very faint sixth copy stay in the administrator's file.

(3) *The Rags to Riches Story.* As in all large institutions, thousands of cleaning and dusting rags were used within a year. One custodian suggested that the mail truck pick up the dirty bagged rags and have them washed at the district's laundry and returned the next day, instead of throwing them away. The result was the savings of thousands of dollars in expenditures each year.

(4) *Every Little Bit Helps.* During a difficult financial time in the district, ECDC and parent support groups sponsored a meeting of the total community to explain the financial situation in the district. Phone calls were made to hundreds of residents. After the initial presentation and question-and-answer period, hundreds of people were separated into sub-

groups of twenty-five to fifty people for discussions of solutions to the problem. The end results were the incorporation of numerous cost efficiency suggestions and the ultimate approval of a tax renewal by the public. ECDC members served as sponsors and as chairpersons for these sub-group discussions.

The responsibility for employee development involved activities that were sponsored by the ECDC and paid for out of the ECDC budget allocation, and they were inclusive of the individual, sub-group and total district levels. In fact, any employee or group was provided an opportunity to fill out a form and attend an ECDC meetings to request funds for training or staff development. Some of the specific employee development activities are listed below; these cover a broad spectrum of activities.

(1) *Give Me the Power.* ECDC sponsored community education employee training in leadership and communication skills, and ECDC also sponsored an inservice session on the "Power of Praise".

(2) *Help, Mother, I'm Feeling Stressed.* Fifty-three employees were given stress management training.

(3) *Look, Ma, I'm on TV.* Two media employees were given a week's training related to the development of cable TV programs.

(4) *Look, Emma, No Hands.* Eighty bus drivers were given a one-half day of on-the-job safety training in handling a bus during a skid.

(5) *How Do I Keep It, George?* Forty employees attended an ECDC sponsored seminar on personal financial planning.

(6) *I Want to Be a Switch Hitter.* A seminar on career alternatives was offered employees who might be laid off due to pupil population decline.

(7) *How's the Climate in There?* One hundred fourteen employees participated with students and parents in a school climate assessment and improvement program.

(8) *Recognize Me, Baby, I'm Valuable.* ECDC sponsored a yearly employee recognition program the first day of each school year. At this time ECDC sponsored, and the board of education presented, employees with theater tickets, dinner tickets, recognition plaques, engraved pen and pencil sets, and

other inexpensive but meaningful awards. The awards chosen were those decided by the ECDC Council, and they were purchased from the ECDC budget or donated by PTA's or by businesses in the school district.

Figures 9.1 (Structural Model) and 9.2 (Process Model) graphically display the overview of the ECDC operation.

Let's end this explanation of the ECDC by stating that the concern about employees, the quality of their work environment and their opportunities for meaningful input are important to the organizational health of any organization. The ECDC plan described constituted a very successful OD (Organizational Development) intervention, which also included many HRD (Human Resource Development) activities [29].

It is important to stress that ECDC is clearly:

- people-oriented
- process-saturated
- success-reinforced

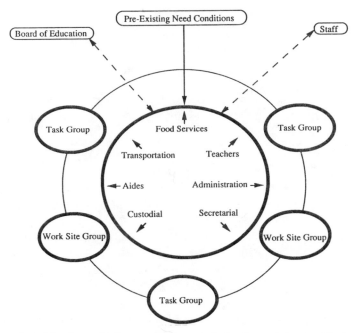

Figure 9.1 Employees' communication and development council structural model.

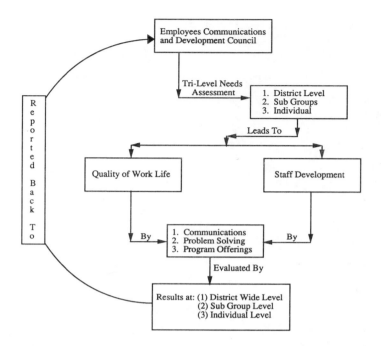

Figure 9.2 *Employees' communication and development council process model.*

SUMMARY

Empowering employees is crucial to the development of any first class organization—including school districts and school buildings. The *how* is not nearly as important as the *why* of meaningful employee involvement. If you believe in people and if you believe that they want to improve themselves, improve other employees, improve the quality of their work, and improve the school district, then you can form means such as vertical teams, horizontal matrix teams, Employee Communications and Governance Councils, or a wide variety of other structures that will work for you.

It is important to the success of any of these means to involve employees and their unions, or other employee group affiliates, in the entire range of planning *before* the program is activated. It is suggested that participation in any scheme should be voluntary, as involuntary participation will likely produce poor products and poor employee attitudes.

The two primary advantages of any employee involvement program are:

(1) It utilizes the intelligence of every employee in improving the school district's work. This, in turn, improves the school district's climate/culture for students; and it lets each employee know he/she is respected, cared for, and valued.

(2) It opens vertical and horizontal lines of communication throughout the school district about mission, vision, goals, objectives, problems, and successes. It fosters both top-down and bottom-up openness [30].

However, when contemplating initiating a new program of employee involvement in a school district that has not historically allowed it, or in a district that has a history of union/management strife, observation of a few cautions are in order:

- Begin with the groups which will maximize a successful start up.
- Remember to let the program *evolve*. There are no set transportable structures or activities.
- Start with challenges that are doable and have at least an 80 percent chance of success. Early failures will likely kill off your program; you can always tackle harder issues, once a history of success has been established.
- It will take a good deal of time and training before true distributed leadership from many employees will evolve, but distributed leadership is the key element in long term success.
- All participants should be volunteers, and they should be told they can drop out of the program at any time. The same rules apply to any formal employee groups.
- Finally, don't start any type of employee involvement and empowerment structure and process unless you REALLY BELIEVE IN PEOPLE. You truly have to believe in the worth, dignity, and intelligence of the humans who educate the children and operate the school district. The organizational health of the school district will greatly improve as an involvement and empowerment bonus.

GUIDELINES

1. Attention must be paid to the overall and individual building and departmental health of the school district, in order to maintain high productivity and effectiveness.
2. The productivity, relationship and "feeling tone" of a school district should be measured by analyzing data from various sources, such as achievement data, climate and culture surveys, and observations; these should be administered district-wide in a confidential manner.
3. These periodic and systematic surveys should be analyzed to reveal trends, provide information for identification of problems and appropriate solutions, disclose group need discrepancies, and provide a "snapshot" of overall district health.
4. Such OD intervention strategies as vertical or horizontal teams should be provided with resources that are appropriate to the groups' "need" assignments.
5. It is crucial to include matrix horizontal teams to meet the coordination and organizational needs of the typical matrix-structured school district.
6. A Quality of Work Life OD intervention approach should be employed to establish an employee involvement *philosophy*, to achieve a *goal* of work environment improvement, and to initiate and sustain a process of effective employee involvement.
7. Prerequisite conditions for an effective involvement program should include—a motivational beginning, districtwide site and campus-inclusive representation, consensus decision making, voluntary participation, appropriate resources, and board support.
8. It is essential that the involvement program have vertical and horizontal district lines of communication.
9. Be prepared for a developmental process of implementation, and aim towards the long term success effect of distributed leadership.

EXERCISES

1. Develop and administer climate/culture survey instruments for your school district, aimed at elementary students, secondary students, parents, and employees.

2. Design a "needs assessment" process for your school district.
3. Suggest some specific charges or assignments appropriate for a vertical team in your school district.
4. Suggest some specific charges or assignments appropriate for a horizontal matrix team in your school district.
5. Design a matrix horizontal team for your district, being sure to include key organizational and departmental functions.
6. Draw a proposed design or combination of structures to display an optimum Quality of Work Life employee involvement plan for your district.
7. List some district assignments or responsibilities that would be appropriate for such an employee involvement program.
8. Suggest some employee development activities that are tailored to your district's needs.
9. Design and conduct an employee audit, consisting of open-ended questions, to assess the effectiveness of an existing district team structure
10. Design a "winning" employee group team attitude instrument, with the intention of analyzing individual member and total group responses. Administer the instrument to an existing district team structure.

SELECTED REFERENCES

1. Webb, L. D. et al. 1987. *Personnel Administration in Education.* Columbus, OH: Merrill Publishing Company, p. 55.
2. Fox, R. S. et al. 1973. *School Climate Improvement: A Challenge to the School Administrator.* Bloomington, IN: Phi Delta Kappa, pp. 1–2.
3. Connor, P. E. and L. K. Lake. 1988. *Managing Organizational Change.* New York, NY: Praeger Publishers, pp. 86–88.
4. Joyce, B. R. 1986. *Improving America's Schools.* New York, NY: Longman, Inc., pp. 94–95.
5. Brookover et al. 1982. *Creating Effective Schools.* Holmes Beach, FL: Learning Publications, Inc., pp. 43–44.
6. Dyer, W. G. 1983. *Contemporary Issues in Management and Organization Development.* Reading, MA: Addison Wesley Publishing Company, p. 126.
7. Meares, L. B. 1986. "A Model for Changing Organizational Culture", *Personnel*, 63(7): 38–42.
8. Meares, L. B. "Model", p. 39.

9. Connor, P. E. and L. K. Lake. *Managing*, pp. 151–156.

10. Connor, P. E. and L. K. Lake. *Managing*, pp. 155–156, 160–166.

11. Connor, P. E. and L. K. Lake. *Managing*, pp. 155–156.

12. Sikula, A. F. and J. F. McKenna. 1984. *The Management of Human Resources.* New York, NY: John Wiley & Sons, pp. 236–238.

13. Webb, L. D. et al. *Personnel Administration.* pp. 252–253.

14. Sikula, A. F. and J. F. McKenna. *Management*, pp. 120–121.

15. Warrick, D. D., ed. 1985. *Contemporary Organization Development,* Glenview, IL: Scott, Foresman and Company, pp. 208–209.

16. Sikula, A. F. and J. F. McKenna. *Management*, pp. 123–124.

17. Sikula, A. F. and J. F. McKenna. *Management*, p. 122.

18. Silula, A. F. and J. F. McKenna. *Management*, p. 123.

19. Ibid., p. 123.

20. Schmuck, R. A. et al. 1977. *The Second Handbook of Organizational Development in Schools.* Palo Alto, CA: Mayfield Publishing Company, pp. 324–325.

21. Lewis, A. 1989. *Restructuring America's Schools.* Arlington, VA: American Association of School Administrators, p. 226.

22. Sikula, A. F. and J. F. McKenna. *Management*, pp. 124–125.

23. Sikula, A. F. and J. F. McKenna. *Management*, p. 125.

24. Hampton, D. R., C. E. Summer, and R. A. Webber. 1987. *Organizational Behavior and the Practice of Management.* Glenview, IL: Scott, Foresman and Company, p. 688.

25. Hampton, D. R., C. E. Summer, and R. A. Webber. *Organizational Behavior*, p. 333.

26. Webb, L. D. et al. *Personnel Administration*, p. 53.

27. Warrick, D. D., ed. *Contemporary Organization Development*, pp. 208–210.

28. Webb, L. D. et al. *Personnel Administration*, p. 57.

29. Warrick, D. D., ed. *Contemporary Organization Development*, pp. 205–206.

30. Lewis, A. *Restructuring*, pp. 229–231.

CHAPTER 10

Implications for the Future Development of Employees and Organizations

> The dominant principal of organization has shifted from management in order to control an enterprise to leadership in order to bring out the best in people and to respond quickly to change [1].

THE AUTHORS TOTALLY concur with this statement, and it is in this vein that we look at the future of OD and HRD, in the face of numerous changes that will impact the school districts of the future. Now let's turn to the task at hand—that of predicting the future and planning for the changes required to accommodate it, from a school district's perspective.

Before we take a journey into the implications for the future development of employees and organizations, let's review what has preceded this chapter. Then, with the present clearly in mind, we will continue our future journey.

Chapters 1 through 9 dealt with matters of "what is" and "what should be" or "what could be" from the frame of reference of the present. Using this orientation towards the present, let's briefly summarize the materials covered in the individual chapters that precede this final chapter.

Chapter 1 presented a model of HRD (Human Resource Development), a listing of external factors that influence HRD operations, and a discussion of internal factors that impact HRD operations.

Chapter 2 presented a model of OD (Organizational Development), a discussion of internal factors that influence OD planning, and a listing of external factors that impact OD planning.

Chapter 3 dealt with the matters of conducting a *needs* assessment, methods of identifying important trends, means of projecting *needs* (gaps between "what is" and "what should be" or "what could be"), and ways of developing strategic plans.

Chapter 4 presented materials related to implementing strategic goals and objectives; defining an action program; answering the Why? Who? When? Where? What? and How? questions of an action plan; monitoring progress; evaluating results; and recycling into new strategic planning activities.

Chapter 5 discussed methods of determining human resource needs; matters related to locating, recruiting, screening, selecting, assigning, and inducting employees; methods of appraising employees' performance levels; procedures for preparing the human resource inventory and projecting future human resource needs; and the requirement of recycling the entire human resource systems approach.

Chapter 6 presented reasons for staff evaluation and staff development or training programs; methods of helping adults learn; tactics for identifying staff development needs (gaps between "what is" and "what should be" or "what could be"); plans for conducting a comprehensive staff development program; and plans for developing a specific staff development activity.

Chapter 7 presented materials related to methods of employee involvement and empowerment; specific empowerment examples of: (1) site level vertical experiential teams, (2) quality circles, and (3) project groups. The chapter also stressed the importance of the beliefs one holds about people and the necessity of acting upon these beliefs.

Chapter 8 discussed the desirability of developing a win-win attitude between unions and management. It specifically discussed: (1) the definition of win-win; (2) the difference between win-win and an adversarial stance during collective bargaining and during the day-to-day operation of the school district; (3) structures that promote win-win, and (4) reasons why a win-win attitude is crucial to the development and maintenance of a healthy school district organization.

Chapter 9 presented materials related to assessing the existing culture and climate within a school district and within each school site, selecting OD (Organizational Development) intervention strategies that help create and maintain a healthy organization, utilizing district-wide vertical teams, and using a comprehensive QWL (Quality of Work Life) approach to developing and maintaining a healthy school district organization.

Chapter 10 now focuses totally on the future as it analyzes existing external and internal trends, projects and anticipates future external and internal trends that might impact the OD (Organizational Development) and/or the HRD (Human Resource Development) activities of a school district and its constituent parts (school buildings and departments), and recommends a unified OD and HRD management system as the most effective means of dealing with both the organizational and the human needs of any school district.

Specifically, this chapter will: (1) analyze those existing and projected external and internal trends that may impact the school district and its strategic plans for the future; (2) predict those impacts that may affect employees and the total school district organization; (3) present a plea for a new model systems approach to OD and HRD entitled the *HOM* (Human and Organizational Management) Model; and (4) develop a vision, a mission statement, and goals related to HOM.

Let's begin our journey into the future by analyzing the existing and projected external and internal trends which may well impact the school district and its strategic plans for the future. These trends are important ones to study for their possible impact on the employees in the future and for their possible impact on the organizational structure of the school district in the future [2].

POTENTIAL EXTERNAL AND INTERNAL IMPACT TRENDS

The potential external and internal impact trends that most likely will influence the way the school district of the future does business, the ways in which employees are utilized and helped, and the ways in which the school district will configure itself to accommodate these trends are listed below. Some will exert external pressure on the employees and the school district to meet needs (gaps between "what is" and "what should be" or "what could be") identified in the eyes of business leaders, industrial leaders, and governmental leaders. Others will cause changes to take place in employee training and staff development and in instructional and managerial structures because of the evolving unique needs of a changed student population, or at least a change in the requirements of that student population [3]. Still others will be motivated by the desire to improve, which will come directly from the employees, their unions, or management personnel.

Potential external impact trends include those that have an immediate or a long term direct or indirect effect on the school district organization and/or its sub-parts (school buildings or departments) [4]. Also, there are those trends of an international scope, which can have a secondary level impact, such as the lack of availability of sufficient funds due to the success of Asian and European countries' manufacturing and economic superiority as compared to many of the United States' industries and businesses' success [5].

Some of the original impact and secondary impact variables to be monitored are those listed below. The specific trend will be first identified and the potential impacts will be listed. We will begin with the predictive trends of John Naisbitt, and we will then list the existing and/or potential impacts that we can discern from the trends.

In John Naisbitt's *Megatrends*, published in 1982, he listed ten major trends that are still continuing in the 1990s. In 1982, Naisbitt listed the following important trends [6]:

- *The trend* is from an industrial society to one based on information. There is also a trend towards high tech/high touch.

  The impact of this trend is continuing to affect school districts by introducing the technology into the schools for use by students, teachers, and administrators, for both instructional and management purposes. Computerized instruction and management, robotics in the vocational curriculum areas, the trend of video disk storage of information replacing printed materials in libraries and media centers, electronic mail, satellite programming from all points in the world as a prime delivery method of global education and comparative civics, interactive video transmissions for such purposes as live discussions with political leaders because of the potential of down-link communications systems, and the predictability of even more sophisticated developments will continue to impact the instruction and management techniques of school district [7].

Three very important and challenging questions face
school district decision makers as they adjust to this
continually evolving technological evolution: (1) How do we
determine the qualitative levels of the burgeoning supply of
information available? (2) How do we *maximize the user-
friendly* quotient of these technologies? and (3) How do we
generate sufficient funds to purchase the newest and best
software and hardware [8]?

- *The trend* is towards a world economy, rather than a
national economy.

The impact on school districts exists today and will
continue as business and industry apply direct and
indirect pressures on the school districts to improve their
student products by forming partnerships with schools, by
lobbying legislatures to intervene by mandate, and by
producing funding reports of what is wrong with our
schools or reports of how to improve our schools. Industry's
target is ultimately to have available to them more highly
skilled graduates, especially in the areas of math and
science [9].

If the school districts cannot successfully meet the
qualitative accountability demands, it is very possible that
business, industrial and governmental officials will create
many alternative educational structures, within and
without the public schools, to compete with those that now
exist in school districts. The 1990 trend towards more
innovative *restructuring* schemes [10] and towards student
and parental *choice* [11] are merely the twin tips of the
potential reform iceberg [12].

- *The trend* is from a society run by short term
considerations to one run by long term considerations.

The impact on school districts is mainly of a two-fold
nature: (1) As more small entrepreneurial companies with
fewer than fifty employees hire a much higher percentage
of the total workforce, and as more business/industry-
educational cooperation (if not partnerships) increase, the
school districts can provide, through community schools'
operations, training and retraining for the small
businesses' employees. In addition, employees of businesses
and industries will assist the school districts by allowing
students to "shadow" employees in their work space, and

they will present lectures and demonstrations in the classrooms of the school district [13]. (2) Many school districts are realizing the importance of getting involved in *strategic planning* (long term planning to reach the district's vision of "what should be" or "what could be") [14]. A greater use of this strategic planning methodology will continue and expand during the 1990's.

- *The trends* are from centralization to decentralization, and from representative democracy to participative democracy.

   The impact of this trend is moving in two primary directions, and these will continue and accelerate if the centralized and historically authoritarian structure of our current school districts cannot demonstrate their effectiveness more successfully than is currently the case. The first direction that is becoming very evident is that of a movement towards *site-based management* [15]; and the second direction is that of *empowering* employees, parents, and the school districts' citizenry in a meaningful way to become integral players within the decision-making processes of the school district [16].

- *The trends* are from institutional help to more self-reliance on the individual, and from hierarchies to networking.

   The impact is evidenced by observing that school districts are assisting individuals to be more self reliant by such means as: (1) providing shared jobs, whereby two individuals who wish to work part time can accomplish their desires; (2) providing wellness programs to assist employees in improving the condition of their health; (3) providing employee assistance, whereby the school district has a confidential referral structure to assist employees who may have problems of substance abuse, or who may require temporary psychological or counseling assistance because of the stress they incur when they experience the death of a loved one, a divorce or some other stress-causing event; and (4) developing child-care provisions for single parents with children, or for two-employee families who have school aged or pre-school aged children [17].

   Networking opportunities are enhanced by supporting employee attendance at meetings or conferences which are also attended by employees of other educational institutions. Thus, employee opportunities are available to meet and link with employees of other school districts or with officials of state, regional, or national organizations. Also, many school districts are fostering networks by joining forces with other school districts and by contributing funds to offer joint district training and staff development opportunities through various networking structures [18].

- *The trend* is movement from North to South.

    The impact in the 1980s was to the "Sunbelt". Should this trend continue, it will have multiple potential impact on the school districts of the nation: (1) while some sections of the country must generate funds to build new school buildings, hire additional employees and provide additional instructional support systems, other sections of the country will have to develop plans to operate with less funds, close school buildings, change student attendance boundaries, pink slip (lay off) employees, and do many other undesirable activities related to downsizing.

- *The trend* from an either/or situation to a multiple options format.

    The impact on school districts is now, and will continue to be, that of offering a much more open system in which students, employees, parents, and citizens will receive more information about their schools and be more highly involved in the decision making processes of school districts [19].

Now that we have dealt with the existing and potential impacts on school districts and their constituent parts as they relate to trends identified by John Naisbitt in 1982, we will turn to some other external trends that will impact the school districts of the nation.

- *The trend* reported by the December 15, 1989 issue of the American Association of School Administrators' *Leadership News* is "According to the National Education Association, by 1993 the needs for teachers will exceed the number of new teacher graduates by 37 percent" [20].

    The impact on school districts will have the effect of causing: (1) a much more intensive recruiting effort; (2) a lobbying of legislators and of state departments of education officials for alternative certification procedures for degreed persons who did not go through the traditional teacher training schools of education. The situation is similar for principals and other categories of school administrators; and (3) the generation of increased sources of income to make teachers' and administrators' pay and fringe benefits competitive with those of business and industry [21].

- *The trend* to create a much more flexible set of working conditions will also come about, and it is related somewhat to the impending teacher and administrator shortage.

    The impact will be the same or similar for school districts as it will be for industry, business, and governmental institutions. Olmstead and Smith outline ten new scheduling options related to the evolving flexible workplace.

    The new scheduling options include: (1) flextime, (2) compressed workweek, (3) regular part time employment, (4) job sharing, (5) phased and partial retirement, (6) voluntary reduced work time, (7) leave time, (8) work sharing, (9) flexiplace (work in different locations—some could be conducted at home), and (10) contingent employment (when job reductions take place) [22].

Let's return now to John Naisbitt's identified *trends* in his book *Megatrends 2000*. The ten trends he predicts as the most important ones that will affect our lives in the 1990s.

- the booming global economy of the 1990s
- a renaissance in the arts
- the emergence of free-market socialism
- global lifestyles and cultural nationalism
- the privatization of the welfare state
- the rise of the Pacific Rim
- the decade of women in leadership
- the age of biology
- the religious revival of the new millennium
- the triumph of the individual [23]

The potential impacts of these trends on the school districts of this country include the following probabilities:

- The emergence of free markets, the global economy, the rise of the Pacific Rim and the global lifestyles and cultural nationalism are all interrelated. They will affect school district curriculums in the areas of business, mathematics, science, and foreign language as we are forced, finally, to teach realistically about the world, and the place of the United States in that world. The school districts will also be affected by the pressures of our business, industrial, and governmental leaders who will insist on students who can compete in the marketplace with students from all parts of the world. Finally, the school districts of this country will be affected financially and directly in proportion to the success of our businesses' and industries' ability to generate profit in competition with the businesses and industries of the other nations of this world [24].

- The privatization of the welfare state will have its effect in that the school districts will have to accept some retraining responsibilities for those people who will enter the work world with little or no required skills, and this function will take place through the school districts' continuing education divisions. Also, as national and state funds are removed from the welfare system, the school districts will have to negotiate with other lobbying groups and with the various legislators to get a good share of the monies released from the welfare programs [25].

- The decade of women in leadership, which is building very slowly, will have an impact on the way school districts are operated. We predict that women will be more student-oriented, and that they will insist on high quality standards. Also, the diminution of the "good old boys" network will be replaced by the "good old girls" network, and this network will have agendas that will differ, in part, from those of the "good old boys" network [26].

- The age of biology will obviously affect the science curriculum of our schools. It also should provide curative and preventive interventions that will assist the schools because they will have a lesser percentage of the student body who have handicapping conditions [27].

- The religious revival may very well have an effect on the curriculum. The obvious battle between the teaching of creationism and science will intensify. More importantly, there will be pressure on the schools to teach values, but conflicts will come as various religious groups argue that the schools should teach their particular values [28].

- The triumph of the individual will affect the school districts as they work to devise structures that will allow students more input opportunities into their education; and this trend will also be recognized as the school districts develop schemes to empower parents, employees, and community members as partners in the planning of goals and objectives of their local school districts [29].

Beyond those trends listed from specific source documents, there are also additional external trends of which the school districts' decision makers must be aware. The districts' decision makers also have to develop plans to accommodate these external trends. The major additional external trends include those listed below.

- A trend towards a continuing aging of our population [30].
- There is a trend towards the concept of knowledge as capital, and the conceptual requirement of developing human capital. That is, knowledge will increase the earning power of individuals in relative proportion to the amount of knowledge acquired. This, in turn, will allow our corporations and institutions to complete more profitably and successfully with the challenging nations of world [31].
- There is an increase of laws and regulations related to education emanating from state legislatures and state education departments [32].
- A trend is evolving towards a market and client driven operation at the individual school building and at the school district levels. That is, the school district's and individual school building's decision makers will have to provide their clients with what the clients require, and these requirements will have to be provided in competition with other schools, school districts, or other education-producing agencies. If the local education decision makers cannot provide the clients' requirements, they had better have some clear and defensible reasons that are accepted by their clients. This is truly site-based and district-based accountability related to the service agencies we call school districts and school buildings [33].

- In the 1990s the human race, out of survival necessity, will pay much more attention to the environment.
- There will be added competition from a wide variety of agencies who will compete for the reduced pool of available taxes—this will be especially true at the local level [34].
- Telecommunications will increase in complexity and availability.
- Political decisions, world-wide, will be focused on economic considerations. This will be a dramatic shift away from armed forces power and away from the conflict between such major philosophical political theories as democracy and communism.

Now that we have discussed the external trends that will impact the school districts, let's turn to those internal trends that will have the potential of impacting our school districts. The internal trends will sometimes impact all school districts, and some will impact individual school districts in different ways. What is absolutely true is that each district's decision makers will have to be creative in the structures they invent and in the responses they make to these internal variables. Since the trends listed below will have a varying impact on each school district, only the trends will be listed—the impact projections will be left to the reader as she/he deals with the trend that exists in her/his local school district.

- increasing or decreasing drop-out rate
- decreasing or increasing academic achievement
- changes in the availability of financing—greater or less money
- changes in the racial, cultural or socio-economic mix of students
- adding or lessening mandates from the national, state or local school board levels
- increasing or decreasing pressure from the community, from area businesses or industries, and from local governmental units
- increasing or decreasing the number of "at risk" students
- increasing or decreasing the number of special education, vocational education or gifted and talented students
- surpluses or shortages in the supply of excellent candidates for the various employees positions that are

vacant. This is especially important in "key man" positions.

- changes in the type of employee, and in the attitude of new employees
- changes in the availability, affordability, and uses of new technology
- changes in the culture of the community or of the school district or of school buildings within the district
- changes (increases or decreases) in school climate measures as observed or as analyzed by school climate instrumentation
- increasing or decreasing community support as witnessed by such means as attendance at school sponsored events, volunteerism, or passage of tax referendums
- increasing or decreasing employee morale as evidenced by the decrease or increase in employee grievances and by morale-judging instrumentation
- changing structure or communication patterns and empowerment patterns within the school district and within the individual school buildings
- changing the amount of "choice" provided students and their parents related to which school the students will attend, which curriculoum choices the students will have, and which teachers the students will accept

Now that we have listed a wide variety of trends and we have projected the probable impact that many of them will have on school districts and on the individual schools, we shall turn to a discussion of our vision of "what should be" in the future related to OD (Organizational Development) and HRD (Human Resource Development) in the school districts of this country.

Let's begin by reviewing the historical development of these two fields, and then we shall project a future model (see Figure 10.1).

Historically, OD was the province of the outside consultant. The consultant would collect data, analyze the problems, recommend interventions, get approval to initiate the interventions, collect data after the interventions, analyze the data, and write and present a report. HRD, historically, limited itself to training functions. The initial Historical OD/HRD is currently outdated, and it is being replaced by an Enlightened Current Model.

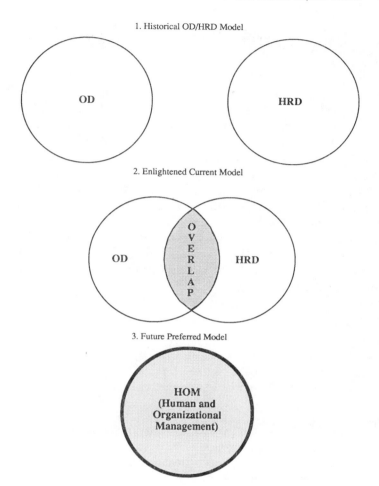

Figure 10.1 *Models of OD (Organizational Development) and HRD (Human Resource Development) Evolution.*

The enlightened current model differs in three respects from the Historical OD/HRD Model: (1) outside consultants have to share the intervention work with internal consultants who are employees of the organization, (2) human resource development is not restricted to training activities; the activities now include such programs as wellness and employee assistance, and (3) the enlightened organization sees overlap between the OD and HRD tasks, and those responsible for them work together on these overlap areas.

The future model we suggest is one which envisions OD and HRD as being completed joined into a single HUMAN AND ORGANIZATIONAL MANAGEMENT MODEL, in which changes in the organization's structures, goals, mission, objectives, strategies, tactics, and tasks are seen as having a direct effect on the employees of the organization. Conversely, changes in the types of employees or in employee skills, knowledge, or attitudes directly affect the structure of the organization. The ultimate *excellent* organization will attend to organizational needs and human needs as one integral requirement. This future approach deals with the *management* of both the organization's and the humans' needs (needs being defined as the gaps between "what is" and "what should be" or "what could be") in a unified manner.

Now that we have outlined the changes in the three models dealing with OD and HRD, let's amplify on the vision, mission, and goals of the future HOM Model (Human and Organizational Management Model).

THE VISION OF THE HOM MODEL

The totally integrated HOM Model will have a series of crucial elements envisioned. Ten major elements of the model are listed below:

(*1*) There will be a continuous *two-way communications system* built into the organizational structure that will monitor the health of students, employees and the organization. The data collection will be arrayed in a manner, that permits easy analysis of problematic areas. Decisions on specific interventions will be made with a full knowledge that whatever change is made that affects one of the parts may well affect the whole. This *management information retrieval system* is crucial to the success of the HOM Model. It will include: (a) internal and external communications, (2) human relations communications, and (3) marketing communications.

(*2*) There will be a *marketing system* built into the HOM Model. This marketing system will be designed to be an information delivery and retrieval system that is individually targeted to each of the organization's client groups or stakeholder groups. It will also be designed to attract the brightest and best candidates to become employees of the organization whenever job openings develop.

(3) There will be an *empowerment structure* wherein employees become an integral part of the planning and decision-making processes of the organization. There will be times when citizens and students will also be involved in the planning and decision-making processes of the organization.

(4) *Employee development activities will be broadly defined*, and they will be geared to the tri-levels of: (a) individual employees, (b) sub-groups of employees, and (c) the total district employees. These activites will be of a long term, not a quick-fix, nature; and the quality outcomes of these development activities will be evaluated. They will include personal needs as well as organizational needs, and they will include health and welfare provisions as well as training provisions.

(5) *Entrepreneurial activities* will be encouraged, and successful entrepreneurial ventures will be recognized and rewarded.

(6) *Intervention structures will be highly diversified* within the organization. Such structures will be placed into action when a defined need (gap between "what is" and "what should be" or "what could be") is identified; and they will include, but will not be limited to, the following structures: (a) focus groups, (b) project groups, (c) labor/management teams, (d) vertical teams, and (e) horizontal teams.

(7) A *win/win labor/management structure* will be utilized to avoid conflict and grievances, and it will be designed to resolve differences and to allow all parties to reach consensus and win. This structure will also be one of many used to analyze needs and to develop interventions to meet those needs.

(8) A *continuous strategic planning process* will be part of the model. The strategic plans of the HOM Model will be integrated into the strategic plans for the entire organization.

(9) It will be *outcome based* in that a built-in measurement, evaluation, and impact process will be completed to measure the quantity of change and the quality of change that has taken place. Quality control will be the goal.

(10) The HOM model will *integrate the elements of human relations* as they relate to the degree of satisfaction of the

employees, it will utilize training and staff development to cause *behavior modification*, and it will use a *systems approach* to all of its activities because the decision makers will understand that the whole affects the parts and the parts affect the whole.

Now that we have discussed the ten basic elements that comprise our vision of "what should be" included in the HOM Model, let's develop a mission statement which will encompass our mission; then we will follow through with a series of goals related to the vision and mission.

HOM MISSION STATEMENT

It is the mission of Human and Organization Management to operate a systems approach that involves all categories of employees within the organization to identify needs (gaps between "what is" and "what should be" or "what could be") related to individuals, sub-groups, and the total organization; and to develop and promote training and interventions to meet the identified needs in a manner that will provide the employees with a positive work environment and a feeling of contentment, while providing a high quality product within a highly productive organization.

Now that the vision elements have been identified and the mission statement developed, we should turn to the development of the strategic goals that will guide the organization in the future. Development of these goals is a crucial process, and communication of these goals is imperative for any organization that hopes to achieve its future vision.

HOM STRATEGIC GOALS

The strategic goals related to the vision and mission of HOM are as follows:

- A productive and satisfying employee environment will exist, and a high quality and productive organization will exist.
- A two-way management information system will be

developed that will include internal and external communications, human relations communications, and marketing communications.

- Employees will be empowered and entrepreneurial activities will be encouraged.
- Employee development activities will be continuous, and they will relate to personal as well as organizational needs. They will also be directly targeted to the tri-levels of the individual, sub-groups, and the total organization.
- Union/management will be based upon win-win problem solving, which will benefit the employees, the organization, and its clients.
- Intervention strategies will be utilized that will have as their base employee development and interventions to meet both employee and organizational needs.
- A systems model of strategic planning will exist that will be outcome-based and that will encompass all the goals listed above.

Now that we have listed the vision elements, the mission and the goals of the HOM Model, let's briefly take a look at the employees of the near future who will benefit from school districts that will utilize this HOM Model. The near-future employees will have these characteristics:

- Administrators will be younger, as a very high percentage of the current administrators will leave their positions in the near future. They will also be more highly educated and be more in tune with the evolving technology [35].
- All categories of employees will be better educated and they will have different job expectations than those of their predecessors. They will be dissatisfied with the conventional job descriptions, and with the degree of input they have into decisions that affect them [36].
- There will be a large increase in the number of women who will be in leadership positions [37].
- Issues like quality of work life, societal responsibilities of the school district, and international culture will be areas of interest and activity for the new employees [38].
- Competition for promotion will be great as there is a large concentration of middle aged employees—many more than can be accommodated by job diversification or by promotion [39].

To successfully deal with the needs of the future employees, those responsible for HOM will have to possess: (1) skills of influence, (2) analytical skills, (3) synthesizing skills, (4) implementation skills, (5) evaluation skills, (6) outcome measurement skills, (7) communications skills, and (8) skills of motivation. Since HOM is a collective matter, the group dealing with HOM will collectively need to possess or acquire skills in these eight areas.

In order to operate a successful HOM one must accomplish the following:

- Keep the work family together and keep the members of the work family happy.
- Remember that the key to organizational success is high quality service to the customers.
- Meet identified needs (gaps between "what is" and "what should be" or "what could be") by strategic interventions.
- Solve problems by allowing flexibility in time and in methods.
- Keep a loose-tight operation, wherein the culturally established quality parameters and activities are varied and productive, and they are selected by various employees.
- Monitor external and internal trends and project their impact on your school district; by remembering that many trends are interrelated and may have multiple impacts on your school district, you can develop strategic plans to accommodate the trends and to capitalize on their positive impacts.

Let's end this chapter by an appropriate quote from John Naisbitt's *Megatrends 2000:*

The most exciting breakthroughs of the 21st century will occur not because of technology but because of an expanding concept of what it means to be human [40].

SUMMARY

The new dominant principle of organization in changing from management control to empowerment and transformational leadership, provides a compelling framework for predicting the future development of employees and organizations. The external impact trends that will likely influence school systems are those originally proposed in 1982 by Naisbitt, and they will be augmented by the needs of a demographically changed society. School districts have, in the years since Naisbitt's trend predictions, continued to: implement emerging technology; to form business partnerships in the spirit of a global and competitive economy; to restructure to meet increasing qualitative accountability demands; to provide alternatives to corporate training and to plan strategically; to empower employees at the site level; to encourage individual and networked flexible support structures for human resource needs; and to meet school demographic changes in labor supply and demand.

The potential impacts of Naisbitt's "Millennial Megatrends" [41] on the school districts of this country include: the continuation of curricular responses to global marketing needs; the retraining of unskilled individuals as the welfare state concept diminishes; the rise of women in school leadership; the impact of science on curriculum and handicapped student adaptations; the continuing classroom conflict over values as a religious revival occurs; and the empowering of individual students and parents as stakeholders and partners in the schooling process. Major additional external trends include the aging of the population, the requirement to maximize human capital, the increase in educational regulation, the press for privatization of the educational process, the demands of the environmental crisis, the shrinking pool of public resources, continuing telecommunications complexity, and the dramatic global political power shifts that are occurring at the end of the decade. Particular internal trends that will impact school districts are related to the major additional external trends, in that they are concerned with academic achievement, dropouts and at-risk students, student cultural and program subpopulations, financing, regulation and mandates, technology, and the professional labor supply. More human resource-oriented trends are reflected in many school districts' collaborative involvement with their communities, with the growing sensitivity to multicultural concerns, and in the active seeking of stakeholder participation and support. School climate issues, employee morale and involvement/empowerment patterns, and the redesign of existing structures are increasing areas of activity and concern.

In light of the forthcoming changes and trends, it appears that the historical OD/HRD models are becoming outdated, and are being replaced by an enlightened current mode—the Human and Organizational Management Model (HOM). An optimum organization using this model would respond to organizational and human needs as one integral requirement. This model has a number of crucial systems—communications, management information retrieval, and marketing. It also incorporates an empowerment structure with broadly defined employee development and entrepreneurial activities. Other structures include highly diversified interventions, win/win labor/management, and continuous strategic planning. The HOM is outcome-based and integrates the elements of human relations through a behavior modification staff development outlook and a systems approach to all activities. It is the mission of Human and Organization Management to use employee involvement in the identification of needs, and to develop strategies to meet those needs through a maximal human environmental process, aimed at the strategic goal of productive, integrated involvement of employees.

The characteristics of the near-future educational employees include a young and an increasingly female leadership group, an increase in preparedness and job/work life expectations of all employees, and a concentration of middle management employees. These conditions will demand a HOM provision of climate maintenance, appropriate and flexible interventions, and close monitoring of the external and internal trends, which were described in this chapter, in order to strategically and positively implement the organizational and human resource merged model called HOM.

GUIDELINES

1. It is important to monitor the original impact and secondary impact trend variables as they appear to be or as they potentially could affect the school district.

2. Adjustment must be made by school decision makers concerning the continually evolving demands of technology, accountability and competitiveness, decentralization, and employee personal and career needs.

3. District strategic planning must consider the pending teacher and administrator shortage, and the need for flexible working conditions.

4. School systems should prepare to address the new trend educational concerns of preparation for global competition, the need for massive skills retraining, the school leadership changes, and the curricular and structural reform implications.

5. District strategic planning should also consider the population demographics, discern any regulatory trends, and be proactively prepared for a move towards client-driven school operation.

6. Districts should expect competition for shrinking resources, devise new ways to address environmental concerns, and consider the curricular and philosophical changes that may come with global political power shifts.

7. The more immediate and existing concerns of academic achievement, students at-risk, special programs and subpopulations, technological shifts, school climate, employee changes in expectations, and community support should be reevaluated in light of the current and anticipated trends.

8. School districts should assess their existing OD and HRD structures, and consider adopting the HOM Model as an integrated organizational system.

EXERCISES

1. What internal and external trends exist in your school district? What will, in your judgement, be the potential of each trend and of the collective trend? What intervention strategies can you use to accommodate and take advantage of these trends?

2. What elements would you include in your Human and Organizational Management Model? Why would you include each of these?

3. Conduct a needs assessment for your district related to the human and organizational needs which exist. What action programs will you initiate to meet these identified needs?

4. Develop a strategic plan for your school district. What specific elements will you include?

5. What is your personal vision for the school district ten or more

years in the future? How will the described existing external and internal trends impact your district?

6. Of the described impacts on the school systems nationwide, which do you consider to be the most significant? How could its effect be dealt with in an integrated school district HOM Model?

SELECTED REFERENCES

1. Naisbitt, J. and P. Aburdene. 1990. *Megatrends 2000*. New York, NY: William Morrow and Company, p. 218.
2. Webb, L. D. et al. 1987. *Personnel Administration in Education*. Columbus, OH: Merrill Publishing Company, pp. 260–261.
3. Flamholtz, E. G., Y. Randle, and S. Sackmann. 1987. "Personnel Management in the Tone of Tomorrow", *Personnel Journal*, 66(7):43–48.
4. Kimberly, J. R. and R. E. Quinn. 1984. *New Futures: The Challenge of Managing Corporate Transitions*. Homewood, IL: Dow Jones-Irwin, p. 2.
5. Webb, L. D. et al. *Personnel Administration*, pp. 267–268.
6. Naisbitt, J. and P. Aburdene. 1982. *Megatrends*. New York, NY: Warner Books, p. 2.
7. Mecklenburger, J. A. 1988. "What the Ostrich Sees: Technology and the Mission of American Education", *Phi Delta Kappan*, 70(1):18–19.
8. Perelman, L. J. 1988. "Restructuring the System Is the Solution", *Phi Delta Kappan*, 70(1):20–24.
9. Twentieth Century Fund. 1983. *Making the Grade-Report of the Twentieth Century Fund Task Force on Federal Elementary and Secondary Education Policy*. New York, NY: Twentieth Century Fund, Inc. p. 14.
10. Lewis, A. 1989. *Restructuring America's Schools*. Arlington, VA: American Association of School Administrators, pp. 3–4.
11. Pearson, J. 1989. "Myth of Choice: The Governor's New Clothes?" *Phi Delta Kappan*, 70(10):821–823.
12. Lewis, A. 1989. *Restructuring America's Schools*. Arlington, VA: American Association of School Administrators, p. 214.
13. Lewis, A. *Restructuring*, pp. 98–107.
14. Kaufman, R. and J. Herman. 1991. *Strategic Planning in Education*. Lancaster, PA: Technomic Publishing Co., Inc.
15. Lewis, A. *Restructuring*, p. 177.
16. Maeroff, G. I. 1988. "A Blueprint for Empowering Teachers", *Phi Delta Kappan*, 69(7):473–477.
17. Webb, L. D. et al. *Personnel Administration*, pp. 260–261.
18. Maeroff, G. I. "Blueprint", pp. 473–477.
19. Lewis, A. *Restructuring*, pp. 245–246.
20. American Association of School Administrators. 1989. *Leadership News*. American Association of School Administrators, (55) p. 2.

21. Shanker, A. 1990. "The End of the Traditional Model of Schooling – and A Proposal for Using Incentives to Restructure Our Public Schools", *Phi Delta Kappan*, 71(5):345–357.

22. Olmstead, B. and S. Smith. 1989. "Creating a Flexible Workplace: How to Select and Manage Alternative Work Options", *AMACOM*, 462.

23. Naisbitt, J. and P. Aburdene. *Megatrends 2000*, p. 13.

24. Benjamin, S. 1989. "An Ideascape for Education: What Futurists Recommend", *Educational Leadership*, 47(1):8–14.

25. Perelman, L. J. 1988. "Restructuring the System Is the Solution", *Phi Delta Kappan*, 70(1):20–24.

26. Whitaker, K. S. and K. Lane. 1990. "Is a Woman's Place in School Administration?" *The School Administrator*, 2(47): 8–12.

27. Adkins, G. 1989. "Megatrends Author Foresees the Millennium", *Educational Leadership*, 47(1):16–17.

28. Spiro, D. A. 1989. "Public Schools and the Road to Religious Neutrality", *Phi Delta Kappan*, 70(10):759–763.

29. MacDowell, M. A. 1989. "Partnerships: Getting a Return on the Investment", *Educational Leadership*, 47(2):8–14.

30. Galagan, P. 1987. "Here's the Situation", *Training and Development Journal*, 141(7): 20–22.

31. Galagan, P. "Situation", p. 21.

32. Porter, A. 1988. "Indicators: Objective Data or Political Tool?" *Phi Delta Kappan*, 69(7):473–477.

33. Conley, S.C. and S.B. Bacharach. 1990. "From School-Site Management to Participatory School-Site Management", *Phi Delta Kappan*, 71(7): 539–544.

34. Pipho, C. 1989. "Full Agenda, Empty Pockets", *Phi Delta Kappan*, 70(10):750–751.

35. Lewis, A. *Restructuring*, pp. 236–243.

36. Flamholtz, E. G., Y. Randle, and S. Sackmann. "Personnel Management", pp. 43–48.

37. Flamholtz, E. G., Y. Randle, and S. Sackmann. "Personnel Management", p. 45.

38. Galagan, P. "Situation", pp. 20–22.

39. Leibowitz, Z. B., C. Farren, and B. Kaye. 1983. "Will Your Organization Be Doing Career Development in the Year 2000?" *Training and Development Journal*, 37(2):14–20.

40. Naisbitt, J. and P. Aburdene. *Megatrends 2000*, p. 16.

41. Naisbitt, J. and P. Aburdene. *Megatrends 2000*, p. 13.

Abramson, L. 1988. "Boost to the Bottom Line", *Personnel Administrator*, 33(7).

Adkins, G. 1989. "Megatrends Author Foresees the Millennium," *Educational Leadership*, 47(1):16–17.

Albrecht, Karl. 1983. *Organization Development.* Englewood Cliffs, NJ: Prentice-Hall.

American Association of School Administrators. 1988. *Challenges for School Leaders.* Arlington, VA: American Association of School Administrators.

American Association of School Administrators. 1989. *Leadership News.* American Association of School Administrators, (55): p. 2

Appelbaum, S. H. and B. T. Shapiro. 1989. "The ABCs of EAPs", *Personnel*, 66(7):39–46.

Beckhard, R. and R. T. Harris. 1977. *Organizational Transitions: Managing Complex Change.* Reading, MA: Addison-Wesley.

Beer, M. et al. 1985. *Human Resource Managment.* New York: NY: Macmillan.

Benjamin, S. 1989. "An Ideascape for Education: What Futurists Recommend", *Educational Leadership*, 47(1): 8–14.

Berger, R. W. and D. L. Shores, eds. 1986. *Quality Circles.* New York, NY: Marcel Dekker, Inc.

Blake, R. R. and J. S. Mouton. 1969. *Building a Dynamic Corporation through Grid Organization Development.* Reading, MA: Addison-Wesley.

Bolton, R. 1979. *People Skills.* Reading, MA: Addison-Wesley.

Brookover, et al. 1982. *Creating Effective Schools.* Holmes Beach, FL: Learning Publications, Inc.

Buchholz, S. and T. Roth. 1987. *Creating the High Performance Team.* New York, NY: John Wiley & Sons, Inc.

Budde, J. F. 1979. *Measuring Performance in Human Service Systems.* New York, NY: American Management Associations.

Burke, W. W. 1987. *Organization Development.* Reading, MA: Addison-Wesley Publishing Co.

Business Week. May 2, 1988. "Perspective of the Problem", *Business Week*, p. 126–127.

251

Byars, L. L. 1987. *Strategic Management.* Second edition. New York, NY: Harper & Row, Publishers.

Carnegie Forum on Education and the Economy. 1983. *A Nation at Risk.* New York, NY: Carnegie Forum on Education and the Economy.

Carnegie Forum on Education and the Economy. 1986. *Report on Teaching as a Profession.* New York, NY: Carnegie Forum on Education and the Economy.

Castetter, W. B. 1986. *The Personnel Function in Educational Administration.* New York, NY: Macmillan Publishing Company.

Conley, S. C. and S. B. Bacharach. 1990. "From School-Site Management to Participatory School-Site Management", *Phi Delta Kappan*, 71(7): 539–544.

Connor, P. E. and L. K. Lake. 1988. *Managing Organizational Change.* New York, NY: Praeger Publishers.

Deutsch, A. 1979. *The Human Resources Revolution: Communicate or Litigate.* New York, NY: McGraw-Hill Book Company.

Donaldson, L. and E. E. Scannell. 1978. *Human Resource Development.* Reading, MA: Addison-Wesley.

Duke, D. L. 1987. *School Leadership and Instructional Improvement.* New York, NY: Random House.

Duttweiler, P. C. 1989. "Components of an Effective Professional Development Program", *Journal of Staff Development*, 10(2):2–6.

Dyer, W. G. 1983. *Contemporary Issues in Management and Organization Development.* Reading, MA: Addison Wesley Publishing Company, p. 126.

English, F. and B. Steffy. 1983. "Curriculum Mapping: An Aid to School Curriculum Management", *Spectrum*, 1(4): 17–26.

Feuer, D. and B. Geber. 1988. "Uh-Oh . . . Second Thoughts about Learning Theory", *Training*, 25(12):31–38.

Fitzgerald, L. and J. Murphy. 1982. *Installing Quality Circles: A Strategic Approach.* San Diego, CA: University Associates, Inc.

Flamholtz, E. G., Y. Randle, and S. Sackmann. 1987. "Personnel Management in the Tone of Tomorrow", *Personnel Journal*, 66(7):43–48.

Fox, R. S., et al. 1973. *School Climate Improvement: A Challenge to the School Administrator.* Bloomington, IN: Phi Delta Kappa.

French, W. L. and C. H. Bell, Jr. 1973. *Organization Development.* Englewood Cliffs, NJ: Prentice-Hall, p. 33.

Galagan, P. 1987. "Here's the Situation", *Training and Development Journal*, 141(7): 20–22.

Gibb, J. R. 1978. *Trust–A New View of Personal and Organizational Development.* Los Angeles, CA: The Guild of Tutors Press.

Greenfield, T. B. et al. 1969. *Developing School Systems-Planning, Organization, and Personnel.* Toronto, Ontario: Institute for Studies in Education.

Hampton, D. R., C. E. Summer, and R. A. Webber. 1987. *Organizational Behavior and the Practice of Management.* Glenview, IL: Scott, Foresman and Company.

Harris, B. M. 1986. *Developmental Teacher Evaluation.* Boston, MA: Allyn and Bacon, Inc.

Harris, B. M. et al. 1979. *Personnel Administration in Education.* Boston, MA: Allyn and Bacon, Inc.

Harris, B. M. 1989. *In-Service Education for Staff Development.* Boston, MA: Allyn and Bacon, Inc.

Herman, J. 1989. "A Vision for the Future: Site-Based Strategic Planning", *NASSP Bulletin*, 73(518): 23–27.

Herman, J. 1989. "External and Internal Scanning: Identifying Variables That Affect Your School", *NASSP Bulletin*, 73(520): 48–52.

Herman, J. 1989. "School Business Officials' Roles in the Strategic Planning Process (Part II)", *School Business Affairs*, 55(3): 20–23.

Herman, J. 1989. "School District Strategic Planning (Part I)", *School Business Affairs*, 55(2): 10–14.

Herman, J. 1989. "Site-Based Management: Creating a Vision and Mission Statement", *NASSP Bulletin*, 73(519): 79–83.

Herman, J. 1989. "Strategic Planner: One of the Changing Leadership Roles of the Principal", *The Clearing House*, 63(2): 56–58.

Hersey, P. and K. Blanchard. 1982. *Management of Organizational Behavior*, Fourth edition. Englewood Cliffs, NJ: Prenctice-Hall.

Hinson, S, M. S. Caldwell, and M. Landrum. 1989. "Characteristics of Effective Staff Development Programs", *Journal of Staff Development*, 10(2): 48–51.

Hopper, L. 1988. "Unstressing Work: What Smart Organizations Do", *Public Management*, 70(11): 2–4.

Hord, S. M. et al. 1987. *Taking Charge of Change.* Alexandria, VA: Association for Supervision and Curriculum Development.

Horwitz, J. and H. Kimpel. 1988. "Taking Control: Techniques for the Group Interview", *Training and Development Journal*, 42(10): 52–54.

Hoy, W. K. and C. G. Miskel. 1987. *Educational Administration.* Third edition. New York, NY: Random House.

Hoyle, J. R., F. W. English, and B. E. Steffy. 1985. *Skills for Successful School Leaders.* Arlington, VA: American Association of School Administrators.

Human Resources Forum Supplement. Sept. 1989. "Entry-Level, Support Staff Need Training, Survey Shows", *Management Review*, pp. 1–4.

Johnson, S. M. 1984. *Teacher Unions in Schools.* Philadelphia, PA: Temple University Press.

Joyce, B., B. Showers, and C. Rolheiser-Bennet. 1987. "Staff Development and Student Learning: A Synthesis of Research on Models of Teaching", *Educational Leadership*, 45(2): 11–23.

Joyce, B. R. 1986. *Improving America's Schools.* New York, NY: Longman, Inc.

Kaufman, R. and J. Herman. 1991. *Strategic Planning in Education.* Lancaster, PA: Technomic Publishing Co., Inc.

Kaufman, R. and J. Herman. 1989. "Planning That Fits Every District", *School Administrator*, 8(46): 17–19.

Kaufman, R. et al. 1975. *Human Dimensions of School Improvement*. Philadelphia, PA: Research for Better Schools, Inc.

Kerman, S. and M. Martin. 1980. *Teacher Expectations and Student Achievement Teacher Handbook*. Bloomington, IN: Phi Delta Kappa.

Kiefer, C. and P. Stroh. 1983. "A New Paradigm for Organizational Development", *Training and Development Journal*, 37(4):27–35.

Killion, J. P., J. P. Huddleston, and M.A. Claspell. 1989. "People Developer: A New Role for Principals", *Journal of Staff Development*, 10(1):2–7.

Kimberly, J. R. and R. E. Quinn. 1984. *New Futures: The Challenge of Managing Corporate Transitions*. Homewood, IL: Dow Jones-Irwin.

Kirshenbaum, H. and B. Glaser. 1978. *Developing Support Groups*. La Jolla, CA: University Associates.

Kohler, L. T. 1980. "Basic Points for Negotiators", *AS & U*, 52(9):40–41.

Laird, D. 1978. *Approaches to Training and Development*. Reading, MA: Addison Wesley Publishing Company, p. 47.

Lawler, E. E. III and S. A. Mohman. 1989. "High-Involvement Management", *Personnel*, 66(4):26–31.

Leibowitz, Z. B., C. Farren, and B. Kaye. 1983. "Will Your Organization Be Doing Career Development in the Year 2000?" *Training and Development Journal*, 37(2):14–20.

Lewis, A., 1989. *Restructuring America's Schools*. Arlington, VA: American Association of School Administrators.

MacDowell, M. A. 1989. "Partnerships: Getting a Return on the Investment", *Educational Leadership*, 47(2):8–14.

Mace-Matluck, B. J. 1986. *Research-Based Strategies for Bringing About Successful School Improvement*. Austin, TX: Southwest Educational Development Laboratory (Office of Educational Research and Improvement, U.S. Department of Education).

Maddux, R. B. 1988. *Team Building: An Exercise in Leadership*. Revised edition. Los Altos, CA: Crisp Publications, Inc.

Maeroff, G. I. 1988. "A Blueprint for Empowering Teachers", *Phi Delta Kappan*, 69(7):473–477.

Matteson, M. T. and J. M. Ivancevich. 1977. *Controlling Work Stress*. Englewood Cliffs, NJ: Prentice-Hall.

McGreal, T. 1989. "Necessary Ingredients for Successful Instructional Improvement Initiatives", *Journal of Staff Development*, 10(1):35–41.

Meares, L. B. 1986. "A Model for Changing Organizational Culture", *Personnel*, 63(7):38–42.

Mecklenburger, J. A. 1988. "What the Ostrich Sees: Technology and the Mission of American Education", *Phi Delta Kappan*, 70(1):18–19.

Metz, E. J. 1981. "The Verteam Circle", *Training and Development Journal*, 35(12):79–85.

Mink, O. G., J. M. Shultz, and B. P. Mink. 1979 *Developing and Managing Open Organizations*. Austin, TX: Learning Concepts.

Moore, J. R. 1988. "Guidelines Concerning Adult Learning", *Journal of Staff Development*, 9(3):2–5.

Morrisey, G. L., P. J. Below, and B. L. Acomb. 1988. *The Executive Guide to Operational Planning.* San Francisco, CA: Jossey-Bass, Inc., pp. 65–66.

Nadler, D. A. 1977. *Feedback and Organization Development.* Reading, MA: Addison-Wesley.

Naisbitt, J. and P. Aburdene. 1990. *Megatrends 2000.* New York, NY: William Morrow and Company.

Naisbitt, J. and P. Aburdene. 1982. *Megatrends.* New York, NY: Warner Books.

Neal, R. G. 1988. "Justice Favors the Well Prepared", *The Executive Educator*, 10(11):17–18.

Nyland, L. 1987. "Win/Win Bargaining Pays Off", *Educational Digest*, 53(1): 28–29.

Oliva, P. F. 1976. *Supervision for Today's Schools.* New York, NY: Longman, Inc.

Olmstead, B. and S. Smith. 1989. "Creating a Flexible Workplace: How to Select and Manage Alternative Work Options," *AMACOM*, 462.

Pearson, J. 1989. "Myth of Choice: The Governor's New Clothes?" *Phi Delta Kappan*, 70(10):821–823.

Pennington, R. 1989. "Collaborative Labor Relations: The First Line is the Bottom Line", *Personnel*, 66(4):78–83.

Perelman, L. J. 1988. "Restructuring the System Is the Solution", *Phi Delta Kappan*, 70(1):20–24.

Peters T. J. and R. H. Waterman, Jr. 1982. *In Search of Excellence.* New York, NY: Harper & Row, Publishers.

Pfeiffer, J. W., ed. 1986. *Strategic Planning.* San Diego, CA: University Associates, Inc. pp. 21–22.

Pipho, C. 1989. "Full Agenda, Empty Pockets", *Phi Delta Kappan*, 70(10): 750–751.

Porter, A. 1988. "Indicators: Objective Data or Political Tool?" *Phi Delta Kappan*, 69(7):473–477.

Rebore, R. W. 1987. *Personnel Administration in Education.* Second edition. Englewood Cliffs, NJ: Prentice-Hall.

Schmuck, R. A. and M. B. Miles, eds. 1971. *Organization Development in Schools.* Palo Alto, CA: National Press Books.

Schmuck, R. A. and P. J. Runkel. 1988. *The Handbook of Organization Development in Schools*, Third edition. Prospect Heights, IL: Waveland Press, Inc.

Schmuck, R. A., et al. 1977. *The Second Handbook of Organization Development in Schools.* Palo Alto, CA: Mayfield Publishing Company.

Schneier, C. E., R. W. Beatty, and L. S. Baird. 1986. "Creating a Performance Management System", *Training and Development Journal*, 40(5):74–79.

Schneier, C. E., R. W. Beatty, and L. S. Baird. 1986. "How to Construct a Successful Performance Appraisal System", *Training and Development Journal*, 40(4):38–42.

Schuster, F. E. 1985. *Human Resource Management.* Reston, VA: Reston Publishing Company, Inc.

Shanker, A. 1990. "The End of the Traditional Model of Schooling–and A Proposal for Using Incentives to Restructure Our Public Schools", *Phi Delta Kappan*, 71(5):345–357.

Shroyer, M. G. 1990. "Effective Staff Development for Effective Organization Development", *Journal of Staff Development*, 11(1):2–6.

Shtogren, J. A., ed. 1980. *Models for Management: The Structure of Competence*. The Woodlands, TX: Teleometrics, International.

Sikula, A. F. and J. F. McKenna. 1984. *The Management of Human Resources*. New York, NY: John Wiley & Sons.

Sloan, R. P. and J. P. Gruman. 1988. "Does Wellness in the Workplace Work?" *Personnel Administrator*, 33(7):42–48.

Sloane, A. A. 1983. *Personnel-Managing Human Resources*. Englewood Cliffs, NJ: Prentice-Hall, Inc.

Smith, P. and R. Baker. 1986. "An Alternative Form of Collective Bargaining", *Phi Delta Kappan*, 67(8):605–607.

Sparks, G.M. 1983. "Synthesis of Research on Staff Development for Effective Teaching", *Educational Leadership*, 43:46–53.

Spector, B. and M. Beer. 1985. *Human Resource Management*. New York, NY: Macmillan.

Spiro, D. A. 1989. "Public Schools and the Road to Religious Neutrality", *Phi Delta Kappan*, 70(10):759–763.

Stackel, L. "EAP's in the Work Place", *Employment Relations Today*, 14(3):289–291.

Stephens, G. and J. Herman. 1985. "Using the Instructional Audit for Policy and Program Improvement", *Educational Leadership*, 42(8):70–75.

Sussman, L. and S. D. Deep. 1984. *COMEX–The Communication Experience in Human Relations*. Cincinnati, OH: South-Western Publishing Co.

Tanker, P. A., 1987. "Why Flexible Benefits Are So Appealing", *Management World*, 16(2):17–18.

Tough, A. 1979. *The Adult's Learning Projects*. Second edition. Toronto, Ontario: Institute for Studies in Education.

Tushman, M. L., W. H. Newman, and E. Romanelli. 1986. "Convergence and Upheaval: Managing the Unsteady Pace of Organizational Evolution", *California Management Review*, 29(1):29–41.

Twentieth Century Fund. 1983. *Making the Grade-Report of the Twentieth Century Fund Task Force on Federal Elementary and Secondary Education Policy*. New York, NY: Twentieth Century Fund, Inc.

University Council for Educational Administration. 1987. *Leaders for America's Schools: The Report of the National Commission on Excellence in Educational Administration*. University Council for Educational Administration.

Warrick, D. D., ed. 1985. *Contemporary Organization Development*. Glenview, IL: Scott, Foresman and Company.

Webb, L. D. et al. 1987. *Personnel Administration in Education*. Columbus, OH: Merrill Publishing Company.

Webster, W. G. 1985. *Effective Collective Bargaining in Public Education*. Ames, IA: Iowa State University Press.

Welsbord, M. R. 1978. *Organizational Diagnosis: A Workbook of Theory and Practice*. Reading, MA: Addison-Wesley.

Whitaker, K. S. and K. Lane. 1990. "Is a Woman's Place in School Administration?" *The School Administrator*, 2(47):8–12.

White, L. P. and K. C. Wooten. 1986. *Professional Ethics and Practice in Organizational Development*. New York, NY: Praeger Publishers.

Yoder, D. and P. D. Staudohar. 1982. *Personnel Management and Industrial Relations*. Seventh edition. Englewood Cliffs, NJ: Prentice-Hall, Inc.

JERRY JOHN HERMAN is professor and area head of the Department of Administration and Educational Leadership at The University of Alabama at Tuscaloosa. Dr. Herman has been a professor at Iowa State University, and has held positions as a professor at Cleveland State University and Western Kentucky University, and as an adjunct professor at the University of Michigan, Michigan State University, Eastern Michigan University, and Northern Michigan University. He has had twenty years of experience as a school superintendent in districts in the states of Michigan and New York and as an assistant superintendent for instruction, elementary and secondary director, elementary and secondary principal, research and developmental specialist, audiovisual coordinator, and teacher at the elementary, junior high, senior high, and junior college levels. He received his B.S. degree from Northern Michigan University with concentrations in history, biology, and physical education. Dr. Herman's M.A. degree in Educational Administration is from the University of Michigan; his Ph.D. was also awarded by the University of Michigan in Educational Administration. In addition, Dr. Herman's vita includes postdoctoral study in business administration at the University of Michigan and work as a consultant to school districts and to industry. Dr. Herman has authored seven books, fifteen monographs, and more than 100 articles on a wide range of educational and business issues. He has recently authored a new text on strategic planning. Dr. Herman has amassed numerous professional honors and awards in the field of administration and educational leadership.

Janice Elizabeth Herman is an associate professor in the Department of Educational Leadership and Instructional Support at The University of Alabama at Birmingham. She has been an assistant professor in the Department of Curriculum and Instruction at The University of Alabama at Tuscaloosa, and was a Cooperative Superintendency Fellow in educational administration at The University of Texas at Austin. Dr. Herman's vita includes Texas State Department of Education experience in school accreditation, elementary school principalship, responsibility for instructional supervision in bilingual and English as a Second Language programs, and experience as a teacher in grades kindergarten through six and in gifted and talented education. She also taught in Thailand at the International School of Bangkok and at the American University Alumnae Association. Dr. Herman received her B.A. from the College of William and Mary with a concentration in Elementary Education, an M.S. in Education from the University of Southern California, and a Ph.D. in Educational Administration from The University of Texas at Austin. Dr. Herman has assisted in the preparation of the State of Texas instructional leadership model; trained teachers, supervisors, administrators, and state department personnel in Texas and Oklahoma in instructional leadership and effective teaching strategies, and provided school improvement training for principals.